Lost Lines

Lost Lines

An anthology of Britain's lost railways

MURIEL V. SEARLE

New Cavendish Books

DEDICATED

To the memory of my dear mother, Ellen Rose (Nellie) Searle, with whom I travelled many of these Lost Lines. In particular, the chapter entitled 'Land Cruise' is lovingly written in recollection of happy times.

M.V.S.

Contents

Introduction	6
Chapter 1 'In The Beginning' (Canterbury & Whitstable Railway)	11
Chapter 2 'Two Grand Dreams' (Port Victoria & All Hallows)	16
Chapter 3 'Sheep Line' (Isle of Sheppey)	23
Chapter 4 'The Shrinking Tunnel' (Ramsgate Tunnel Railway)	31
Chapter 5 'Into Oblivion' (Hythe Branch)	35
Chapter 6 'Fight for Survival' (Westerham Valley Branch)	42
Chapter 7 'Screaming Alice' (Crystal Palace)	50
Chapter 8 'The Bordon Valley' (Bentley to Bordon & Longmoor)	58
Chapter 9 'Oh! Mr Porter!' (Basingstoke & Alton Light Railway)	63
Chapter 10 'The Hayling Billy' (Hayling Island Branch)	68
Chapter 11 'Vehicles of Vectis' (Isle of Wight)	76
Chapter 12 'Across the Sea Bed' (Somerset & Dorset Joint Railway)	87
Chapter 13 'Lost Lines of Avon' (Somerset & Avon Branches)	99
Chapter 14 'To the Twin Villages' (Lynton & Barnstaple Railway)	107
Chapter 15 'Farthest West' (Liskeard & Caradon Railway, Cornwall)	114
Chapter 16 'Kings and Bloaters' (The Norfolk Coast)	118
Chapter 17 'The Oxford Accent' (Blenheim & Woodstock Branch)	128
Chapter 18 'Mid Stations and Palaces' (Derbyshire)	133
Chapter 19 'Wye Wanderings' (The Wye Valley & Forest of Dean)	143
Chapter 20 'Exalted Valleys' (South Wales)	150
Chapter 21 'Land Cruise' (North Wales)	159
Chapter 22 'The Signal in a Field' (Yorkshire & Humberside)	169
Chapter 23 'Easygoing Easingwold' (The Easingwold Railway)	176
Chapter 24 'Murder on the Line' (Railways of Blaydon & Consett)	181
Chapter 25 'Into Lakeland' (Coniston Branch)	187
Chapter 26 'Across Scotland' (Dumfries to Portpatrick & Stranraer)	192
Chapter 27 'Speyside' (Around Elgin)	198
Bibliography	205
Acknowledgements	206
Index	207

First edition published in Great Britain
by New Cavendish Books, 1982.

Copyright © – New Cavendish Books – 1982.
All Rights Reserved.

This work or parts thereof may not be reproduced without prior permission in writing from the publishers.

Design, John Cooper.
Editorial Direction, Allen and Narisa Levy.
Printed and bound by Robert Hartnoll in England.
Setting and Monochrome illustrations, Western Printing Services Ltd, Bristol.

Lost Lines
ISBN 0 904568 41 5

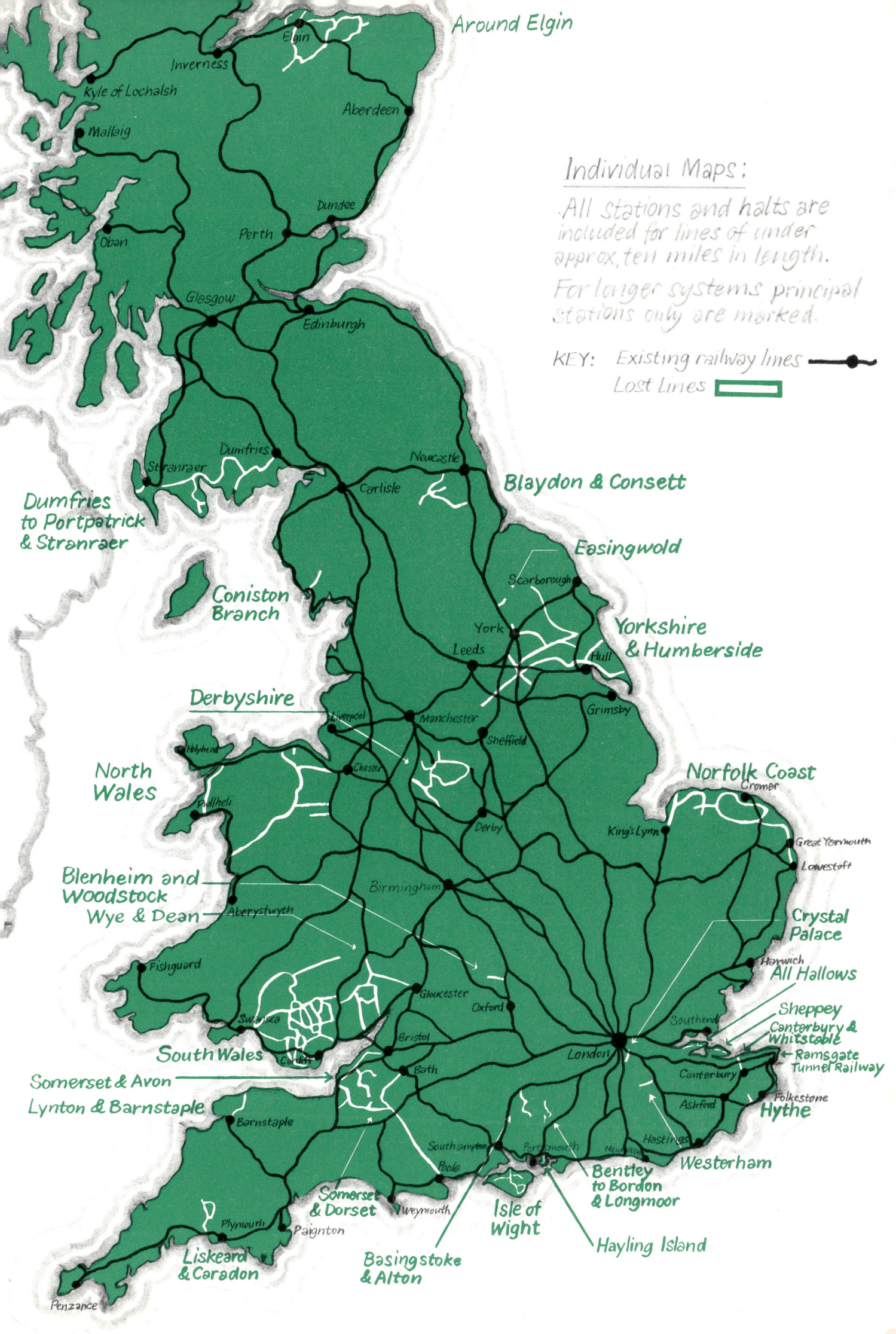

Introduction

What was the essence of Britain's generally steam hauled pre-Beeching branch lines and compact regional systems; can we ever recapture it; and if so, where?

Certainly not on railways still extant, under diesel or electric motive power. Nor, despite their surface promise, on lines that have been preserved as tourist attractions. Without these, true, no present day child or teenager would ever have known the sounds or distinctive scents of steam at all; and without them no adult would be able to revel in those sounds and smells of his youth again, breathing them in with great gulps of nostalgia. Yet their reality is sometimes perhaps not quite genuine. The trains puff satisfactorily enough, but are dedicated to pleasure instead of running a genuine everyday transport service, for which they were built. They carry tourists, but not farmers to market and housewives to the shops; pet dogs on leads, but not crates of live hens; a modicum of holiday baggage in certain instances, but not punnets of Cheddar strawberries to Bristol, or crates of Clarks shoes to John O'Groats.

Perhaps the essential flavour that seems to be lost is best recaptured by seeking out lines that are themselves lost. Preferably totally lost and lifted; otherwise, closed to passengers for many years, and only momentarily disturbed by a latter day goods train creeping past ruins of ghost stations before relapsing into silence heavier than ever.

Why? Because they *are* lost, and imagination and memory must go to work, as one stands on a derelict platform or looks down a grassy trackbed.

The mind's eye and ears can be vivid if we really use them.

Lean against that broken down gate leading up the ramp onto a crumbling platform, somewhere between here, there and nowhere, and will the past to return. It becomes easy to recall how lineside housewives ruled their days by a combination of ancient rolling stock and saddle tank known simple as *The* Train, and ordered their families' meals by it morning, noon and evening. *The* Train was their clock, very different to the trains most familiar to we who have always lived close beside a busy main line, which we only notice when strikes, accidents or engineering works stop them and an unnatural silence falls.

Look at one solitary water tank mournfully marooned amid ornamental flower beds, in the centre of a caravan park that has spread until it swallowed the very site of the tracks that once served it. Gaze at a broken nameboard which kind nature has draped with roses, and return in spirit to the same platform when waiting for a Sunday School special to rumble in.

Yes, here are the railways of yesterday, waiting like television waves of the air to be picked up and translated into pictorial actuality by a sensitive receiver. In this case, not a box on legs but a human imagination linked to experience if one is old enough to remember backwards from the early 1960s, or by book learning if too young to have seen the line in action.

Time and changing requirements created more of these lost lines than can be compressed into one volume, except too briefly. The present volume makes no such attempt, but instead explores a representative selection ranging from little branches with only two stations to self contained cross-country systems, taken from all corners from Kent to Cornwall, the Isle of Wight to Yorkshire, Wales to Scotland.

Each has been chosen because it had some interest beside locomotives and rolling stock – the initial industry or planners' dream it served, whether or not it came to fruition; some place in railway history, such as the spawning of the world's first railway commuters; its terrain, in one case a former sea bed; literary aspects; links with royal trains; even a famous film.

Tracks have been lifted in the majority of cases, leaving trackbed, stations and lineside features languishing in creeping undergrowth to challenge railway historians or those who use the old embankments and cuttings as walkways. Freight trains use fragments of others for a few miles, but demolition of stations and complete removal of track at the very points they chiefly served makes them ghost lines, lost the rest of the way. All Hallows, the big new seaside resort that never was, with its two lost steam connections, affords an excellent example.

Railway mania, spreading throughout the land during the half century following opening of the pioneer Stockton and Darlington Railway, brought most of these lines to birth, though a few were still opening into the 1930s. Some lasted a full century, others for scarcely thirty years. Most died in a complete reversal of railway mania that was sudden and drastic.

The spirit of desolation descends on an abandoned station: up-ended rusty porter's barrow; encroaching brambles; and grass where a platform once stood.
M V Searle

Gates from nowhere to nowhere, closed for the last time years ago. Bushes grow up as abandonment deepens.

Universal relic of long-dead days. Railway notices of pre-Amalgamation companies have suddenly become more scarce than a decade ago, as bridges span empty trackbed.
M V Searle

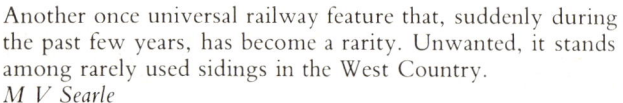

Battered warehouses; a minuscule public room half overgrown with self-propagated sycamore; one post without the platform backing wire it supported; yet another abandoned station droops towards oblivion.
S Levy

At first glance an almost impenetrable copse. This, twenty years ago, was a Yorkshire branch line.
M & J Harris

Another once universal railway feature that, suddenly during the past few years, has become a rarity. Unwanted, it stands among rarely used sidings in the West Country.
M V Searle

Everywhere, railway trackbed in level countryside is being returned to the land whence it came. Trackbed allotments in Yorkshire, with rough fencing replacing a once-smart level crossing.
M & J Harris

Rusted metals awaiting lifting. Another stage in the death of a railway.
M V Searle

Bleak weather; bleak countryside. They emphasise the spirit of lost lines everywhere, snaking across fields and vales. Standing here, only in imagination can we now watch the trains go by.
M & J Harris

Hang out the washing on the railway line; the ultimate in domestic adaptation of a once busy GWR station.
NCB

Decline towards extinction began with the pre-war improvement of public road services and resultant closure of certain rural routes, but gained its main momentum with the phenomenal post-war upsurge of private family motoring, fallen to the financial level of Everyman from its former exclusivity. The apparent immediate answer, increased fares, merely drove more onto the roads, undermining railway finances still further except on profitable main lines, starting a vicious spiralling circle that still exists. Electrification or dieselisation of lines deemed profitable into the future left many suburban or country routes behind the times, too costly to modernise in view of their traffic, still under steam when steam was undoubtedly doomed. Beeching's 'Axe' administered the final *coup de grâce*.

By the mid-Sixties it was all over. Short branches and complete systems alike lay suddenly silent, eerie without the familiar noises of steam, clanking couplings, slamming doors and guards' whistles.

Only a limited number were preserved for posterity by enthusiasts' groups, commerce or councils. Otherwise our railways, previously divided chiefly into steam and Southern Electric, became further divided into steam (rapidly disappearing), electric, diesel, preserved, and lost.

CHAPTER 1

In The Beginning
CANTERBURY & WHITSTABLE RAILWAY

'Make a joyful noise unto the Lord'. Choristers had been flinging those words to Canterbury Cathedral's lofty vaults for centuries.

But on the radiantly sunny morning of May 3, 1830, it appeared that all Canterbury, including its centrepiece cathedral, was atheistically making a joyful noise unto a work of man. Some said, to a work of the Devil, that stood symbolically outside the venerable grey city walls, puffing and snuffling to itself as if it were alive. The new idol, towards which the population from city fathers to errand boys was being drawn from all quarters, was named *Invicta*.

Past public buildings decorated with flags came the mayor, his chest resplendent with all the stiff shirting, velvet and chains of office of Victorian pomposity, with his councillors and corporation, followed by excited crowds. Hundreds more cheered as they went through the massive West Gate, boundary of Canterbury, towards a new temple of Mammon discreetly sited a mile from the cathedral across a river. A temple known as a railway station.

From the cathedral bells pealed out, and from the West Gate's tall round towers guns boomed in salute. More crowds cheered, flags fluttered, and a band struck up. The opening of the new Canterbury and Whitstable Railway was imminent.

Similar scenes were afterwards repeated during some forty ensuing years as railway after railway opened, but in 1830 they were unsullied with familiarity. No steam locomotive had ever been seen in the south. Only the Stockton and Darlington and the Liverpool and Manchester, far away across horse-drawn England, pre-dated this, the world's first railway specifically designed for passengers rather than a mixed traffic of passengers and freight.

Small wonder that excitement was tinged with apprehension. What would be the sensation of flying faster than a running man? What would trains do to lives and businesses geared seemingly forever to reliance on the horse?

Invicta, named after Kent's county motto, and five years older than the line itself, was built in 1825 by Robert Stephenson, and is generally accepted as the earliest locomotive expressly designed for passenger working. Others of similar date had origins in goods and quarry haulage as well as people. She was the only conventional locomotive the Canterbury and Whitstable ever possessed in its own right.

Of a simple 0-4-0 wheel arrangement and superficially similar to Stephenson's more famous *Rocket*, the *Invicta* nevertheless already showed certain prophetic design improvements. With pounding outside cylinders, at the leading end, she was technically the direct forebear of every steam locomotive for the next 120 years.

At the controls was Edward Fletcher, driver throughout *Invicta*'s first months of service, later to become locomotive superintendant of a giant system as yet undreamed of, the North Eastern. Behind the engine, all in open four-wheeler 'boneshakers', rode a bevy of directors and chief engineers, each wearing a red or white rosette, manfully enduring showers of soot and sparks. Next rode the aldermen and city councillors, likewise coping with flying 'blacks', as did the well dressed ladies in carriage number three. On the fourth rode a band, playing determinedly cheerful, patriotic tunes all the way to Whitstable, occasionally marred by overblown squawks as their wagon jolted and jerked. Behind the band rode more wives and daughters, and dignitaries collectively described as 'three hundred proprietors and their families'.

All along the embankments and cuttings, even sitting atop the entrance to the only tunnel, waited curious countryfolk watching the newfangled contraption rattle past, flags streaming. Several hundred yards short of Whitstable itself, *Invicta* was uncoupled, letting the train complete its journey under triumphal 'manual traction'.

More than five years' planning lay behind the opening of this pioneer link between Canterbury and the sea. As far back as Henry VIII's day plans were mooted for improving the Stour navigation, principal outlet for agriculture and brewing, all of which came to nothing. Neither did proposals for a canal in 1811. The suggestion of 1823 to the city by William James, sometimes called 'the father of railways' rather than George Stephenson, that a line should be built northwards to the tiny village of Whitstable and a harbour be constructed there, fell on ears more attuned to practicalities.

Following James's second survey of a route (he had already once surveyed for feasibility before submitting actual schemes) and the passing of a Bill both for the railway and for Whitstable harbour, the Canterbury and Whitstable Railway Company was formed under a Local Act of 1825, the year of the Stockton and Darlington opening. Doubtful, however, of the sufficiency of James's £25,000 construction estimate, Canterbury called in George Stephenson for a second opinion, resulting in a revised estimate of £31,000. Cost escalation before building even begins is nothing new.

For several reasons James was soon replaced by Stephenson as engineer but Stephenson's reign, despite the credit heaped on him locally by posterity, lasted for exactly one visit. The rest of the layout was undertaken by his assistant, Joseph Locke, and by John Dixon.

At Whitstable a harbour was dredged out of the muddy shore to accommodate coasters and colliers, serviced from a network of sidings, an instance of a port being created entirely as an integral part of a railway system instead of, more commonly, a railway being built to serve and expand an existing harbour. Predictably, the whole scheme became known as the Oyster Line, after Whitstable's famous product.

Equally predictably, because of its very early date, the line entered railway and local history with an impressive list of 'firsts'. Chief of these was the tunnel through Tyler Hill near Canterbury, 1,012 yards long. Quite apocryphal, however, was the persistent tale that Stephenson added it purely because Canterbury citizens, enthralled with trains, insisted that no railway could seriously be called a railway without one. On the contrary, hilly terrain made it unavoidable, as well as posing other engineering challenges, such as where an 836 yard stretch had to climb a forest summit at a gradient of 1 in 31.

At either end the Tyler Hill tunnel had massive doors, securely locked at night against curiosity consumed trespassers. Those who chugged through it on opening day, smothered in soot and choked with fumes, became for their ordeal the first passengers in England to travel through a tunnel by steam operated locomotion.

On the following day the Canterbury and Whitstable became the world's first line to sustain passenger traffic in regular timetabled service by steam haulage.

In 1834 the line pioneered a new subscription fares system with the first season tickets, known as Family or Personal tickets, thereby creating a new human creature, the commuter, who would quite literally go forth and multiply until he was numbered in hundreds of thousands, descending on vast city termini into whose concourses alone both the Canterbury and Whitstable's two stations could have been dropped and almost lost. The world's earliest commuters are commemorated in a small plaque just outside the entrance of the present Canterbury West station, reading: 'Near here was the terminus of the Canterbury and Whitstable Railway, 1830. George Stephenson engineer. The world's first railway season tickets issued here 1834.'

Effects on both human mobility and trade were immediate. Passengers could cheaply and quickly join the many timetabled Thames steamers at Whitstable plying to London, Margate, Deal and even across to France and Belgium. Before anyone else south of Liverpool, they discovered how trains liberated the hitherto parochial citizen for pleasure as well as business. Produce flowed out of Kentish farms and orchards, whilst coals and chattels came in to revive Canterbury's flagging industries and create new ones.

Progress eventually overtook little *Invicta*, Robert Stephenson's original 0-4-0 locomotive. After nine years she was sold, having proved on the whole inadequate even on the easy level stretches outside Whitstable, and making hard work of the inland gradients. For a while the line was operated by stationary engines for four miles and a normal engine for the other two, or by stationary engines alone. An atmospheric traction system, then much in vogue, albeit experimentally, was also tested, on the taxing climb towards Tyler Hill tunnel.

By 1846 profits justified jettisoning the original four-wheel 'boneshaker' wagons, open to smuts, sparks and all weathers, in favour of covered wagons, far from comfortable by later Victorian standards but nonetheless a great improvement for passengers. Within two decades the line had also firmly established itself from the freight aspect. 'From Canterbury there is a short branch to Whitstable . . . Whitstable Bay is frequented by a considerable number of colliers, from which Canterbury and the surrounding places are supplied with coal', observed a copious gazetter of every railway extant during the year of the 1851 Great Exhibition, referring to the line's chief goods traffic.

Halfway through the nineteenth century the company was bought out by the South Eastern Railway and reverted to conventional traction. Because of limited overhead clearance in Tyler Hill tunnel, built to take only the small *Invicta*'s thin smokestack, South Eastern and Southern locomotives allocated to Canterbury and Whitstable working were perforce adapted with a shorn-down chimney and lowered driving cab roof. The R1 class 0-6-0 T's, often pictured working this route, were the chief example.

The line was absorbed at the great amalgamation

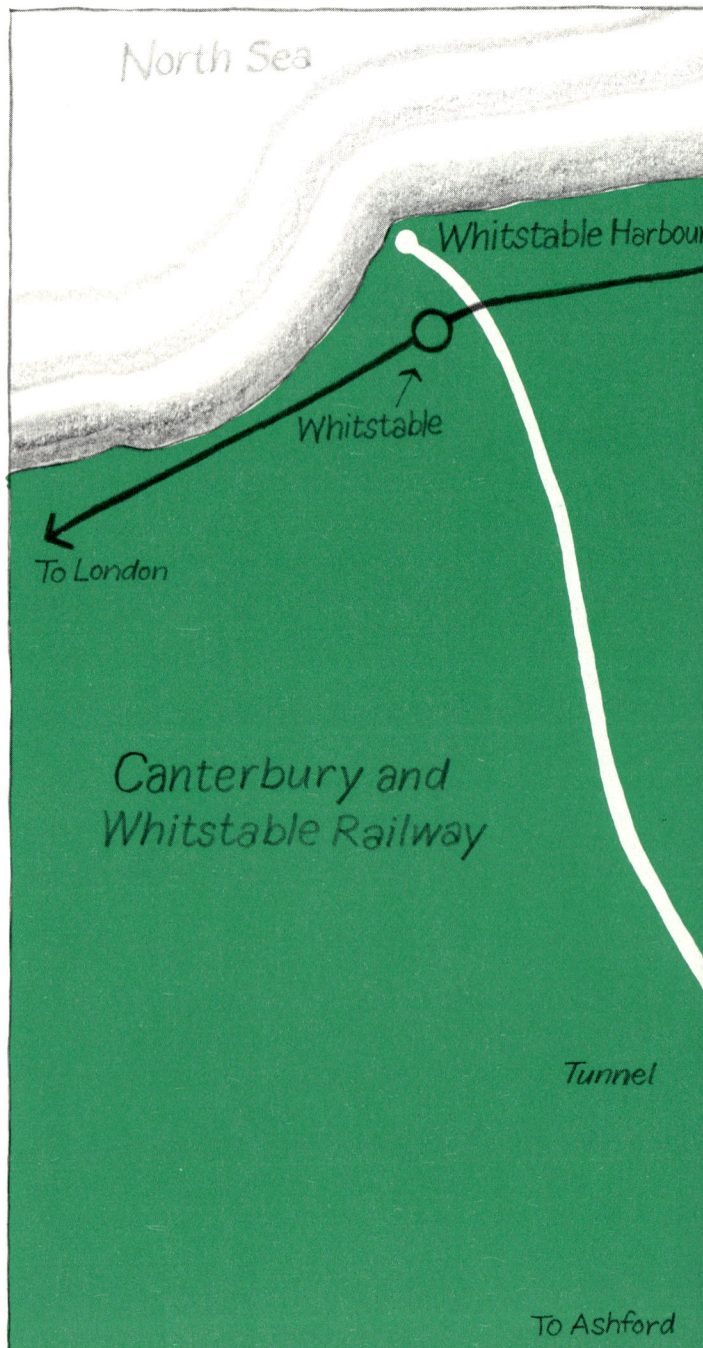

into the Southern Railway and ultimately, by then reduced to freight-only working, into British Rail, who also became owners of Whitstable harbour before selling it to Whitstable Council for the meagre sum of £12,500 – half the cost of a small house in Whitstable today.

Altogether passenger services lasted almost exactly a century, from May 1830 to January 1, 1931, when passenger trains ceased running, improved bus services and the first upsurge of private motoring having destroyed the trains' monopoly.

Freight traffic continued another twenty years or more until December 1, 1952. Even then, full closure proved premature. The next January, Whitstable came to bless the disused railway, when the entire town, grown to great residential size, was marooned and cut off from outside supplies by disastrous floods, and was almost unreachable by road.

The line, mostly embanked and therefore above flood level, was hastily reopened to bring in coal – its original prime freight of a hundred years ago – supplies, and materials for urgent repairs. This service continued for several months before another and final

Plaque to the world's first railway commuters, Canterbury West Station. *M V Searle*

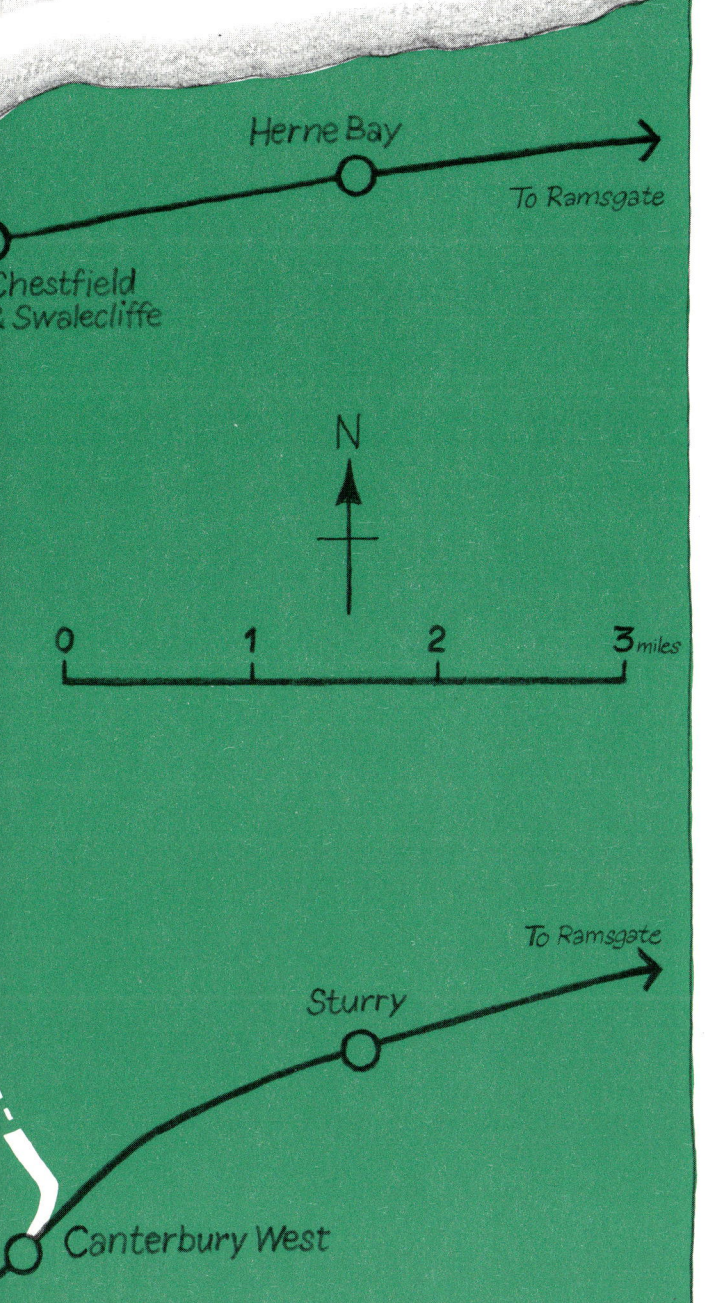

closure, since made almost certainly irreversible by demolition of the bridge carrying the Canterbury and Whitstable over the later London–Ramsgate main line. All remaining permanent way was lifted, leaving only grassy ways for walkers to adopt.

What else is left of this pioneer railway? Quite a lot. At Canterbury West are the First Commuters plaque, and the disused Whitstable bay complete at time of writing with buffers and rusted metals half embedded in overgrowth, a repository for thoughtless travellers' litter and thoughtful sentimentalists' memories. They still snake towards the points and main line. At Tyler Hill survives the old tunnel, half a mile long, boarded up but sometimes penetrated by local university students and others. Nearby stands, still inhabited, the engine man's cottage as a memento of the stationary engine period. The course of the line itself, but for the Whitstable bridge, is easily traceable, including the long embanked descent to the harbour. On Canterbury West station approach is another reminder, a public house inevitably named *The Railway*, whose sign is the red painted *Invicta* in her heyday. An impressive bridge of 1935 carrying Thanet Way over the lost line remains; a few cut stones high above Station Road at Whitstable identify a halt that was added to encourage new traffic; and a shop in South Street still trades as 'The Halt Stores', thirty years after the said halt was abandoned. As we go to press a miniature railway is under discussion, utilising a tiny fragment of trackbed at the seaside resort end of Whitstable.

For a time, eternally surrounded by tourists, stood little *Invicta* herself, preserved – totally exposed to the elements – outdoors in the Dane John Gardens of her home town, regularly repainted the familiar dull red. In 1979/80 she was externally restored at York, for return to Canterbury in a special indoor setting.

In her technical specification and early birth date she was the ancestor of all the great latter day locomotives that roared through Canterbury, up to the great *Battle of Britain*, *West Country* and *Merchant Navy* classes. In *Invicta* and the Oyster Line, Southern steam had its very beginnings.

Opening of the Canterbury and Whitstable Railway, 1830. One of the best known early railway prints, T M Baynes' lithograph showing the final stretch towards Whitstable, near where the main London–Ramsgate line subsequently crossed under it at right angles.

Kent Coast main line express runs underneath a bridge of the Canterbury and Whitstable branch. An unusual shot showing both lines occupied during the branch's last freight-only days.
R S Joby

Invicta in Dane John Gardens, Canterbury. A plaque inside the railings briefly recounted the history of this pioneer line.
M V Searle

The same bridge, shorn off today after closure of the C&W ↗ branch, filmed from a main line electric express in 1977. Whitstable station platform at extreme left.
M V Searle

Abandoned C&W embankment cut down for pushing through of a new minor estate road, seen in 1978.
M V Searle

Stirling R1 class 0-6-0 T No. 1147, as rebuilt with pop safety valves, new smokebox and chimney. On Whitstable branch, in about 1941.
NCB

Entering Tyler Hill tunnel.
R S Joby

CHAPTER 2

Two Grand Dreams

PORT VICTORIA & ALL HALLOWS

A completely new and profitable seaside resort, closer than any other to populous London, and therefore hopefully a serious rival to Southend; a deepwater international ocean terminal expected to lure passenger and freight traffic away from Dover and London . . . these were the ambitious dreams of both Victorian and twentieth century planners which centred on a spit of undeveloped and remote marshland projecting into the Thames Estuary, then inhabited only by birds and scattered countrymen. They would be born entirely of railways. Additionally, an upsurge of industry and agricultural production was envisaged for the countryside traversed by the lines.

Thus, the story of the twin-pronged, fork-shaped system out of Gravesend to Port Victoria and the Isle of Grain, and later onwards to All Hallows, is an unusual reversal of most railway sagas. More commonly, trains would come as the result of existing coal, agricultural or manufacturing industries, or embryonic seaside resorts, that were ripe for expansion given this new form of rapid communication.

Down in Kent the trains came first, into an expanse of nothingness, where neither stick nor stone of a port or resort existed, introduced with a Victorian confidence that both would develop satisfactorily around the rails.

The magnate behind Port Victoria, earlier of the two schemes, was Sir Edward Watkin, whose long term plans extended right across Europe, into London via the prospective port, and thence by direct railways right up to the industrial Midlands.

Proximity to commercial London was the kingpin of this new proposal, twelve miles nearer even than Sheerness at barely forty miles. The Medway provided deep anchorage at all tidal states, given quite short jetties. London's notorious fogs, imprisoning ships for days, were less dense downstream, another powerful factor; trains could carry goods to town following a ship's arrival, whereas in fogbound Woolwich they lay untouched.

In 1882, after months of railway company rivalry, ambition became fact, with completion of this Hundred of Hoo Railway. A new wooden pier carried the line forward over the water to a small terminal station.

Opening day brought the customary flurry of flag-waving, self-congratulation, and public jubilation. '250 ladies and gentlemen assembled in a marquee where a most sumptuous repast was provided', it was recorded of one lineside spot never to see much excitement for the rest of its operative life, Sharnal Street. Patriotism being at its Land-of-Hope-and-Glory zenith, the terminus was named, without further ceremony, Port Victoria; an imperious name for one timber jetty supporting one modest station, and a few miles of rails and sleepers terminating at a mournful riverside.

Initially, trains served regular ferries across to Sheerness, a drastic shortening of this journey on which hopes of early revenue were pinned. However, wider transoceanic operations than those of the ferries *Myleta* and *Edward Williams* occupied ruling minds. 'It is no secret that the Hundred of Hoo line is being constructed to serve a more ambitious purpose than merely to supply local needs' wrote a correspondent in the opening year; 'It is the intention of the directors to establish a service of steamers with the Port of Flushing'. This European connection would transform insignificant Port Victoria into 'an entrepot of vast importance'.

For passengers' convenience an ostentatious harbourside hotel was envisaged, but initially an all-wooden huddle of rooms seemed sufficient. This, with the disproportionately grand name of Port Victoria Hotel, was never actually replaced, a ramshackle bungaloid contraption which, incredibly, outlasted both port and rail until 1952.

Expansion efforts continued with blandishments to the Zeeland Steamship Company, followed in 1885 by a cleverly contrived interview with the Belgian king, which it was hoped would lead to an Ostend service. It did – but Tilbury grabbed it and kept it. Attempts to steal Erith's prosperous trade in imported locomotive coal likewise foundered.

Arrival of the powerful Royal Corinthian Yacht Club in 1890 revived hopes of grandeur. The railway was the attraction, enabling rich members to sail by day and return by train to their London clubs in early evening.

Visions for the intervening lineside districts also fared badly. Halts were opened in 1900 at High Halstow, Beluncle and Middle Stoke, but attracted only handfuls of passengers and a few crates of farm produce. Only a major uralite works, nearer Gravesend, fulfilled the railway's industrial hopes, and continued to the end.

Trains connecting with excursion steamers brought fair trade, but more prestigious was Queen Victoria's adoption of her namesake port for embarkation on the Royal Yacht. Often the lavish Royal Train trundled onto the jetty to transfer a regal entourage to the *Victoria and Albert*. Her patronage was based on the very property that ultimately was the line's downfall, its remoteness; ever mourning Albert, she loved the peace and privacy of this scarcely developed spot, served only by rail without even one road. Other monarchs followed Victoria's lead, notably the German Kaiser whose yacht *Hohenzollern* tied up here while he took the train for London; he recognised the place with a handsome commemorative gift to the little Isle of Grain church. Royal trains continued until 1913, when the Norwegian royal family arrived. Victoria herself, ageing, made her last appearance being lowered from the train in a bath chair and hoisted by crane, still in the chair, straight to the yacht's deck. Railwaymen watched half fearful, half amused, but dared not snigger.

Fortunes temporarily improved when rival Queenborough pier burned down, the Flushing mailboats being re-routed for four years. European travellers poured through the tiny pier station for the shortest boat-train run between any port and London. Decline thereafter truly set in. *Victoria and Albert* came no more, and the wooden railway jetty became deeply gnawed by destructive marine worms. Encasing the piles in concrete was of no avail. Attempts were made to sell both port and railway, and the Admiralty was offered it as a coaling stage. The Admiralty declined. The pompous Corinthian yachtsmen departed for Burnham-on-Crouch. World War I was imminent. In 1915 the minelayer *Princess Irene* blew up, and flying iron chunks slashed into the rotting wood, ruining the already rickety pierhead.

Peace brought a new neighbour whose significance was not fully appreciated, a small oil refinery, the first industrial construction to bear out the original belief that this railway in itself could attract industry, the site being chosen on account of the existing line. By 1931 passenger trains no longer rumbled onto the pier itself, declared totally unable to support them, and a replacement platform was built on the landward side, with a rudimentary shelter extravagantly described as a station. Port Victoria was slowly and inevitably dying. The Victorians believed that birth and death cancelled out each other. So it was with the Isle of Grain railways. As the Port Victoria line languished, a second railway-linked development was gestating. A new Westcliff-on-Sea, directly facing that resort across the sea, was to be created on a virginal strip of foreshore consisting only of a delightful beach, miniature cliffs, and ozone-rich air. Build a new railway, reasoned the planners, and the envisaged town would ripple out from the station into roads of boarding houses, chapels and pubs. All Hallows-on-Sea would be its name, from the inland All Hallows village.

On Whit Sunday, 1932, the first trainload of trippers puffed in, along a new branch line running north and ruler-straight off the old Port Victoria line. No seaside beach stood nearer London, not even Southend, a point duly emphasized in railway posters.

The station welcomed tiny two-car sets of carriages behind modest tank engines. For many years it was served by the ubiquitous H-class 0-4-4 locomotives that continued to the end. Yet it already had the air of a terminus, as if anticipating becoming the nucleus of a town, with its capacious all-over roof for sheltering swarms of arrivals and baggage, and its long platforms. Unusually, the signal box stood on the platform.

Encouragingly, people came even if there *was* no town, lured by newness and the sea. Bigger things, they understood, were imminent. All Hallows Estate Company poured £20,000 into the railway (some £500,000 in present day value), and made generous land gifts, for development. Additionally, a miniature railway ran right down to the beach, and the most prominent landmark for miles was built, the British Pilot pub, recognising the fact that Londoners expected a pint with their picnics. Before more could happen, war broke out again. Port Victoria briefly perked up with searchlights on its half derelict pier, but All Hallows went to sleep for the duration.

After the war, the practicability of both the original schemes was discussed afresh, in totally different contexts. At Grain a new oil refinery of staggering size was proposed – and built – on the basis of the same facilities as the failed Port Victoria: deepwater anchorages, and access to London. Derelict Port Victoria was bought by the Kent Oil Refinery, lock, stock, and mouldering barrel, including the still extant 'temporary' hotel and rotting railway property. All buildings were demolished, but a section of line was retained to serve the works.

Linked with the huge refinery was a development plan, to turn All Hallows into a town of 25,000 inhabitants served by an electrified and modernised railway which would also remove the refinery's growing concern as to sparks from steam trains. Not the original planned resort, but a dormitory town for refinery workers. Again, it was not to be. Workers declining to live within sight-and smell-of their jobs could afford, with the phenomenal rise in personal motoring in the 1950s, to favour Chatham instead. Prospects of an electrified line were abandoned. Still undeveloped, All Hallows reverted to a day trippers' and caravanners' centre. Summer brought more and more behind the usual 0-4-4 Ts and such occasional visitors as the Qls, to open up ever expanding legions of caravans.

One train ingeniously served both All Hallows, due north, and Grain, due east, by virtue of the simple Stoke Crossing, two miles inland, enabling it to run out from Gravesend; on from Stoke to Grain; back to Stoke; up to All Hallows; and again back to Stoke and home. A minuscule smoke plume marked its marshland progress for walkers on the sea wall, enabling them exactly to time their return to the station.

Yet again change was in the air. The continuing upsurge in private motoring throughout England destroyed the trippers' century-old reliance on trains. Beeching's axe was poised over Kent's picturesque carriages and steam locomotives, and fell with a resounding chop.

In 1961 the final passenger train puffed away from All Hallows. The Port Victoria to Grain Crossing line had already been closed to passengers for ten years. The remaining section from Grain Crossing to near Gravesend also closed to passengers in 1961.

What remains? At Kent Oil Refinery, vast expanses of shining pipes and drums, and great jetties receiving giant tankers; between two of these, like a mouse crushed between an elephant's paws, a tiny offshore curve of rotted stumps is visible only at low tide; all that survives of Port Victoria railway jetty. But locally and coloquially these modern berths are still spoken of as Port Victoria.

Behind All Hallows' refreshingly green seafront, rank upon rank of caravans and chalets, some highly elaborate, are approached through well trimmed gardens. Conventional residential development is expanding back along the Chatham road. The booking office and waiting rooms of the disused station serve two or three large camps as a general store with stockrooms, selling food and necessities, the only shop in this area. The outer platform beyond the buildings has been bulldozed, roughly chopped off. Wooden shacks selling sweets and tobacco to arriving passengers survive, boarded up; their trade died with the railway.

The conspicuous locomotive watering tower and tank, visible through binoculars across the sea from Southend, is thoughtfully preserved, embanked with flowers and marooned among ranks of expensive mobile homes, sprawling over the trackbed site. A single planted row of frail saplings along this camp's outside edge marks where the railway fencing ran off into the marshes. Tracks were lifted to Stoke Junction many years ago.

Beyond Stoke the 'handle' of the two-pronged Hoo 'fork' exists as a ghost line, flanked by ruined station sites; in 1977 the author arrived too late to photograph Sharnal Street, finding bulldozers in the act of munching the last bricks. Past these old halts a fair number of freight and oil trains rumble irregularly from KOR, an infuriating sight to working residents of scattered villages who dream of persuading BR to create easy rail commuting for them. If part of the line takes oil why not stockbrokers and bankers? Like so many things, a railway becomes highly desirable when it is closed.

During 1977 Medway commuters began campaigning, with newspaper support, for reopening of at least part; perhaps as far as Hoo. Concerned about the future relevance of this chapter, I approached BR for a ruling on possible reopening. The answer was definitive: 'The passenger service between Gravesend-All Hallows-Grain was withdrawn because it was uneconomic. We are not aware of *any* development which would justify its restoration.' Scattered communities supporting too few genuinely regular London-bound travellers in practice, rather than in the cloud-cuckooland of petitioning; and astronomical costs of improving track and signalling, new rolling stock, electrification to passenger standard, and costly rebuilding of halts used only morning and evening, are but the

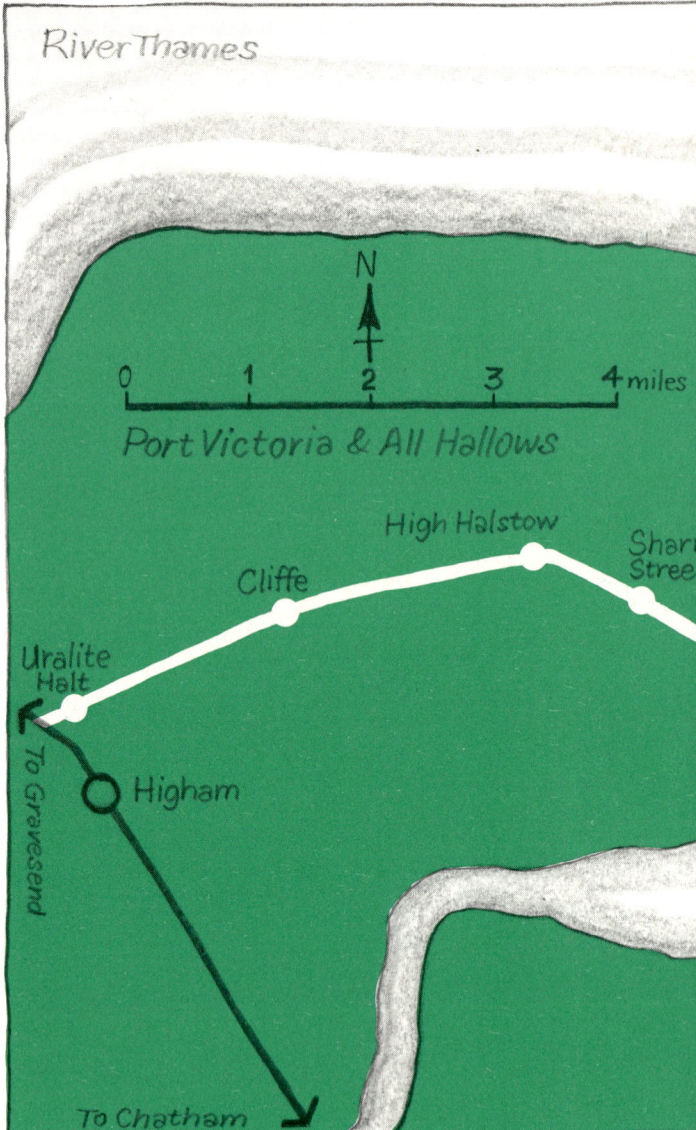

principal reasons behind official disinclination to outlay 'several million pounds' on restoring train services for about six out of every twenty four hours, on a line presently suitable only for freight on part of its length. Only total local authority financing and support, it appears, could persuade BR to think again.

Railborne seasidedom lies outside all three parties' interests. All Hallows grows apace, but some 9 per cent of campers and trippers arrive by car, the rest by excellent bus services. Early in 1982 it became highly likely that the Isle of Grain refinery itself would soon close.

The delightful ride through miles of cornfields to All Hallows behind an old-fashioned large-domed tank engine seems quite definitely a past pleasure. Even a ghost train cannot now reach the terminus, short of running right through the lounges of chalets built across the trackway.

Port Victoria in 1930, one year before closure, with former SECR Wainwright 0-4-4-T No. A311.
H C Casserley

All Hallows station as a shop in 1977; note scales visible on inside counter.
M V Searle

The big old water tank preserved and maintained among the holiday chalets now entirely covering the All Hallows station approaches, seen in 1977.
M V Searle

Stumps of Port Victoria station jetty, visible only at low water off KOR Jetty No. 8. This curved line is all that remains of the jetty branch, demolished for the extension of the Kent Oil Refinery.
KOR

Southern A311 at Port Victoria in April 1930 with train about to depart for Gravesend, taken shortly before closure of station and approach due to instability.
H C Casserley

All Hallows to Gravesend train approaching Stoke Junction. The spirit of marsh, sky and a tiny train, so familiar to All Hallows day trippers, is beautifully captured in this shot of November 1961.
G Daniels

All Hallows station entrance as day visitors best remember it. June 1960.
G Daniels

Refilling at the tank completed, No. 31512 prepares to shunt back into All Hallows in September 1960. The tank is preserved today.
G Daniels

Sharnal Street, one of the few stations as opposed to halts on the Grain/All Hallows branches, seen in 1960. Now totally demolished, but track at this point is retained for freight only.
G Daniels

CHAPTER 3

Sheep Line
ISLE OF SHEPPEY

All Hallows, Lee-on-the-Solent, Selsey and Leysdown never loomed large on any map of Britain's booming nineteenth- and early twentieth-century seaside resorts. Holidaymakers living outside the southern Home Counties have often never heard of most of them. None seems likely now to seriously rival the major tripper towns.

Yet, had a quarter of the dreams of their various speculative promoters come true, All Hallows should have been a high class Southend; Lee a new Bournemouth; Selsey a second Brighton, and Leysdown a minor Margate.

Of the two Kentish examples All Hallows, as has been mentioned, ended as a pleasant caravan and chalet centre surrounded by green grass instead of concrete, seeing its best days after trains deserted it. Its neighbour some twelve miles away, Leysdown-on-Sea, mirrored almost exactly All Hallows' history of grand vision that never materialised. Its initial growth was also to depend on the railway and once again its final use is as a caravanners' and campers' retreat.

Both these places were originally conceived as arising from similar countryside, on island peninsulas jutting into the Thames Estuary; All Hallows on the Isle of Grain north of Rochester, Leysdown at the extremity of the next island downstream, the Isle of Sheppey. Both were aimed at trainloads of spending Londoners, All Hallows automatically attracting a generally peace-loving type, whilst Leysdown lured an earthier East Ender or South Londoner, to whose descendants it is still 'Lays-dahn', plus a small contrasted group of retired couples preferring an undeveloped new settlement to the then gout-ridden cliffs of Folkestone.

Those early characteristics cling on today. All Hallows sails and enjoys quiet ball games, while Leysdown plays Bingo. Common to both places was their origin in the minds of speculators dedicated to prising profit from virgin beaches, and whose plans were reliant almost entirely on railways. They believed that cash automatically flowed at the wave of a magic wand held by a fairy godmother dressed as a railway developer. Speculative builders were certainly to adopt this philosophy in following the railways into the Isle of Sheppey.

In addition, so far as Sheppey was concerned, it was felt that extra revenue could be expected from the island's numerous farms, once these were persuaded that a rail outlet could bring their produce more quickly to market. Cattle and sheep movements were to be an integral part of the new line's workings, with special sidings provided even at the remotest stations. Sheppey, railway promoters reminded themselves, meant Isle of Sheep.

Sheppey Light Railway, operationally and in outward appearances, was very little different from a normal branch line. It came into being under an Order one year before the nineteenth century ended, and was designed to cross the entire low lying island from west to east off the Sheerness line, branching at Queenborough. On a map its course appears aimless, but in truth it was carefully planned, taking in part of Sheerness, a possible new dormitory town (Minster) and rich agricultural countryside, en route to Leysdown. These would hopefully keep it solvent when summer crowds deserted the latter resort.

Two schools of thought joined battle over prospective courses for the initial two miles; one favoured departure out of Queenborough, then more thriving than it is today, and the other a junction at Sheerness, convenient for its important Naval dockyard and, for civilians, connecting with ferries across the Medway to Port Victoria and thence to London, cutting some twelve miles off a journey otherwise made via mainland Sittingbourne. Compromise was finally reached. The SLR – colloquially the Sheppey Light – terminated at Queenborough, but about two years later an electric tramway was constructed north-west to the London Chatham and Dover's Sheerness station, across marshland from the Sheppey Light Railway's Sheerness East.

Other stations as first built provided the barest minimum of facilities as, apart from Eastchurch and Leysdown, all were erected with an eye to economy. Wagonloads of disused sleepers, wrenched up as outworn by main lines, were transported down to Sheppey for forming fronts of platforms, placed upright and side by side. They showed signs of rotting within a few short years, dragging platforms out of true as they warped and subsided. Cheap open wooden trellis fencing fared the same against harsh marshland winters. Replacement of the former by concrete platforms, and of the latter by iron railings, became essential. Sheppey, trying to save money, merely found itself doing the same job twice, at double expense.

At country halts accommodation was usually a corrugated iron shelter, resembling a comfortless bicycle shed. Initially, no platform at all was planned for some halts, the promoters seriously debating whether their customers would clamber up from ground level, by means of an additional carriage step.

The only ambitious plan for this economically-minded line, without one bridge and with only the gentlest gradients, was for a railway-owned hotel for all those holidaymakers the promoters saw descending on Leysdown once trains had made it accessible. None but a dreamer or a Victorian developer would have visualised a counterpart of the luxurious Royal Station Hotel at York or the Charing Cross Hotel in London, in such a spot. Had it ever materialised, one suspects that the Railway Hotel of Leysdown would have been, rather, a cousin of the wooden bungaloid contraption across the Medway whose only grand feature was its name, Port Victoria Hotel.

Sheppey Light Railway – without hotel – opened on August 1, 1901, bringing the island's rail routes to three: this one across to Leysdown; northwards to Sheerness; and a little branch serving the then busy Queenborough Pier, built in 1876 for Flushing-bound steamers. Fares were fixed at a pricey 3d. a mile First; 2d. Second; and the old Parliamentary rate of 1d. Third.

Next year the ambitious directors entered another field of speculation, over-enthusiastically and prematurely as usual. They aimed at attracting London commuter traffic without considering how unlikely was the average city man to make a two hour morning journey, with up to two changes. A new station was opened at East Minster to this end, cashing in on the efforts of estate agents dedicated to making Minster a dormitory suburb.

In conjunction with purveyors of muddy, virgin building plots, the SLR laid on Viewers' Specials for buyers, much as hawkers of Costa del Sol villa plots charter aircraft today. Special trains were an astute move, giving buyers a false impression of comfortable through-train commuter life between seaside homes and London, instead of the wearisome reality of crawling just two stops by light railway, changing at Queenborough, and possibly again at Sittingbourne into the real London train.

Sheep on this Sheep Isle fared distinctively better than business men. They travelled 'through' by wagon, from sidings built into even the smallest halts for attracting lucrative agricultural traffic. Only by guiltily sneaking aboard a Flushing boat-train at Queenborough could anyone wearing spats instead of trotters reach London in under two hours. And then, only just.

Slightly better served were travellers from Sheerness East, again a hopeful dormitory development. After 1903 they had two alternatives; SLR to Queenborough, or their new electric tramway to the London Chatham and Dover Railway's terminus at Sheerness, roughly equidistant.

Early SLR locomotion was no more distinguished than the stations, though adequate enough for a rural railway. From the Brighton company was bought one of the useful little *Terriers* (No. 654, *Waddon*, renumbered as 751 by her new owners), already thirty years old at transfer. She was affectionately dubbed *Little Titch* on Sheppey, after the much loved music hall performer of that name.

1905 brought forth one of the hybrid railmotors much favoured on leisurely country branches, a cross between train and bus wherein engine and carriage were combined as one unit.

As on other country lines introducing railmotors, economical little vehicles ideally suited to branch working, new halts were opened at Brambledown Halt and Harty Road to serve communities which had hitherto been too remote. The sign boards at Harty Road at least told non-local arrivals the truth; this halt stood beside the road *to* Harty, a handful of cottages and one inn about three miles distant along bus-less lanes. Even today this hamlet is one of the loneliest spots in Kent. Railmotors lasted only five years, and were replaced by an SECR tank locomotive in 1910, but the new halts remained.

Contrast was Sheppey's keynote as World War I approached; utterly remote Harty; Minster of the developers' largely unfulfilled dreams; Leysdown of the tripper take-over; naval Sheerness; and bustling Queenborough on its own miniature branch, playing a role now stolen by Sheerness with its 'South Eastern and Chatham Railway/Royal Mail Express Service to the Continent . . . Queenborough–Flushing'. Many a travel guide carried that advertisement for Queenborough, a holiday gateway if not an objective in itself; but few included Leysdown. Though 'South for Sunshine' exhortations lauded such lesser hopefuls as Lydd, Hythe, New Romney and Littlestone-on-Sea alongside Margate and Folkestone, the nearest they came to Leysdown was Sittingbourne on the Kent mainland, itself no resort.

In 1917 the short lived tramway from Sheerness East to the main Sheerness station quietly expired after only fourteen seasons' service. Residents were forced either to use the light railway or take to the roads.

Day-tripping and weekending reached a climax with the cheerful 1920s, as more workers became entitled to holiday pay – but not enough to venture far afield – and Bank Holidays reached their peak.

Old plans for cashing in on this trade were revived. Ambitious as ever, despite sometimes shaky finances, the local railway company announced a new hotel for Leysdown to cater for a hopelessly impractical 1,200 people; more than the biggest established resort could support, with the exception perhaps of London itself.

All that the Londoners descending on this beach wanted, or could afford, were a rapidly expanding colony of tin huts, wooden shacks, converted buses, caravans and chalets. For transport they showed a marked preference for little black Fords and spluttering motorcycles, rather than the Sheppey Light.

Some, of course, did arrive by rail, enough to keep the trains in business; between the two wars they were faithfully served by small 0-4-4 Ts, generally of class R1, first under SECR ownership and latterly in Southern livery. Southern's No. 697 was among the regular workers here. The stock was undistinguished but interesting; two of the withdrawn railmotors shorn of their built-in motive power and adapted as normal carriages.

With Leysdown's character established, the Southern, who absorbed the SLR in 1923, thought again of entry into the accommodation field. Profit, it was believed, was still to be made as long as realistic provision was made for the type of holidaymaker who came here; happy-go-lucky, often Cockney, slightly impecunious, but dedicated to extracting a bob's worth of amusement from every hard-earned tanner

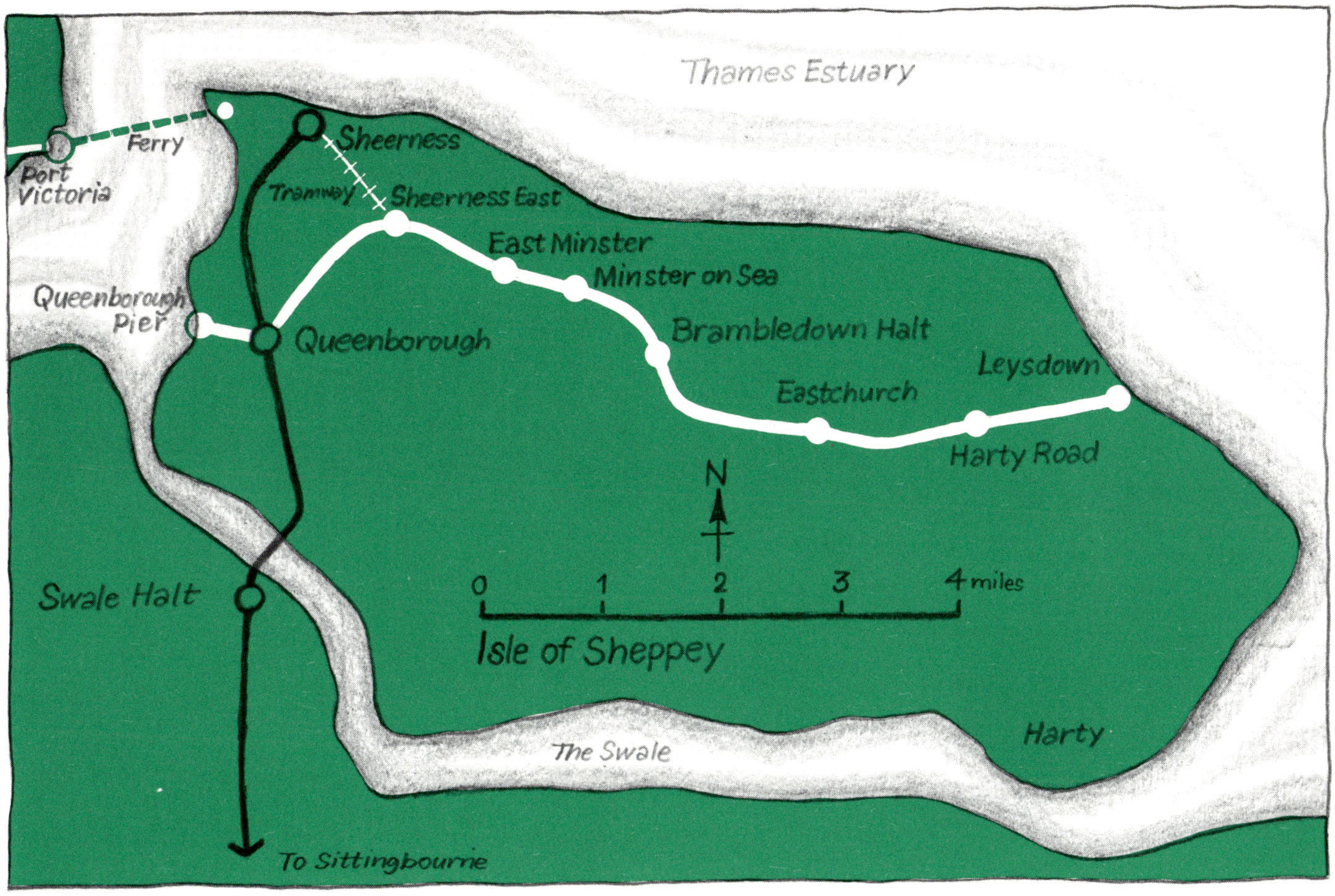

Queenborough station in 1950, showing how its appearance has since changed. The waiting room block, now seemingly at the back edge of the platform, was then a central feature.
E Course

Queenborough station showing buildings formerely in centre of double platform, and now apparently at the edge, as are the seats. Leysdown side, overgrown, at right. *M V Searle*

he forked out. A formal hotel was not his natural environment, even if he could afford it.

Much more practicable, therefore, was the latest proposal, a railway owned holiday camp adjacent to the station. If families did not come by train, at least they would pay for sleeping on railway property. Had not another war intervened before ideas could become reality, this scheme might well have succeeded.

When World War II ended, a new generation had sprung up; half of it somewhat contemptuous of the Leysdowns of this world compared with the lure of the emerging 'foreign' holiday; the other half content with England, but in their post-war affluence no longer satisfied with modestly provided caravan and chalet colonies. In travel, too, they demanded improvement. The former flow of small cars and motor-cycles expanded into legions of bigger cars, and special long distance coaches were sent down from London direct to the Leysdown camps, throughout the summer. More and more came to open up larger and more solid holiday homes than their parents knew, but few of them bothered to change at Queenborough onto a slow island train and enjoy the pleasures of leisured trundling across refreshing open marshland white with thousands of sheep and lambs. Speed was the god of a lemming-like motoring race, rushing ever faster even in seeking relaxation.

Minster, too, rapidly grew away from a railway which had always passed too distantly on the far side of that hilltop town. Minster grew, as earlier planners predicted, but around motor roads and buses climbing up to the place itself, diverted into developing estates of expensive houses paradoxically facing unmade ear-

Leysdown showing platform raised on disused mainline sleepers, visibly sinking, and fenced with rotting wooden trellis. *Lens of Sutton*

Brambles encroach on present Up platform at Queenborough from deserted Leysdown bay on right. A small building erected since closure is also now on the derelict side of the fencing. *M V Searle*

Leysdown with replacement concrete platform and iron railings. But the fragile wooden seat in middle distance remains. *Lens of Sutton*

thy roads, deep with winter mud. East Minster, its more speculative neighbour, drifted towards bungalow growth, for weekenders, retirement and local residence, again reliant on buses and cars rather than trains.

Agriculture, always expected to be a financial mainstay, followed suit, sending sheep and cattle by lorry instead of patronising the convenient sidings installed at almost every halt, however small, for farmers' benefit. Supplies in general became definitely road-borne, adding to the financial problems of a little line which had rarely paid.

The war had been over only five years when the old 0-4-4 tanks made their last passenger runs on December 4, 1950. Only the Sittingbourne–Queenborough–Sheerness line remained, solvent enough to justify electrification and improvement. To accommodate eight-car electric trains, composed of two four-car units, platforms were lengthened. At Queenborough, while the Sheppey Light half of the Up platform sank under grass and weeds, additional platform length was constructed from its northward end. The original double platform, where shelters, seats and lamp posts formerly occupied the middle to serve both sides, became only single, with those installations now appearing along the back against a fence. New outbuildings geared to electrification arose, straddling both halves; but now they, too, are on the wrong side of that fence between yesterday and today.

Beyond Queenborough the course of the Sheppey Light track curves away across open country, easily discernable; but all the former SLR stations have vanished, some completely into oblivion.

Harty Road and its cattle siding might never have been, nor tiny Brambledown Halt. Queenborough Pier branch closed as far back as 1914.

Briefly a 2ft guage so-called Sheppey Light Railway was launched as an attraction over a short stretch at Leysdown. Rushton Hornby diesels of 1936 vintage were used, but it did not last long.

Leysdown station site is a car park. It seems symbolic of the fate of branch lines everywhere, caught up by the motoring age and unable to retaliate with Inter-City speed.

Southern No. 697 on Sheppey Light Railway.
Lens of Sutton

Eastchurch station, with points and sidings, in contrast to the more primitive Sheppey halts.
Lens of Sutton

Railway Routes

SOUTH EASTERN & CHATHAM RAILWAY.

ROYAL MAIL EXPRESS SERVICES
TO THE
CONTINENT
VIA

Dover	Folkestone	Queenboro'	Dover	Folkestone
Calais	Boulogne	Flushing	Ostend	Flushing

LONDON & PARIS IN LESS THAN **7 HOURS**

BY THE
SHORT SEA AND MAIL ROUTES

Turbine Steamers cross the Channel daily between Dover and Calais, also between Folkestone and Boulogne.

PULLMAN CARS IN CONTINENTAL SERVICES BETWEEN LONDON, FOLKESTONE, AND DOVER.

FRIDAY, SATURDAY, and SUNDAY to MONDAY or TUESDAY TICKETS
ARE ISSUED FROM
CHARING CROSS (West End), WATERLOO (Junction), CANNON STREET, & LONDON BRIDGE
TO
Bexhill, Canterbury West, Deal, Dover, Folkestone Central, Folkestone Junction, Hastings, Hythe, Lydd, Maidstone, Margate, Littlestone-on-Sea, Ramsgate, Rye, St. Leonards (Warrior Square), Sandgate, Sanaling Junction, Sandwich, Shorncliffe, Southborough, Tonbridge, Tunbridge Wells, Walmer, and Whitstable.

ALSO FROM
VICTORIA (West End), HOLBORN VIADUCT, and ST. PAUL'S to
Bexhill, Birchington, Broadstairs, Canterbury East, Deal, Dover, Faversham, Hastings, Herne Bay, Maidstone, Margate, Ramsgate, St. Leonards, Sheerness, Sittingbourne (for Milton), Tunbridge Wells, Walmer, Westgate, and Whitstable.

For Fares and further particulars respecting the Cheap Tickets, see Excursion Programme.   FRANCIS H. DENT, *General Manager.*

Series, 1913-14.]

Harty Road halt 'serving' (at three miles distance) Sheppey's remotest part.
Lens of Sutton

← Queenborough's great days. Its once flourishing Flushing service (now revived, but from Sheerness) is here advertised by the SECR in 1913. Both Queenborough Pier and its service loop vanished decades ago.
Ward Lock Ltd

Ruins of Leysdown station in April 1956.
NCB

SR No. 1021 (4-4-0, class B1) with set of ex-SECR railcars at Leysdown in 1936.
Locomotive & General

← The lonely peace of Sheppey, despite the presence of one house and a car, is demonstrated in this shot of a SLR rural halt.
Lens of Sutton

Easygoing Brambledown Halt on the last day of operations in 1950. Obligingly the crew wait for the photographer to climb back aboard.
E Course

Arrival at Leysdown, December 2, 1950. *E Course*

Leysdown, general view. *E Course*

Leysdown train arriving at Queenborough on last day of steaming, 1950.
E Course

CHAPTER 4

The Shrinking Tunnel

RAMSGATE TUNNEL RAILWAY

We remain in Kent for the curious instances of a standard gauge line that physically shrank before becoming lost, and of a station now entered by hundreds of thousands every summer, but never to catch trains.

Few holidaymakers realise, when patronising the imposing amusement hall 'Pleasurama', at the centre of Ramsgate's golden beach, that they are in fact inside the former Ramsgate Sands (or Ramsgate Harbour) station. Those, more local, who do know, still bitterly regret its loss to railway usage over fifty years ago, replaced by a mainline station about one and a half miles inland – a prime reason why many day excursionists prefer Margate, with its station in sight of the beach, and rarely go to its sister resort.

Ramsgate Sands, actually alongside the sands, was opened by the London Chatham and Dover in 1863, a vast improvement for passengers and harbour goods on the rival South Eastern station, again far inland. But usefulness was achieved at a high price in labour, requiring tunnelling downwards from clifftop to sea level for nearly a mile, inside heavy chalk, at a steep angle of 1 in 75. Only at the last moment, half a minute's run from the platforms, did trains burst with a roar from this 1,124 yard long tunnel, one of the finest sights on the coast.

Amalgamation of both LCDR and SER into the Southern precipitated the building of the present Ramsgate station, farther than ever from the seafront. The LCDR/SER approaches were joined and the town run-in was smoothed near the tunnel's upper entrance. Southern, unconcerned that families bound for the seaside wanted to land near the sea, closed the splendid older terminus at the water's edge.

It was not, however, destroyed. Taken over commercially, it became the resort's chief amusement centre for many generations, under various names, initially including a funfair and small zoo. The tunnel was also turned into a public amusement. Inside the standard gauge double-track tunnel, metals were lifted and replaced by two-foot narrow gauge single track, a shrinkage leaving cavernously eerie wide spaces each side of the small open-sided electric trains which ran under the title of the Ramsgate Tunnel Railway.

From an upper terminus at Hereson Road, near Dumpton Park, the pleasure line (which it was mistakenly hoped, would also attract local shoppers from the buses) descended to the promenade. To become a paying attraction, it was realised that the trains must offer visitors more holiday orientated scenery than interminable soot encrusted bricks whilst rattling through this claustrophobic eternity under ground. Night illuminations being the wealth of Southend and Blackpool, Ramsgate decided to do likewise, in the eternal RTR night. Colourful illuminated set-pieces and tableaux in lights were created either side, filling the depressing emptiness of a tunnel too big for its diminutive trains. The promoters artfully stopped them after a quarter mile, it being hoped that by then patrons would be conditioned to endure the rest by the trains' lights alone.

To reopen privately the disused LCDR tunnel, a steep extension tunnel was cut, of only eight feet clearance and six feet wide, just sufficient for the electric cars. Caught in their moving lamps, the meeting point of midget and giant was as startling as a plunge from Oxford Street into a low narrow alley.

On August Bank Holiday, 1936, the RTR ran its first rides, with four-car trains powered from overhead wires like trams, capable of splitting on occasion into two- or one-car units. Top and bottom cars, as on a funicular, moved off simultaneously, crossing at a passing loop for which there was ample space in the full sized tunnel.

But only three more seasons remained for establishment of the RTR before World War II put Ramsgate off the holiday map and into Hell Fire Corner, almost facing occupied France. Beaches were barbed wire no-man's-lands, but the tunnel entered yet another new life, as a popular and safe public air raid shelter, accommodating almost as many as the more famous Chislehurst Caves, also in the Kent chalk, nearer London.

In 1945 came peace, and the following year the RTR reopened. Its lighted set pieces looked somewhat battered by then and by about 1955 were removed. Chalk falls closed the line altogether in 1957, but one more attempt was made in the following season to revitalise it, with new concrete platforms. Even so, five minutes incarcerated in this eerie cavern, careering downhill in sideless cars, had little appeal for the new sophisticated motoring generation. On September 26, 1965, the RTR closed for good.

The Romney, Hythe and Dymchurch, ever alert for material matching its own narrow gauge, took over most operational assets; not only colour-light signals, but points, track, and even sleepers. Little but ballast and rusty supports of forgotten tableaux remained when the tunnel's massive maw was finally bricked over.

Differences in the built-up cliff wall's colour, material and texture immediately east of 'Pleasurama' make the blocked up entrance easily recognisable, with massive remains of railway company brickwork. Near a local synagogue, a fine air vent is said to exist. From steps by the tunnel mouth one can still see exactly the view our grandfathers shot with their Box Brownies half a century ago, with the station itself

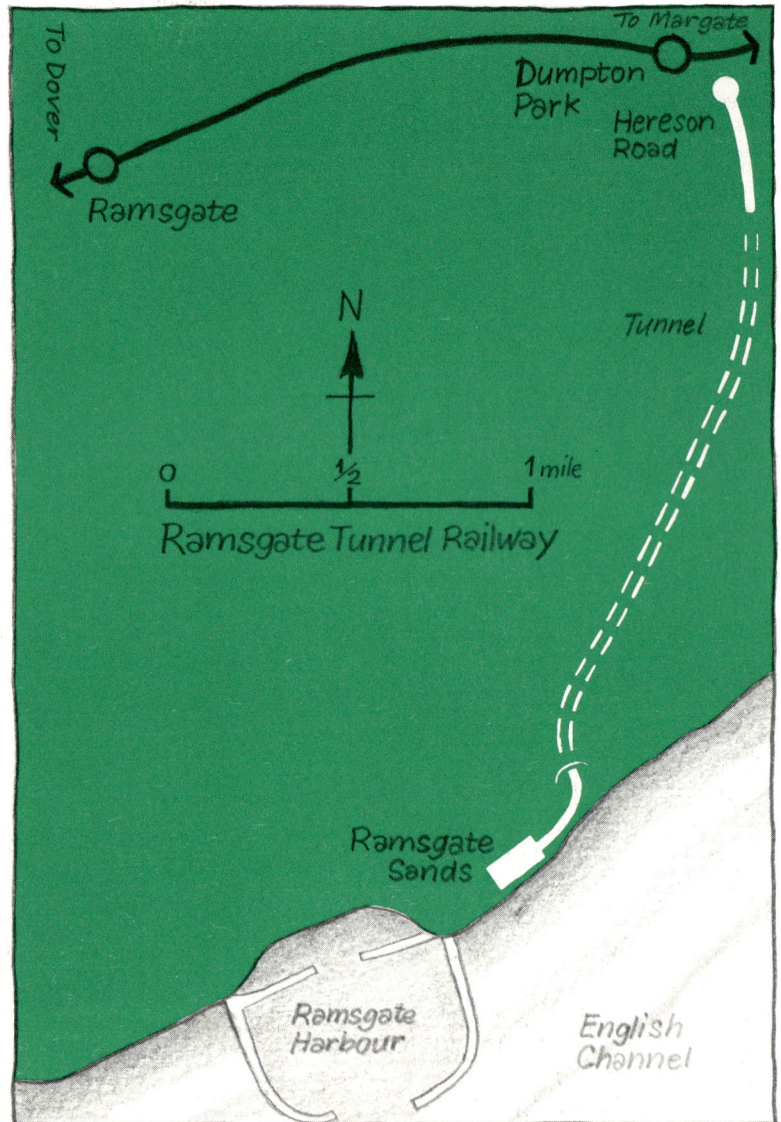

Railcar powered by overhead cables about to enter Ramsgate Tunnel Railway for a pleasure run in 1953.
John H Meredith

easily identifiable as such from this angle. The trackbed, asphalted over, accommodates fairground amusements, a helter-skelter, and stalls.

Strolling back beside this former trackbed we return to Ramsgate Sands station, today a rendezvous for uncerebral fun for the multitudes. It is not, on the surface, much like a station, being entirely cased outside with modern walls and additions. But inside the hall, anyone lifting his eyes up from Bingo can still see a railway character about the high roof above. The smaller structure added against its western wall, again given to amusements, marks the site of a goods yard. Hereabouts, near Ramsgate's casino and whelk stalls, is the site of the old LCDR turntable, identifiable from the road's unusual curvature.

Railway enthusiasts find fascination in identifying these telltale signs. But who else, stopping between Bingo sessions or feeding pennies into bandits to grumble (rightly) about the excessively long walk back to Ramsgate station, now realises that he *is* standing on a station – a station abandoned fifty years ago?

Classic view of Ramsgate Sands station, as displayed in several local public buildings, including modern station buffet.
Lens of Sutton

All the shunting and movement of a busy seaside station in the height of the season fifty years ago. An engine running light is entering sidings beyond the tunnel mouth (right), whose site is still identifiable. *Lens of Sutton*

Ramsgate tunnel at right, open station with over-all roof in the distance, and sidings beyond the tunnel, alongside the promenade, seen about half a century ago. *Lens of Sutton*

View from the identical situation in January 1978. Masonry of the tunnel entrance at right, sidings site concreted over in the foreground, and station, adapted as a modern amusement hall, in the background haze. *M V Searle*

Blocked up entrance to Ramsgate Tunnel Railway, with massive original piers remaining each side, January 1978.
M V Searle

Site of trackbed between tunnel opening and terminus, concreted over and currently housing a small funfair with helter skelter. *M V Searle*

Ramsgate Sands station today, in the guise of 'Pleasurama'. Side walls faced, and additional end walls added. Yet it still has the basic outline of a solid seaside terminus. *M V Searle*

CHAPTER 5

Into Oblivion

HYTHE BRANCH

Between about 1830 and 1930, reasons for building minor branches could be as varied as human life itself – industry, port development, mining, tourism, military requirements, whims of powerful landowners, and pure railway mania dictating that every town, however thinly populated, ought to possess at least one station.

Down on the Kent coast at historic spread-out Hythe, five reasons lay behind a projected link through its neighbour Sandgate to Folkestone in one direction, and to the nearest London bound main line in the other: military encampments; one of England's grandest hotels; local desire to join more fully with a world set on the move by trains; hopes of creating a completely new seaside resort to cash in on an ever increasing boom; and the need for improved boat-train access to Folkestone and thence onwards through Boulogne and Calais into Europe.

Well into the nineteenth century, the ancient Cinque Port of Hythe, mainly set back from the seafront against protecting inland hills, was larger and more prosperous than Folkestone, a few miles away; a fact difficult to appreciate today when comparing quiet little Hythe with that crowded clifftop resort and almost over-active gateway to France.

About the year of the Great Exhibition, Folkestone was only just yawning awake, jolted by the alarm clock of railways and improved roads, thanks to which it was set to become a premier port. 'A few years ago (Folkestone) was one of the most straggling and miserable looking towns in England, but it has lately risen into importance to the detriment of Dover', wrote a chronicler in 1851. Folkestone had made excellent progress since June 28, 1843, when the railway first invaded that scruffy fishing village of barely more than four thousand souls, coming in to a rough temporary station on the outskirts because the immense approaching Foorde Viaduct was incomplete. Its harbour, semi-derelict in 1840, was acquired in 1843 by the South Eastern Railway as a vital part of its combined rail and Channel linking operation, foreshadowing its modern position uniting British Rail and Sealink.

Much admiration was heaped upon the SER's work with difficult shingle beaches in excavating foundations and erecting facilities, available regardless of hour or tide; all accomplished in three short years. 'We may be allowed here to refer to the advantages derived by travellers to the Continent from the exertions of this Company (the SER) to render the harbour at Folkestone available at all tides' applauded an important railway gazetteer of 1851; 'That terrible shingle, which has so long baffled the exertions of infant science, and even now, at Dover, braves the exertions of the British Government, has, at Folkestone, at length yielded to the natural lights of scientific experience, under the tutelary genius of commercial enterprise.'

Natural barriers were undoubtedly prolific hereabouts, not least the long steep incline between Folkestone station, high behind the town on a hilltop looking across to Boulogne, and the point of embarkation.

Today this point is noticed by every boat-train passenger as his express halts at the junction east of Folkestone Central, hangs around infuriatingly awaiting signals, reverses, shunts onto special outside lines, and crawls down past streets clinging to cliffs to harbour level. Yesterday the same gradient was a prime reason for Hythe, next resort along this coast, cannily entering the battle of the boat-train planners, as the chief intermediate point on a proposed alternative approach to Folkestone Harbour via Sandgate, leading in over more level terrain. Before electrification no fewer than four 0-6-0Ts often hauled one Up boat-train. Sandgate and Hythe would also reap more direct benefit as emergent holiday resorts, given trains. For final good measure, a further resort as a source of profit could be created from scratch between them to be known as Seabrook, and facing the intriguing outline of France from this exhilarating stretch of coast.

Only a year after arrival of the main line at Folkestone, Hythe and Sandgate duly got their own railway, branching off at Sandling a couple of stations west. It opened on October 9, 1874 for ceremonial purposes and on October 10, for normal time-tabled working. The only disappointment was that the branch served neither Hythe nor Sandgate in practice, coming only to the lip of Hythe's background hills before running parallel to the coast, but well inland, towards Sandgate. There, it again stopped short of the all-important sea front seemingly almost out of spite. Distance from a town centre discouraged from the start any intensive use by locals bound for Folkestone, or trippers coming in. A long walk to the beach, and a weary uphill slog homewards, was not the average family's notion of a picnic. For the military, from camps around Hythe which complemented the major Shorncliffe Camp, the haul was made worse by heavy army boots.

More useful to many was the Folkestone, Hythe and Sandgate Horse Tramway, or Horse Railway, built by the SER, trundling through the streets of Hythe via the town square, to serve the nationally famous Hotel Imperial, the eastern promenade, and emergent Seabrook – a resort fated never actually to materialise – before running onwards to Sandgate; there it stopped not high up above the town, like conventional trains, but where the public expected to pick up transport – at the seaward end of steep Sandgate Hill.

Obviously, therefore, some link between this convenient seafront railway and the two inconvenient back-of-town stations was a logical future project; but in actuality nothing came of the talked of contact.

The only uphill railed transport (not connecting with a station) was a picturesque steep-grade railway of 1893 from the foot of Sandgate Hill up to the western outcrop of the Folkestone Leas, operated by two cars on cables.

In 1876 powers had been obtained for the further extension eastwards of the standard gauge railway from Sandgate to Folkestone Harbour, in order to bypass the long stiff gradient down from Folkestone Central. This line ran far more gently down from Sandgate to a virtually level final approach. Like so many schemes in this locality, the continuation never materialised. Its failure is still a matter of some regret, now that boat trains in summer follow each others' tails down to the Sealink ferries on a scale undreamed of by those who first visualised an alternative run in.

Nevertheless, cross Channel traffic from Folkestone steadily increased, with ever bigger and better steamers being launched. NEW! was the advertiser's favourite word in 1907 as much as it is today. A typical SECR slogan read: 'NEW! New Turbine Steamers *Invicta*, *Onward* and *The Queen* cross the Channel Daily, between . . . Folkestone and Boulogne'. Kent and trains were thus early intertwined by name, '*Onward*' being the old SER motto, and '*Invicta*' the country motto of Kent.

Hythe and Sandgate obstinately continued the holiday war, minus further rail improvements, picking up a minor share of trade from visitors unable to afford more than a few days, and for whom their reasonable proximity to London meant moderate fares. As elsewhere, it paid companies to angle for weekend custom, when so many found a full week beyond their pockets. 'Friday, Saturday and Sunday-to-Monday or Tuesday Tickets are issued from Charing Cross (West End), Cannon Street and London Bridge to . . . Deal, Dover, Folkestone, Hastings, Hythe . . . Sandgate, Sandling Junction, etc' incited the SECR in about 1906, with a personal exhortation from the general manager to join his trains: 'For Fares and Further particulars respecting the Cheap Tickets see Time-Books and Programme. Vincent W. Hill, General Manager.' It all sounded alluring enough, though the branch conveying passengers to their final destinations rarely offered anything more spectacular than two carriages behind a labouring old Class R1 0-4-4T or similar, making hard work of a miniscule branch.

World War I put a full stop to the holiday life, though military usage of the line naturally increased. For the duration the seafront horse railway was closed, not to be reopened until some time after the Armistice in 1919, worked by teams of army mules from Hythe or Shorncliffe. Not a few patrons revived former regrets that steam had never replaced beasts of burden, despite periodic schemes; how controllable was a locomotive compared with unpredictable '0-4-0' mule-power! The Sandgate–Leas cable railway closed down at the end of the war, never to reopen.

In the Twenties another development arose, which was destined to put Hythe on a wider touristic map. In 1927 the quickly celebrated Romney Hythe and Dymchurch Railway, the 'Smallest Public Railway in the World', was opened from a special Hythe terminus, a mile or so from the main Hythe station, to run in the opposite direction towards New Romney. Despite the gap between stations, thousands arrived to admire the RH&DR's marvellous scale model locomotives in immaculate livery. Thereafter a sizeable proportion of all visitors came solely for the RH&DR, and joining the latter with a main line, allowing direct transfer of passengers without erratic bus connections, became a project worthy of consideration. Sandling rather than Hythe was most favoured, being little farther across country and with the benefit of a single instead of double change, probably from a special adjacent bay.

In the event, however, the RH&DR instead invested in further mileage away from Hythe, over shingle and marsh to Dungeness, beyond its original Hythe–New Romney section. This section had been proposed as a light railway by the SECR but never actually developed.

While the miniature RH&DR prospered, the standard sized Sandgate branch steadily languished, as the bus boom eroded its traffic; not surprisingly in view of the awkward positions of the seaside stations. Hythe could barely support such an amenity; Sandgate, dependent on seasonal trade and suffering more badly under the great Depression, could no longer justify a service. This section gave up the unprofitable ghost and closed on April 1, 1931. Many railwaymen noted gloomily that this was April Fools' Day.

Irony of ironies, the bus company that helped kill the line bought the disused station at Sandgate for future development. Most of it was demolished except for part of the Up platform – retained for the sake of its built in 'Gents' as a useful busmens' accessory. On the rest of the site was built a bus garage, still operative today.

The remaining Sandling–Hythe section was reduced to single line working, another nail in the coffin of eventual closure. Running down was thereafter the order of the day.

From 1943 the line closed altogether, a victim of war here in Hell Fire Corner, and although peace brought brief restoration, services continued to decline. The more trains were axed from a now pathetic timetable, the more passengers were driven to buses or cars, spinning a vicious circle of diminishing services and shrinking revenue ever faster.

Faithful to the end the usual R Class engines kept the line going – No. 31660 was regularly in harness – shuttling along wearing a slightly disconsolate air with half empty carriages. December 3, 1951, brought inevitable closure. The 'Sandling for Hythe' platform notice no longer spoke the truth.

Only at Sandling Junction do substantial reminders exist of an always backwater line, some thirty-one years after closure and over half a century after the

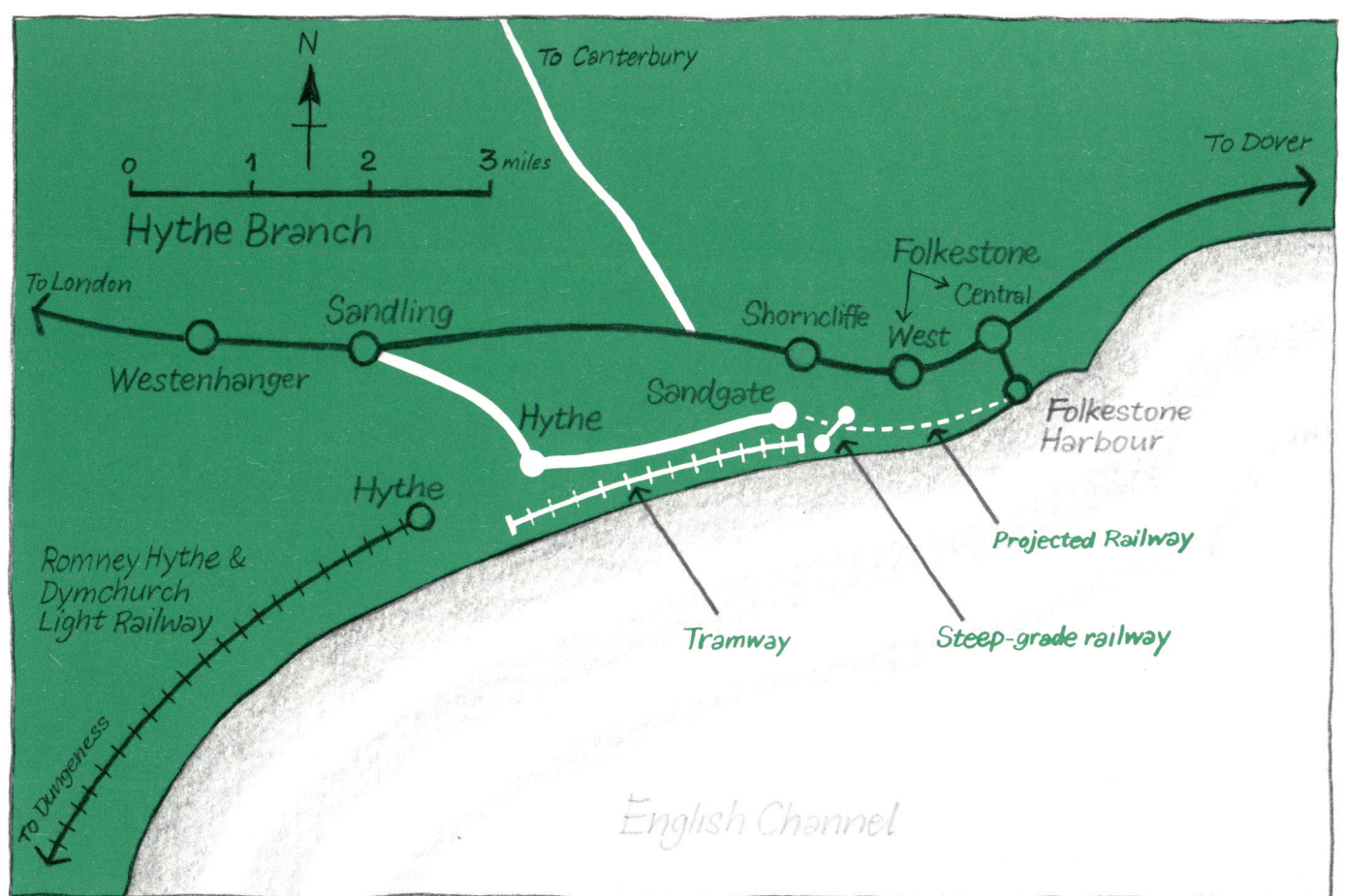

Sandgate part sank into oblivion. The old Hythe bay, at roughly a 45° angle off the present Up platform, remains in good preservation, though its adjacent yard has inevitably become a car park.

A few days before Christmas in 1977 the author travelled down specially to take pictures of the line's remains between Sandling and Hythe. It should have been a dreary pilgrimage, to a place once alive with men and steam, now interred in a cemetery of memories. December fog would surely heighten the impression of gloom.

Instead, this proved the most pleasant in a series of photographic sorties. At Sandling the disused platform was remarkably well preserved, almost scrubbed-looking but for a few tufts of gold autumnal grasses between three or four cracks; presumably it had received some attention, as the approach to two existing mainline platforms. Original blunt-headed iron railings, draped with brambles, divided the platform from a narrow dip, an old siding where marks of sleepers still showed clearly between banks of wild plants which stopped short of the trackbed, as so often happens where ballast inhibits growth. Below the Hythe platform track was in position, rusty but clear of weeds; it appears to have been relaid as an occasional siding for Sandling, running a few yards to a small white crossing gate, closing off the branch from the main Folkestone–London road.

In the opposite, or Hythe direction, the line ended after perhaps a hundred yards at a massive superimposed buffer block. Beyond it there was nothing but a rural path of most alluring beauty. It might have passed for a 'ride' on a forested estate, rather than the bed of an abandoned railway. Straight ahead it ran, under identifiable embankments all red, gold, green and brown, past weathered field gates where hikers formerly waited for trains to pass. The trackbed was smooth and clear, almost completely covered with soft, brilliant emerald mosses, stretching towards a prospect formerly only seen by the engine driver dead ahead: banked-up, wooded hillsides swathed in white winter mist.

I went to Sandling to find pathetic fragments of railway archaeology. I found beauty and tranquility, sitting on one single wooden sleeper in the middle of a disused track, watching mists come down. Only a rusted porters' barrow, propped against a fence, reminded me that this used to be a place of work.

Further remains exist down the line, less picturesque than at Sandling and less easily identifiable. Hythe station has totally vanished, but at Sandgate the modern bus garage marks a spot on railway maps of the past. The former horse tramway succumbed long ago, but much of its course is recognisable in the raised line of the Princes Parade promenade which runs from the luxury Hotel Imperial of Hythe towards Sandgate.

Folkestone Harbour annually accommodates more and more holiday boat trains, labouring up the slow weary incline to the main line high up above the sea at cliff top level. How logical would have been the once discussed alternative approach from Sandgate alongside the shore, but in the current economic climate, how unlikely is any revival of such a plan! More than unlikely; destruction by housing and roads of much railway property between Hythe and Sandgate makes the reopening of the essential railhead at Sandling virtually impossible.

Sleepers in various states of decay at Hythe line siding, Sandling, in 1977.
M V Searle

'South For Sunshine'. Southern Railway's popular advertisement of the 1920s, featured the modest Hythe and Sandgate among 'The finest resorts in the world'.
Ward Lock Ltd

Meeting point of 'then' and 'now': Sandling Junction with present London Up line (left) and gate shutting off disused Hythe platform and its rusting track, 1977.
M V Searle

Beauty where permanent way once ran, between Hythe and Sandling, with double gates to lost footpath crossing place. In December mist, 1977.
M V Searle

End of the line – literally – a few yards out of Sandling.
Beyond, just a pretty grassy trackbed to Hythe.
M V Searle

Ruins of Hythe station looking towards Sandgate as it appeared in 1954.
E Course

Remains of trackbed and platform at Sandgate in 1954. Note 'gents' at right, retained for use of busmen whose vehicles ousted the trains.
E Course

Lost line in a landscape, (1981): ivy-hung bridge and telltale rows of lineside houses betray a route closed fifty years ago, at Sandgate. *M V Searle*

Sandgate station, South Eastern Railway, in 1891, showing middle-road. *Lens of Sutton*

On the Hythe branch in the 1930s.
Lens of Sutton

An old picture postcard showing Sandgate station and the line climbing (right) towards Hythe, with Royal Military Canal and Hotel Imperial at Hythe in distance.
Lens of Sutton

Sandgate horse tramway in about 1918. Standard gauge Hythe and Sandling branch ran above and behind houses on left.
Pamlin Prints

41

CHAPTER 6

Fight for Survival

WESTERHAM VALLEY BRANCH

'Westerham station! Westerham station!' called the driver as my bus rattled down into the charming little town of Wolfe and Churchill, pulling in as usual to the tiny forecourt, otherwise occupied only by a wall pillar box and a broken off railway trespass notice. It all seemed very ordinary and normal, as the bus disgorged its load in the customary place – except that there was *no* Westerham station, and had not been for ten years. Thus do old habits and expressions cling among those who all their lives were accustomed to this curious combination of country branch and outer suburban commuter line.

The bus went on, leaving me to explore the forlorn rough space where formerly had stood a neat little station. There was the gap where once had been the front passenger entrance off the still extant forecourt, and traces of its cobbled brick walk-through onto the platform. The platform itself was discernible, too, although its form was unusual for this country; like a French or Spanish station platform, it rose barely a foot above where the permanent way ought to have been. Not because it was built *à la français*, but because the site of the tracks had been almost filled in. Only the asphalt surface and the lip of the edge was left. Across the point where the terminal buildings ended was a forbidding fence, grown with weeds, but beyond it the uncovered platform still stood, not filled in like the section nearest the village, stretching away into a scrubby field occupied by spikey bushes, young trees and more weeds where trains had formerly pulled in and out. The whole scene was made the more forlorn by a spray of November drizzle. It was a good place to go back over a hundred years of activity, to when the first rails were laid.

Westerham's lost line was fifty years younger than its Kentish precursor, the Canterbury and Whitstable, having its beginning in three sets of South Eastern Railway powers, of 1864, 1867 and 1870, which all came to nothing. These were followed by a Bill promoted in 1876 by a group which included rich local businessmen anxious for better communications with London, and one of whom sank £30,000 into the scheme.

The line was to be built in two parts, from Dunton Green, a little way north of Sevenoaks on the main London line, to Westerham; and onwards from Westerham to Oxted, linking with the principal lines south from Croydon. Its path would be the lovely valley snuggled between the North Downs and Pilgrims's Way, and the ridge where Chartwell lies. The SER, however, remained adamant that if it was to back the plans of the Westerham Valley Railway Company no link to Oxted could be added, a requirement the SER pursued into Parliament when in 1876 the Westerham Valley Railway Bill was hammered out.

As happened wherever a new railway was planned, there was at least one member of the local ruling classes who protested that it would despoil his ancestral estate with its polluting fumes and noise. His complaint was that the smoke from the engine – horrible sight – would be visible from his grounds, puffing across country all the way from the branching off point to Westerham. Not surprisingly the diehard gentleman's objection to so obnoxious a vision as a little branch line train was overruled, and in July 1876 the company was incorporated. The scheme then stagnated for another three years, until in 1879 agreement was reached with the South Eastern for actual construction and working.

The directors had plentiful experience behind them, including as they did such notables as Sir Edward Watkin, the light behind Port Victoria and other Kentish dreams and schemes, and to whom is attributed the somewhat exaggerated statement, 'I know of no place in the World that wants a Railway more than Westerham'. And there was William Tipping, a squire hailing from Liverpool, whose knowledge ranged back to the dawn of railways in the Liverpool and Manchester Railway, with thirteen other directorships under his belt. He was described as tall, bald, bewhiskered, and adorned with a 'Newgate frill', hair under the chin so termed because it covered the place where a hangman's rope might run.

Building began late in 1879 on the short single track branch of under five miles, westwards from Dunton Green, and allowed for only one lineside station purporting to serve the attractive village of Brasted though it passed a mile from the centre, and half a mile from the nearest house.

Unrealistic estimating soon bit into the promoters' funds, the initial estimate of £65,000 rising by £5,000 as a result of unforeseen problems in the terrain. Here, the squelching, muddy and marshy land of the valley bottom through which the line ran on a steep incline absorbed every rivulet off the hills on both sides as well as storm water from Westerham itself. The station's position was again determined by the land, being the nearest point to which trains could run on the level.

No extension beyond Westerham towards the Surrey border was ever undertaken.

July 6, 1881, saw opening day, comparatively late in the railway building calendar but no less enthusiastically received for the delay. 'Success to the Railway!' proclaimed a triumphal arch across the main street, heavy with branches of evergreen and fluttering with flags, in a manner popularised elsewhere on Queen Victoria's jubilee progresses. Also inscribed was the one-word motto of the South Eastern Railway, 'Onward!'.

Special trains ran up and down all day free of charge – the only time, it was said, that the notoriously extortionate SER gave anything for nothing – loaded with local schoolchildren and puffed up directors and dignitaries, smiling like contented cats full of railway company cream.

Sir Edward Watkin, now the local as well as SER railway king, presided at a Town Hall banquet, displaying a fair minded determination to leave nobody out by proposing toasts ranging from Her Majesty to the Archbishop of Canterbury, whose personal connection with the Westerham Railway appeared decidedly tenuous. Possibly enlisting the Almighty's aid, through His ministers, was an insurance against future calamity.

More far seeing as an omen was the opinion expressed by some that, given trains, Westerham would in effect become an outer London suburb, by virtue of its businessmen turning into daily commuters, though that particular term had not yet been invented, and a carrier's cart still plied for those suspicious of trains.

Next day, July 7, full passenger services began to the main line at Dunton Green, allowing Westerham men to change there and reach their offices in about one and a half hours, slow by railway standards but an improvement on the roads. By November it was possible to patronise the tiles as well as the offices of the metropolis thanks to the addition of a once-weekly special late night service arriving back at nearly one o'clock in the morning, considered an outrageous invitation to levity by sanctimonious residents who reckoned to be in bed before this train even left town.

It is probable that the railway, soon given fully into SER ownership, was initially worked by *Folkestone* 2-4-0 engines. With the 1890s comes historical certainty and the 2-4-0 *118* class and simple four-wheeler rolling stock, plus the universal Stirling Q-class 0-4-4T, a locomotive much favoured in the London suburbs.

For a short period that strange hybrid of bus, tram and train, the 'rail motor', took over, a combination of tank locomotive and single carriage divided into smoker, non-smoker, baggage and guard's van (also tried on the suburban Hayes and Elmers End lines). They were leisurely creatures, so slow that the previous ten minute timetable was revised to over a quarter of an hour, a reversion of progress unpopular with railwaymen and public alike. For this service a new halt, the only other station the line would acquire, was opened to serve Chevening.

Soon the old Q class engines were back, with rolling stock stepped up to three-car sets, to the relief of passengers jammed into the inadequate road motors. Little P classes 0-6-0 tank engines also appeared.

In the early 1920s a new departure fast gained hold in south London and west Kent – electrification.

Electrification was considered essential for speeding-up the ever increasing traffic of daily workers to London; travelling from earliest morning on cheap 'workmens' tickets requiring them to be in town by eight or even earlier, until past nine. Such an operation would allow more trains than ever to serve any given line within a short time. Early in the electrification period, geared to the third-rail system that remains characteristic of the Southern, this improvement came as near Westerham as the Orpington and Tonbridge route. Indeed, its country offshoot with its increasing populace of season ticket holders would appear to have been an obvious candidate for similar treatment. In the event, however, electrification passed Westerham by, a decision which virtually ensured its ultimate demise though, like King Charles, the railway was to prove 'an unconscionable time a-dying'.

Amalgamation into the Southern Railway in 1923 brought few immediate changes, locomotives continuing in old South Eastern and Chatham livery for about a year. The line, steam-hauled, continued to be something of a backwater between the morning and evening rush hours. Its somnolent days were enlivened by the carriage of milk churns, this lovely agricultural valley being a leading producer of milk and cream, as it still is today. Old London Chatham and Dover stock sufficed for passengers, now hauled chiefly by classes B and Bl 4-4-0 and 01 0-6-0, including carriages having only waist-high divisions between half-open compartments, alpine style, similar to the two car sets used on the All Hallows branch right up to its closure; those, far more than the all-purpose locomotives which could be seen almost anywhere on the Southern, were for many the most essential ingredient of the Hoo line's latter day charm. On the Westerham branch, it is said, they even provided passengers with the doubtful luxury of a spittoon.

Westerham went placidly on, its conventional steam-hauled life broken only by the brief advent of a rail-bus originally ordered for the steep ascent of Devil's Dyke near Brighton but banished from that demanding climb because of inadequate braking. Even on the gentle Westerham branch this train disgraced itself, regularly breaking down between stations and having to be pushed ignominiously home by a normal locomotive. Quietly it disappeared in favour of the more familiar 0-4-4T.

During World War II the line coasted on, disturbed by no more hardship than blacked out trains and blue lamps on stations and halts. Worse was to come in peacetime than in war, with a drastic cut in services during 1955 when trains, undermined by universal increases in motoring, were completely axed outside the rush hours, precipitating Westerham into the world of mornings-and-evenings-only commuterdom. Only its commuter traffic staved off total closure of the service sarcastically yet affectionately nicknamed the *Westerham Flyer*. In these late days the line was worked mainly by H class 0-4-4T and R/R1 0-4-4T locomotives which, like the line itself, were patently doomed as the railway world moved ever more irrevocably towards electric or diesel traction. Even to the end over a hundred city bound workers, sometimes as many as two hundred, picked up the *Flyer* daily, a large number for a compact little town so far out of central London. They were a powerful factor in the argument of those who pleaded the line's value as a necessity against the voices of those who now openly preached the gospel of closure.

The fight for survival was on. It would be a long battle.

Abandonment was temporarily held back by recommendations of the Central Transport Users' Consultative Committee, despite BR's statement that losses topped £11,000 a year; but in 1961 the Minister of Transport personally decided that two hundred workers a day were insufficient reason for delaying closure any longer. Human necessity, in a community geographically near London but by road facing a long and weary haul by unreliable bus and coach, counted for little against official reasoning based on ticket office takings. October 28, 1961, was fixed as the final day of operation. Thousands of signatures to a petition and hundreds of column inches of newspaper protest availed nothing in the face of BR's argument that losses had mounted to £26,000.

In golden October sunshine the two-car pull-and-push *Westerham Flyer* flew her last runs up and down to Dunton Green behind Class H or D1 engines, as did a six-coach special for enthusiasts pouring in to attend the obsequies choked with cameras and tape recorders. Many were compelled to clamber aboard from track level, as the train was too long for a tiny platform rarely expected to cope with more than local two-car combinations.

Even then the battle for preservation and reopening was not over. For a new group of railway lovers and everyday passengers it was, they hoped, but the beginning.

Westerham Valley Railway Association was formed in 1962, pledged to buy the five miles of line from British Railways provided that the nationalised concern's stipulation that genuine commuter services should be run, as opposed to enthusiasts' and pleasure trips, was maintained. In the other corner of the ring in which the fight for survival took place was Kent County Council, another heavyweight, determined to put a new motorway – or even three – through this peaceful valley alongside the Pilgrims's Way, utilising

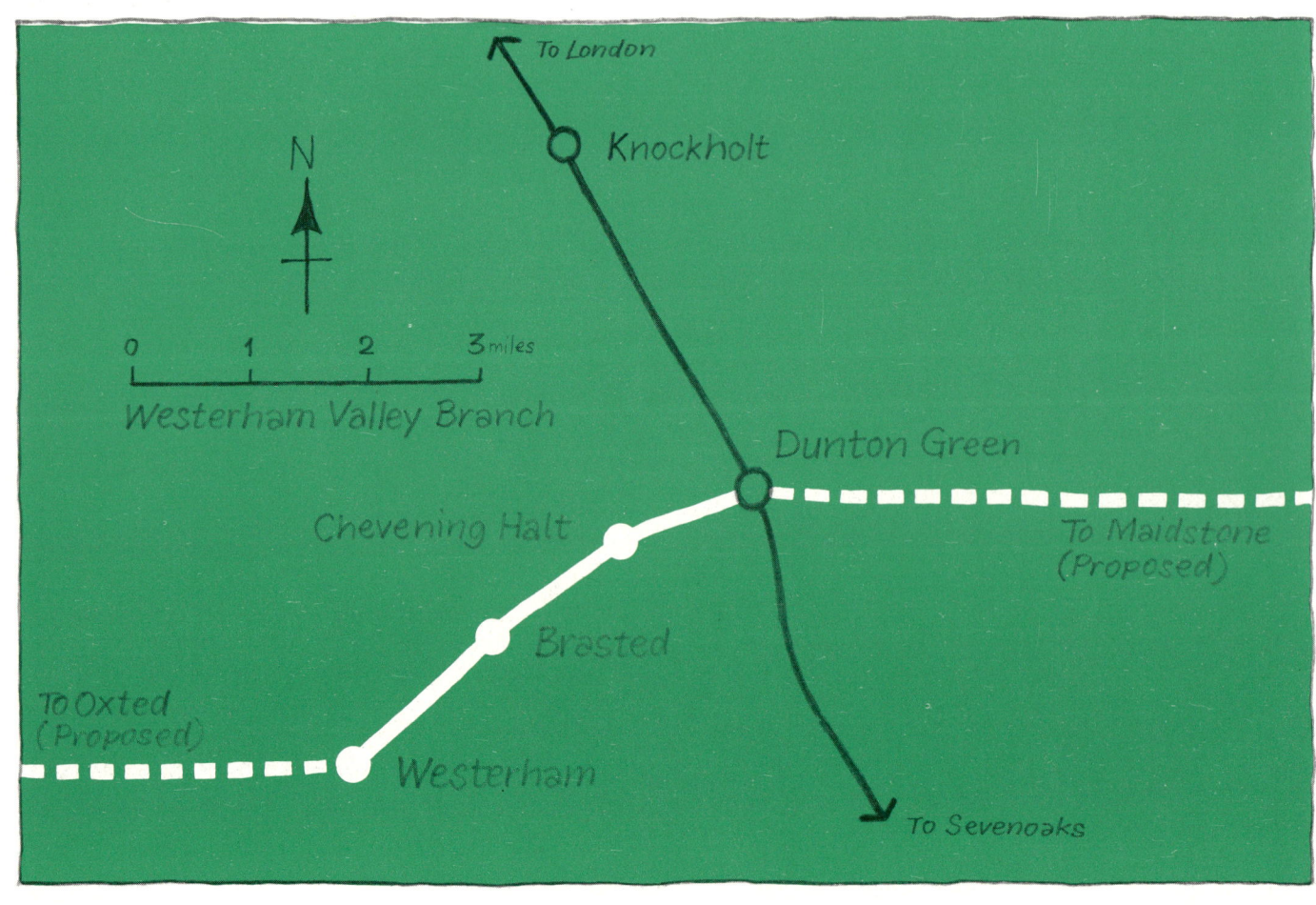

Westerham forecourt in use for buses, as it has virtually always been, showing gap in wall where once was the station entrance. *M V Searle*

most of the line as a readymade basis.

Nevertheless the swelling band of helpers worked on. Westerham station was patched up as their working and social headquarters, its wooden entrance door adorned, if memory serves aright, with notices proclaiming their title and object. Enthusiasts descended in legions at weekends, keeping points clear of weeds, signals in working order, and buildings in tolerable condition in preparation for the day when trains would run again.

Two Class H engines were earmarked for purchase at the low price of £1,000 apiece, less than the cost then of two cars, as well as a Q1. On the Western Region some useful diesel railcars were found, and London Transport was also canvassed, for three old Metropolitan coaches.

As stock was actually being assembled for possible reopening, however, a new blow fell. Kent County Council, doubly determined to wrest the railway from Westerham for road building, threatened compulsory purchase. The only loophole was the condition that the locals could have their line if they financed a special road bridge to carry the proposed artery across the railway near Chevening. At over £26,000 it was an impossible demand. It had to be admitted that hopes of saving the railway were fading.

Today they are dead. At a cost of £40,000 the motorway planners won their land, and broad bands of excavation were driven along the route formerly plied by trains. No less than three roads are involved, the giant South Orbital, the Sevenoaks bypass and Westerham Link Road. Such land as was not required was sold off for others to develop in tune with improved road communications.

In many ways the new roads undoubtedly benefit an area whose traffic increases year by year. All the same, those who regret the loss of the *Westerham Flyer* cannot but wonder what would have been the reaction of the country gentleman who, only a few miles away, had described a railway engine as 'this snorting, spluttering, hideous iron machine, belching forth smoke and steam', if he could have seen a motorway in turn replacing the iron horse.

Disused platform cut into two by a fence where station buildings ended. Beyond it, the rest of the platform survives among weeds and grass.
M V Searle

Westerham in summer 1959.
NCB

Brasted Halt, looking towards Westerham.
G Daniels

Interior SECR railmotor, Westerham, summer 1959.
NCB

Westerham station and forecourt in 1959.
NCB

Devil's Dyke Sentinel railcar, of type brought from that steep-grade hill railway to Westerham.
Pamlin Prints

Evening train from Dunton Green to Westerham, at Chevening.
G Daniels

Branch train at Westerham in 1957.
G Daniels

Cab view from Westerham branch railmotor in 1959.
NCB

Westerham signal box, summer 1959.
NCB

'Change here for Westerham branch'.
Sign at Dunton Green.
G Daniels

Westerham in 1959. Yards are all filled in, bulldozed or otherwise abandoned today.
NCB

Southern No. 31518 at the terminus in Westerham's last days.
Pamlin Prints

CHAPTER 7

Screaming Alice

CRYSTAL PALACE

Scuttering on audible clawed feet a squirrel jerked back and forth among rustling autumn leaves, periodically stopping to chew a scrap held in tiny paws. His setting was a forest of young oak, plane and silver birch, falling abruptly away down a wooded hillside, grown up of its own accord in only a few years. Beyond the trees, golden leaved in November sunshine, stretched a panorama of blue distance.

Immediately below me, so overgrown with trees and bushes that even in thinning foliage it was well nigh impossible to photograph, lay the boarded-up entrance to a disused tunnel, its arch decorated in sham-Norman manner by a long dead builder, conscious of the architectural masterpiece his now derelict railway was to serve. It appeared the type of scene that is familiar enough to seekers after lost lines deep in the Peak District or the wilds of Wales, yet 'remote' was the last word one could apply to this site. Only a pavement's width separated the woodland squirrel from a constant stream of red double decker London buses and an endless procession of cars and lorries, flowing only five yards behind my back as I leaned on a still extant length of station wall. I was barely four miles from London Bridge, on top of Sydenham Hill, with on one side a vast open emptiness where the Crystal Palace stood for eighty years and on the other another yawning gap where its own station used to be. The Palace site was recognisable, occupied by a caravan camp, a public open space overlooking the superb panoramas for which the Palace was famous, and a motorcycle training track; but the High Level station might never have been, except for that tell-tale tunnel mouth, so thoroughly overgrown that the place begins to resemble Sydenham Hill before the Crystal Palace was rebuilt there in 1854, three years after housing the Great Exhibition of 1851 in Hyde Park.

Railways had a definite influence on the Exhibition's initial success, as well as on the choice of a more permanent site for the enlarged Crystal Palace. The Palace, indeed, was literally born on a railway station, brainchild of a man intimately involved in railways from their earliest days, Joseph Paxton.

At the time Paxton was a director of the Midland Railway, in which capacity he was engaged full time while 233 other architects were battling for adoption of their designs for a building to house the forthcoming Great Exhibition. None appeared suitable, to the despair of the organisers, with only ten months to go.

At the last moment Paxton, told of the dilemma by influential friends, agreed to send in a design of his own. Despite his considerable reputation as an architect, notably of the giant Great Conservatory of Chatsworth, railway matters, nonetheless, perforce came first, including a disciplinary hearing of an errant Derbyshire pointsman over which he, as Chairman, must preside. Sitting in chairmanly majesty in a Midland Railway meeting room at Derby station, Paxton appeared more engrossed in doodling on his blotter than in the case. Was he interested, a colleague huffily enquired? 'I know all about the pointsman's case', was the historic retort. '*This*, gentlemen, is a design for the Great Industrial Exhibition.' The Crystal Palace, little different from its finished conception, had been born. The outcome we all know. The design was accepted, the news being conveyed home by railway company telegraph headed 'Manchester, Buxton, Matlock and Midlands Junction Railway' and reading 'a message from London to say that Mr Paxton's plan has been approved by the Royal Commission'.

The Great Exhibition proved more effectively than any other event the amazing manner in which railways could open up the world. Never had such thousands been able to see London, many for the first time, pouring in by special trains; clergymen with parish parties, officers leading Portsmouth ratings given special educational leave, and ordinary folk from all over England. Among the exhibits astonishing them were the latest railway engines, immortalised in Thackeray's saga of a goggle eye 'Oirishman':

> 'There's steam engines,
> That stands in lines,
> Enormous and amazing,
> That squeal and snort
> Like whales in sport,
> Or elephants a-grazing.'

Even more astonishing than the exhibits themselves was the huge glass building which housed them. Long before closing day plans were afoot to save it for permanent public resort.

In two ways railways and railwaymen decided the new location. Good communications were already available, although not to the actual site, in a section of the London Brighton and South Coast Railway, the London and Croydon. It passed the lower edge of the earmarked estate through Anerley, so named according to lineside legend from its lone Scotsman resident in 1839 and his reply to railway developers enquiring the name of the place they wanted to buy, 'this is the annerly hoose' (the only house).

Other lines were planned. 'Rails for the new Crystal Palace Railway are now in a forward state. The railway traveller . . . may notice on his left between Sydenham and Anerley stations navvies hard at work preparing the ground. The space through the wood for the line of rails that is to run into the Palace is now cleared of trees, and presents a picturesque woodland scene, the timber lying across the way in happy confusion.'

So wrote one passing by in 1852, with building of both lines and Palace in progress. This line is still used intensively, serving suburbia.

Additionally the London and Brighton laid down extra track alongside its existing line, 'Crystal Lines' exclusively for 'Crystal Traffic'. Locomotives were specially built for the steep gradients. Before 1857 was out, countryside described in 1827 as a 'cathedral of singing birds' was invaded by a cathedral of shining glass with its attendant rails, roads and property developers.

Even before this opening up of Sydenham, local railways were ahead in experimental working, the London and Croydon having installed a Samuda principle atmospheric system – direct forerunner of one of the Palace's own two lost railways – said to afford remarkably smooth riding by power sucked up from a 15″ conductor pipe between the rails, at speeds of up to 100 mph. It foreshadowed third-rail electrification of eight decades hence. Carrying the atmospheric over the Brighton line was the world's first railway flyover, a timber viaduct called the 'Flying Leap'.

A second factor in influencing choice of site was that Penge Place, atop Sydenham Hill, was owned by Leo Shuster, chairman of the Brighton Railway and Crystal Palace Company, and close friend of Paxton, willing because of his combined palace and railway interests to sell the Place and 200 acres to a syndicate including himself for a reasonable price. Shuster was also among those putting up funds to buy the original Palace.

Opening year, 1854, saw the Palace management thinking of additional transport, with a special private shuttle service worked by a small tank engine and discarded LBSCR stock, bringing main line passengers in significant numbers. Eventually the LBSCR took this private line, as a section of a larger system.

1865 was to be the most important date in local railway history. The High Level line, specifically for the Crystal Palace, was opened on August 1, branching off at Nunhead on the Catford Loop, a line built, it is said, for the benefit of Queen Victoria whose aversion to the lengthy Penge tunnel under Sydenham Hill was well known. It ended in an imposing new terminus on the opposite side of the boulevard-like Crystal Palace Parade, only yards from the entrances.

Charles Barry, designer of the Houses of Parliament, created this splendid glass roofed station with its distinctive Gothic towers. Like Paxton and Shuster, he was a local worthy, resident at 'Lapsewood' on the hill, near Paxton's 'Rockhills'. Sleekly elegant instead of ponderously oppressive like so many stations, the High Level was equipped with copious roofing covering all platforms, heavy wooden flooring, four tracks and a turntable. Hearsay adds statues in niches, intended to turn frivolous minds towards the arts, for which the Palace was intended as a home.

Most impressive was a subway connecting Palace and terminus beneath the road, enabling suburbians from miles around to travel out, change trains and walk from carriage to main doors without raising an umbrella in winter. Known to posterity as the Paxton Tunnel, it resembled a miniature Gothic chapel.

One uses ecclesiastical terms deliberately, for the Paxton Tunnel was constructed by imported Italian craftsmen specialising in church crypts and vaults, on the grounds that none in England possessed training in such delicate work. Warm red and fawn brick was used in Byzantine style for the walls, with stone shafts supporting an exquisite vaulted roof so strong that traffic still roars eternally above it. Upward steps led directly to the Palace.

This was a demanding line for locomotives of the 1850s, Sydenham Hill being over 600 feet above sea level. Though the station lay in a huge hollow excavated under the lip of the hill, it was still some 550 feet above the Thames. Final stretches were through a long tunnel, the only major work still surviving, which provided one of the Parade's favourite spectacles. Visitors loved to watch from a parapet almost directly over the mouth as steam engines burst from the dark maw with an abrupt roar of white smoke, billowing from inside. Trains remained an entertainment so long as the 'Land 'em, smash 'em and over' (London, Chatham and Dover) served 'Screaming Alice' (Crystal Palace) by steam. 'It is needless to particularise the railway facilities; the Crystal Palace is now in connection with nearly all the Metropolitan lines' it could be written by 1873.

Additionally the Crystal Palace acquired a short railway within its own grounds, which today is surely Britain's most lost of all lost lines: the short-lived atmospheric railway. Indeed, so lost that archaeologists have been seeking it for several years without success though it is clearly marked on contemporary maps. Its exact course is undiscovered, so completely has time buried it beneath the Palace park. It linked Low Level and High Level stations and the Palace itself from a terminus alongside the former, whence it climbed steeply uphill. It is of double interest as the prime precursor of the London Underground.

The atmospheric line was opened in 1864, ten years after the Palace, running afternoons only at a fare of sixpence return. At 600 yards long, and with a steep gradient inside a curved tunnel, it was no mean engineering achievement.

The single carriage, of full broad-gauge width, was surrounded by diaphragms fringed with bristles, foreshadowing modern hovercraft, brushing the tunnel's inside walls. Gravity controlled its descent from Palace level, two airtight doors closing as it entered its tunnel, wherein it was propelled forward by air blown in by a stationary engine. Less than a minute sufficed for the journey. In reverse a vacuum was formed ahead of the car, and at the top end it ran under momentum only into the station.

So promising was the idea of a locomotiveless train in a tunnel that next year a similar tube under the

Thames was mooted, from Waterloo to Tottenham Court Road. It failed and work was abandoned, but the embryonic tunnel reputedly survives under the river as London's first Tube.

Between 1914 and 1918 'Screaming Alice' aided the war effort, becoming for thousands of sailors and Marines *HMS Crystal Palace*, technically designated as a ship from which men joining the many bus and tram routes (the High Level railway was closed for the duration) were technically going on 'shore leave'. Tens of thousands passed through on demob parade. With peace the public came back, at train fares by then raised to 1s. 6d. (7½p) return from London, First class, through 1s. 2d. (6p) Second to 1s. (5p) Third, 'plus War Supplement'.

Third-rail electrification came to this area early, the useful line through Low Level to Beckenham Junction (still open) being among the first thirty track miles of LCDR line to be electrified after the 1923 amalgamation, operative from July 1925. The High Level line followed suit, but steam also continued using this route, notably the fine 0-6-0 all-purpose Southern tender locomotives, often seen on the turntable. Electrification was the last railway landmark before disaster.

On the night of November 30, 1936, after closing time, a tiny flame flickered into light in a small Palace room reserved for the convenience of the public, hesitated, and burst out with greater enthusiasm. Discovering that eighty-year-old wooden flooring with a foot-thick layer of explosive dust beneath was to its taste, it probed a little further. Within minutes night staff were on the scene, but already it was too late. So dry was the timber that the gargantuan building, over a quarter mile long, was doomed. Flames roared so fast towards the concert hall where a local orchestra

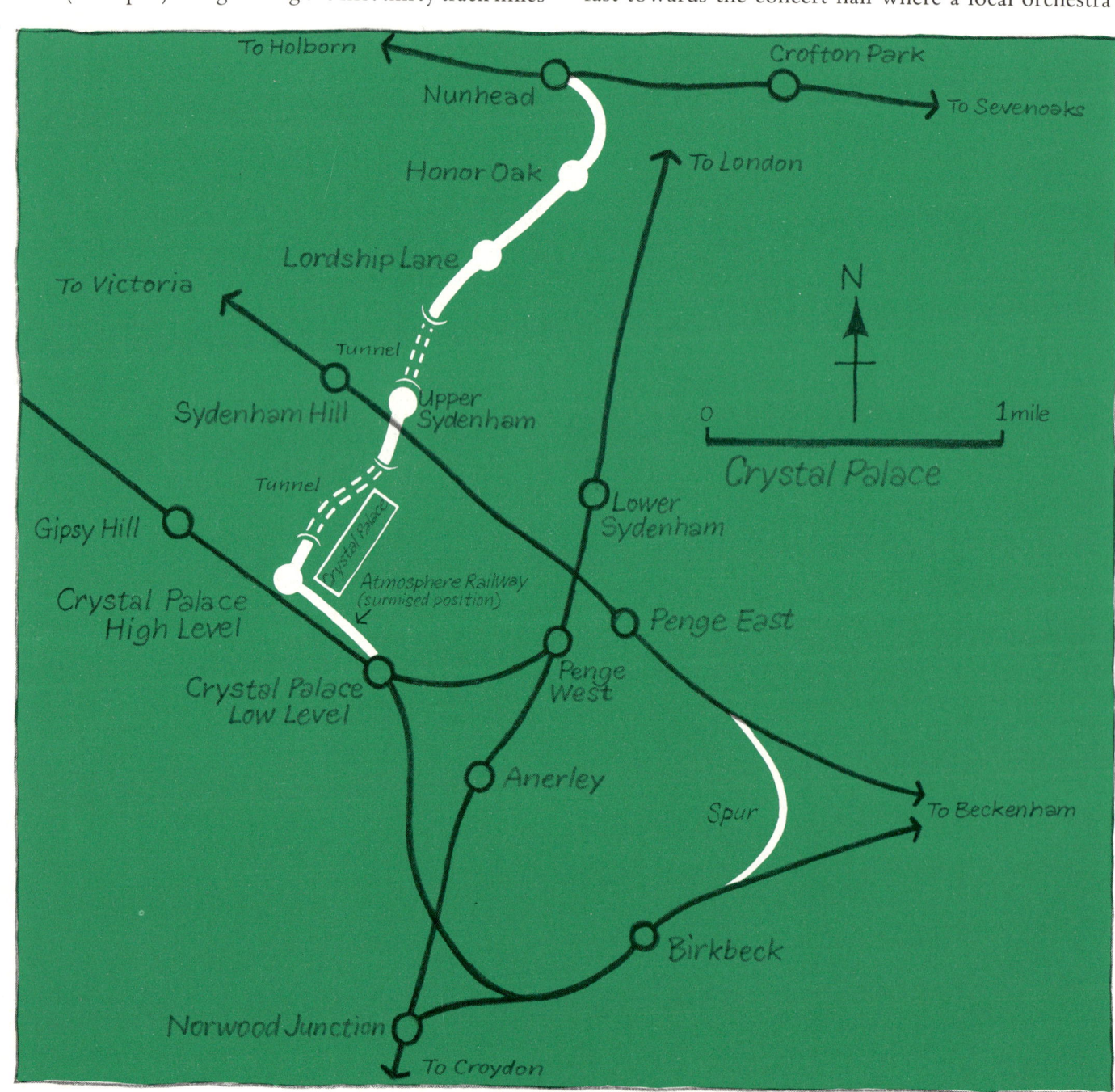

was rehearsing that a firefighter's shout, 'run for your lives!' barely reached them in time. So quickly did the famous hall catch fire that the last fleeing players actually heard the organ's death throes, groaning with unearthly sounds as hot air rushed into the pipework. The most spectacular London fire since 1666 was under way. Five miles off the falling great transept was heard as 'gunfire of the Great War'. Halfway across the North Sea pilots reported the huge glow.

It was a fitting end for a Palace larger than life, that rather than continuing in its by then slightly tattered condition, or becoming an enormous white elephant too big for modern taste, it should die with a flourish.

More than the Crystal Palace expired that night. A whole district, dependant on it for existence, was also condemned to lie without further development until the 1960s; and a whole railway was also dealt a mortal blow.

Lost Atmospheric Railway, seen operating in about 1864. Note stationary engine and shed. *Pamlin Prints*

Southern No. 31576 on turntable. This fine table delayed many families visiting the Crystal Palace, unable to drag their children – or themselves – away from a constant succession of incoming trains being prepared for departure. *Lens of Sutton*

A special behind No. 31576. The buffer plaque reads: 'Last Train on the Crystal Palace High Level branch'. *Lens of Sutton*

'The Palace Centenarian'. Last day of operation on the High Level branch, with steam brought back to this electrified line for the nostalgic occasion. *Lens of Sutton*

Tunnel entrance and approaches to station. Banks on right are now totally tree-covered and the tunnel scarcely visible from that angle. *Lens of Sutton*

Before half-hearted discussions on rebuilding the totally irreplaceable could bear fruit, war broke out again. The High Level line closed for the duration, as in the earlier conflict; but in any case there was little now to bring outsiders to Sydenham Hill. The residents themselves were more than amply served by numerous bus and tram routes that continued terminating and interchanging on the Parade.

A flicker of life remained, enough to justify the reopening of this line up through hilly Honor Oak and Lordship Lane, but it was a wavering flicker. The district, minus the Palace, had degenerated and lost its residential appeal, though enough old snobbery remained on the exclusive Dulwich side, among big houses, to say 'No' when proposals were made to extend to High Level a bus route previously ending at Honor Oak, down below, as replacement if the line were closed. It was not then known that many of these small mansions would soon be destroyed, too expensive for upkeep, replaced by innumerable flats whose large numbers of inhabitants might have brought new trade to the line.

Track was lifted and stations closed, the final train running on September 19, 1954, less than ten years after post-war reopening. Ironically, new talk of another Palace was finally shelved, in favour of the National Sports Centre, sited nearer the remaining Low Level station, on the grounds that High Level transport facilities were insufficient! The grand terminal station was totally demolished, and little temporary prefab bungalows took its place. So big was the site that they numbered scores, with ample room for individual lawns and two or three approach roads, one sliced through the station wall.

High Level station's handsome interior. Note the ornate globular lamps. Probably about 1920.
Lens of Sutton

Lifted and abandoned 'Crystal Line' leaving Nunhead, seen from a Catford Loop electric train on adjoining track. 1977.
M V Searle

High Level after third rail electrification, taken in about 1950.
Lens of Sutton

Frontage of the Gothic style station at High Level built for the LCDR.
Pamlin Prints

During 1978–9 the prefabs in turn were boarded up awaiting destruction, lying deserted in a beautiful leafy glade, almost unrecognisable as a station site. Now in 1982 the prefabs are gone and the site is again derelict, its future use uncertain. The Paxton Tunnel, reputedly in a wonderful state of preservation underneath the road after thirty years' disuse but for a wartime stint as an air raid shelter, has been bricked up as a protective measure against vandalism. Proposals for putting it on weekend show have so far foundered, owing to problems of safeguarding it for the rest of the week, in a district where tourists are few in any case.

Land here is too valuable to lie idle for long. All along this steep suburban line, great chunks of embankment and cutting have vanished, bulldozed away to nothing or filled in for building yet more flats. This is clearly seen from Catford Loop trains passing the abandoned 'Crystal Lines' and their empty bridge arches south of Nunhead, where high embankment suddenly drops away for a new estate, built over its flattened former course. Only at the High Level site is there any real indication of the old larger-than-life scale of things, in massive remains of the station presently uncovered by road works, and in what must surely be one of Britain's longest station walls, stretching the full length of the Parade, almost out of sight from one end to the other. Otherwise desolation reigns; on one side yawns a vast gap where the Crystal Palace stood, on the other is the void of its lost station.

At least we can see from its former ground plan how big was Barry's handsome terminus, the scale of its approaches, and the place of its turntable and tunnel. Of the other lost Crystal Line, the atmospheric railway, nothing meets the eye. For several years now transport archaeologists and local historians have been systematically searching for it, with a wonderful prize as bait; could the single car train, locked up for the last time before they were born, be there still inside its forgotten tunnel? It would be the transport find of the century.

Its exact location is said to be uncertain, surveys having been made in the direction of Norwood Junction or between Penge and Sydenham, hoping for evidence of its underground hiding place. Yet, curiously, readily available evidence exists to show its likely position, exactly where any railway enthusiast would expect to find it, close alongside the remaining Low Level station, where passengers would have transferred from one train to the other by some adjacent link. This link, and the course of the railway itself, appear clearly marked, down to the words 'station entrance', on a detailed plan of Palace and grounds of 1864. Hopefully, this piece of railway history will ultimately be uncovered.

As 'Screaming Alice' burned in London's greatest funeral pyre its last general manager reputedly said, unashamedly in tears, 'My Crystal Palace is finished. There will never be another.' The same can now be said both of the railway that climbed near the top of the hill, and the railway that served it by atmospheric pressure under ground, in its gargantuan heyday.

The bare site of the station, tracks and yards after total demolition, seen in 1965. Its huge emptiness exactly complements the desolate vastness of the Palace site itself, across the high road in the background. *NCB*

Only the long outer wall survives to indicate the size of High Level and its approaches, probably one of the longest station walls in England, at about 3/8 mile long. Tunnel opening under masonry at right.
M V Searle

The same site in December 1977. Sydenham Hill has reverted to its pre-Crystal Palace natural beauty. The glade-like station space is filled with prefab houses. Now they, too, are boarded up awaiting destruction. What next? *M V Searle*

CHAPTER 8

The Bordon Valley
BENTLEY TO BORDON & LONGMOOR

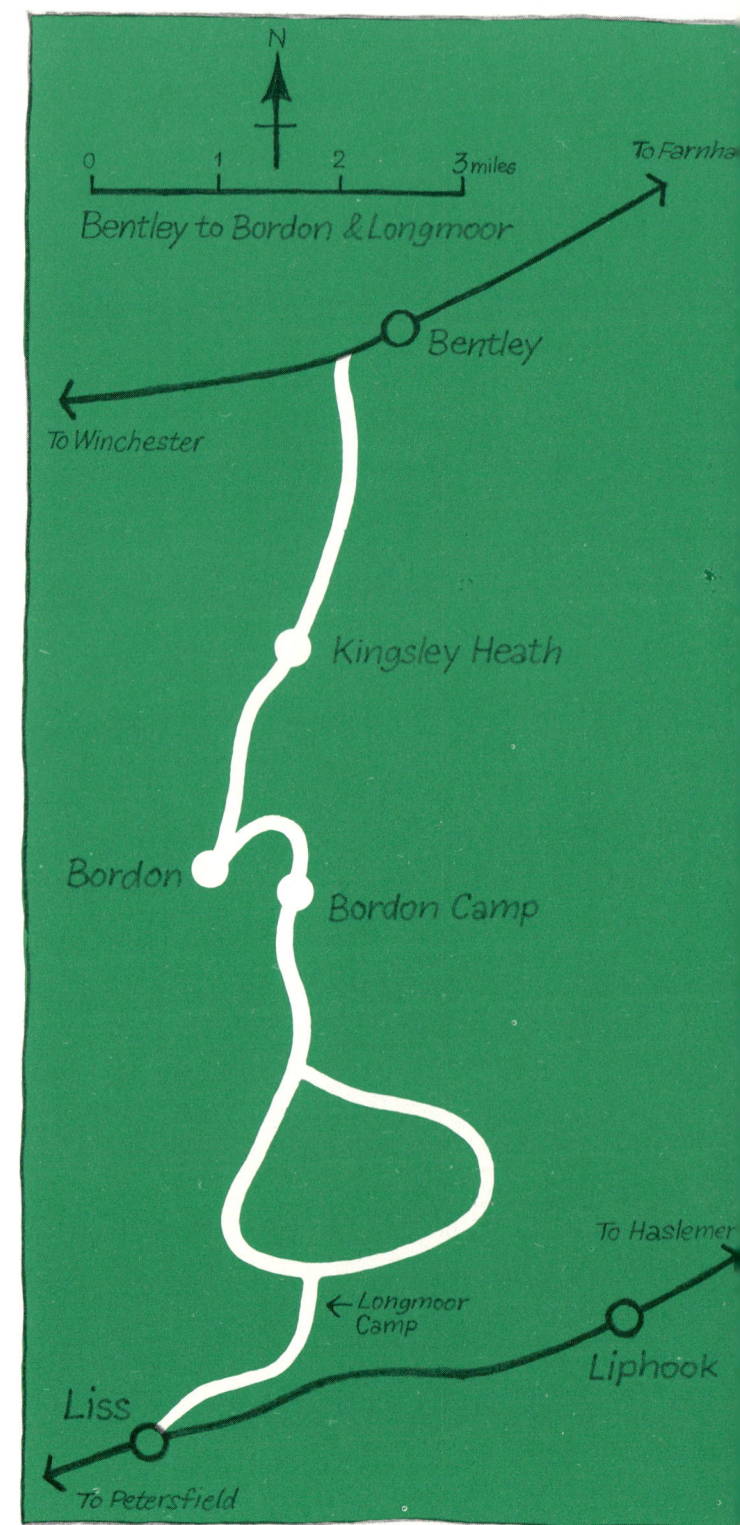

Little lines as well as large concerns make up the total picture of Britain's forgotten railways. Some, like the Canterbury and Whitstable, were big in historical import if not in size; others were of lesser historic importance but had unusual offshoots and within their own localities were a fact of life, taken for granted until they came to an end.

Just such a line was the brief branch off the main London to Farnham and Winchester line running from Bentley to Bordon, and which, so to speak, kept its head always in Civvy Street but its feet in Army boots.

It lay where the forested and scenic, often spectacular, Surrey Hills fall off into the gentler pastoral countryside of eastern Hampshire, skirting near the boundary of the spreading Alice Holt Forest before penetrating deeper from the main line towards another stately southern woodland, Woolmer Forest.

Technically this little branch with big military connections was designated a light railway, a point rammed home to civilians embarking at the Bentley branching off point by a prominent notice, 'Change Here for Bordon Light Railway'. In practice it was a normally worked standard gauge minor branch line, bearing little difference to the rest of the London and South Western which brought it to fruition. It was one of two LSWR light railways in the same vicinity, sister to the lengthier and better known Basingstoke to Alton.

This line's parent Bordon Camp was, like Tidworth, Black Down and Longmoor in the same army-oriented area, built to accommodate soldiers repatriated from the Front after the Boer War. Some link between it and Longmoor, only about four miles south, was a logical development, the germ both of the LSWR Bordon branch, with which this chapter is mainly concerned, and the Longmoor Military Railway or LMR. Initially an 18 inch line was laid between the two camps, but replaced in 1907 by standard gauge track. The LSWR and military authorities were also agreed on the construction of a standard connection by normal public railway up to the nearest main line, namely the Bentley to Bordon, which faithfully served both parties for fifty-two useful if erratic years. Primarily a normal country branch, the Army was its best customer and *raison d'être*.

Only four and a half miles long, the branch was first brought into being through a Light Railway Order of 1902, but was not opened until three years later, on December 11, 1905. Early one-engine-in-steam operation quickly gave way to standard working.

Only one other station was built, as Kingsley (or Kingsley Heath), at roughly the halfway mark. For a brief time immediately after opening, lineside Kingsley indulged in extravagant dreams of a full station instead of its primeval platform, lonesome lamp and solitary seat; even of its own goods siding, but the scheme was too grandiose for so minor a halt, and was soon shelved. Kingsley, still without even a roof, went to sleep again; a snooze broken in future only by brief stops of the regular train and sporadic troop movements.

Bordon itself was, in local parlance, a 'proper station', not only for the public benefit but also as an interchange between civil and military railways. It made at least minimal pretentions to terminus status with a signal box, siding, and even a small engine shed.

At Bentley on the main line passengers would change for Bordon, although they rarely comprised more than a slightly dispirited handful bound for the place itself, Kingsley, or the even more remote Oakhanger, deep in spreading farmland. Their change was made at an otherwise little frequented bay on the Down side at Bentley, separated from the main Down platform by a range of iron railings, like a leper on the wrong side of a colony wall, giving the impression that the main line was resolved not to be associated with the branch. Through trains, all the same, were forced at intervals to tolerate the interloper's presence as the Bordon train, lacking any outside track of its own, necessarily shared the main line for some distance from Bentley before branching off into its own territory.

Neither Kingsley nor Bordon were initially sufficiently populated to justify a new railway in their own right, even in the over enthusiastic early 1900s, when railway mania still had considerable life. Its most important service was to the sprawling Army camps of Bordon itself and Longmoor, complementary establishments to Aldershot, some miles north, of which defence regulations preclude more than cursory mention. For every civilian carried up to the Second World War, the line often transported a wagon load of troops. Trains were transferred from Bordon to the camp lines by private loops to the Longmoor Military Railway, then known as the Woolmer Instructional Military Railway, a self-explanatory appellation.

Older residents still tell of thousands of soldiers passing along the Bentley branch between 1914 and 1918, lustily singing *Keep The Home Fires Burning* with outwardly cheerful faces, knowing that every clack of the wheels brought them nearer the ghastly ordeal of 'going over the top' and probable death in the choking mud of Flanders. Between wars troop movements were naturally more sporadic, but considerable goods traffic was maintained.

The civil Bordon branch was only twenty-two years old when, despite Army traffic, the first signs of a run down appeared, with reduction of Bordon signal box facilities in 1927. On the other hand, another military extension was opened in the opposite direction down to Liss, allowing a complete north-and-south link by 1933 with two main lines running parallel with each other but about twelve miles apart, the London–Winchester and London–Haslemere–Portsmouth.

For a second time in its half century of life Bordon branch burst into intensive activity in World War II, as soldiers came through for training before embarkation; this time they departed singing *Hang Out Your Washing On The Siegfried Line*.

Over 25,000 men, it is locally said, trained on private railway stock before leaving to deal with bombings and blastings on the real thing.

Branch line quietness and greenery at Bordon in August 1957. *G Daniels*

Afternoon train from Bordon in 1957. It used the main electrified Waterloo–Alton line for a brief stretch. *G Daniels*

Returning peace brought a definite decline of non-mainline railways in general, which neither the Bordon branch nor its military extensions could escape. Road transport, in military circles as well as Civvy Street, increasingly took over from rail work. No longer was a private system like the LMR justifiable for training purposes.

Ordinary passenger services between Bentley and Bordon ceased fairly early in the calendar of nationwide closures that continued unabated until about 1966; the final train ran on September 16, 1957, though freight continued to the camps for another decade until April 4, 1966. Track was lifted in 1967.

In the post-war period, the only time recalled by most residents, total rolling stock comprised one small M7 tank and two ancient ex-LSWR carriages, barely fitting the tiny Bentley bay. The LMR, no longer

The once-important signal box early in 1978, photographed from an Alton bound train. Four days later it was due for destruction, removing one of the best visible reminders that here was the entrance not only to a country branch, but to the military camps of Longmoor and Bordon, and to the Longmoor Military Railway. *M V Searle*

Approaches to Bordon Station in 1957. *G Daniels*

← Charming Kingsley Halt of the poplars and peace. Pull and push for Bentley arriving, backwards, in 1957.
G Daniels

30027 leaves Kingsley Halt for Bordon on an August afternoon in 1957. G Daniels

reachable via Bordon, relied on its southward outlet at Liss on the Portsmouth route before its own closure.

The Bentley bay was where I started looking for remains one frozen February day in 1978. Like a low trough the deserted grassy bay lay trackless, backed by bushes. Time had bitten chunks from the crumbling platform lip. Traceable by eye was the branch outlet towards the main line and the crooked old deserted signal box once controlling heavy troop trains as well as local shuttles out to Bordon. 'You want the signal box, of course?' a helpful Bentley railwayman said when I telephoned asking what could be photographed, before making a special visit; 'You'll have to come in the next four days – the Army are going to demolish it this Saturday.' I went down quickly, and caught it from a speeding Alton train. Now it is gone, another step towards oblivion, making it harder to spot the branch turning. When I found it, it lay under thin snow rippling like regular waves to reflect outlines of sleepers that were no longer there, only their beds. Bordon and Kingsley station sites have both been built over.

Except in localised recollection, Bentley to Bordon is among our least remembered abandoned branches.

Notice of closure, the publicly posted death certificate of many branches in the 1950s and 1960s, here pasted up on the Bordon branch.
G Daniels

The shallow, overgrown bay at Bentley, still showing some railway evidence.
M V Searle

The point where the Bordon line (left) ran out towards the signalbox guarding its departure southwards towards its namesake town, 1978.
M V Searle

Time and disuse have bitten a jagged chuck from the Bentley platform edge, as found by the author early in 1978.
M V Searle

CHAPTER 9

Oh! Mr Porter!

BASINGSTOKE & ALTON LIGHT RAILWAY

'An ancient town situated near to the canal bearing its name, and communicating with the rivers Thames and Wey, which with the railway facilitate a brisk trade in corn and malt'; that was Basingstoke when Queen Victoria had sat on the throne for about fifteen years. It was just coming awake in the light of its first mainline railways, its other chief features being 'a sixteenth century church, a free school . . . several other charities, a market hall, town hall, and a jail'.

The London and South Western, serving Basingstoke, was to become increasingly uneasy about maintaining its monopoly between here and the south as the century progressed and the rival Great Western set increasingly covetous eyes upon its territory. For the GWR Basingstoke would be a most convenient springboard, enabling the company to gatecrash this geographically non-Great Western countryside and thus force its way through to Portsmouth and its remunerative traffic.

It was clear to the LSWR, that the course most likely to be grabbed by the GWR in such an event was the as yet unopened valley via Alton, and thence southwards to the port. Only by acting fast and taking this valley route for itself could the LSWR forestall for certain its rival's plan. Parliament, the LSWR felt certain, would never countenance a second line through the same territory, once a first had been built.

Thus this serene agricultural district acquired a light railway offshoot of the LSWR despite the fact that its scattered farmers and villagers neither needed, wanted, nor were likely to financially support such a line.

In 1896 the standard gauge Basingstoke and Alton Light Railway became the earliest to be raised under the then new Light Railways Act of the same year. No time was lost in leaping aboard the bandwagon of the Act in order to halt the GWR.

At Butts Junction, about a mile out of Alton, the new line turned off, in its finalised form being equipped with but three intermediate stations (Cliddesden or Cliddesdon, Herriard, and the combined Bentworth and Lasham), plus an additional private halt to a large local hospital, operative but never shown in timetables. Its total cost was relatively low, at £67,000 for about 13 miles of permanent way, thanks to the unusual willingness of landowners to sell cheaply in the mistaken hope that a railway would increase property values in future.

Most stations were rudimentary affairs of corrugated iron, similar to those on Sheppey. Their water supply came from windmills or windpumps. More comfortably served than the passengers were company employees, for whom the LSWR erected substantial cottages and stationmasters' houses. No signalboxes were built; usually trains were simply flagged out by platform staff or a stationmaster.

Beauty rather than possible trade prospects was the single track line's most noticeable characteristic. It meandered through shallow pastoral vales following convenient contours, whose wanderings dictated its 'veritable serpentine character', as a witness of opening day commented. The resulting sharp curves imposed initial speeds of only 10 mph, balanced by a seemingly breakneck 20 mph at other points. Often woods clothed the slopes right to the valley bottoms, enabling travellers to hear singing birds en route. Crossings were frequently ungated, guarded by cattle grids to prevent cows actually wandering onto the track.

Railway mania, with its old-time guns, bells, flags, triumphal arches and civic banquets, had long since evaporated into familiarity before the Basingstoke and Alton's opening on June 1, 1901. Farmworkers briefly left their fields to watch the first train pass, behind 0-4-4T No 203 of the LSWR, but only one cottager is said to have produced a flag. Progress occupied almost exactly an hour for the thirteen miles, making an average speed including stops of 13 mph; small wonder that lineside cattle merely looked up instead of running.

Most passengers travelled as official guests. Only a handful bothered to invest in tickets for the novelty, and barely twenty official spectators witnessed the train's departure, without raising a single cheer. Allegations of great enthusiasm for this line in Alton, said to be capable of mushrooming expansion as a result, proved the proverbial damp squib.

Such passengers as did adopt the new line discovered at least one useful advantage. The formerly roundabout journey to Basingstoke via Winchester, a two-hour drag costing about 3s. (15p) in fares, was reduced to roughly half the time and less than half the fare. Less palatably, light railway services departed only three times a day – morning, noon and teatime – giving neither early business nor evening return facilities. No trains at all ran on Sundays, as if to preserve dated notions that pleasure seeking on the Sabbath was as sinful as keeping late hours on weekdays. Unpopular, too, was an initial habit of attaching coal trucks to trains, delaying passengers considerably with their shunting.

In 1903 a further railway beyond Alton was opened, the pretty Meon Valley route, finally scotching all GWR hopes of intruding across Hampshire to Portsmouth.

On the B&ALR, steam railmotors were tried in 1904, of which the LSWR possessed about fifteen for use on rural runs lacking enough custom to justify full length trains. None of this stable, however, proved fully suitable for this line's curves and gradients, nor to its mixed passenger and goods trains.

Services were improved to six a day around 1912, still without Sunday working. Separate freight trains were run instead of the disliked mixed combinations.

Nevertheless, this line built to forestall a rival company instead of for genuine public service continued losing money, encouraging the LSWR to cash in on the Great War as an excuse for closing it down in 1917. For LSWR main lines, starved of manpower as more and more employees were drafted into the forces, salvation lay in transferring staff away from uneconomic backwaters.

Hopeful of thus avoiding any necessity of reopening the line, now that GWR threats were settled, the company reinforced its point by tearing up track and shipping it to wartime France for repairing bombed front line links.

Human cussedness, however, forced second thoughts. People who had never needed nor used their line when it was there, were loudest in clamouring for restoration in peacetime.

Southern, who absorbed the line in 1923, initially reiterated that proven pre-1917 losses of £4,000 annually precluded reopening, but were later reduced to making a vague promise to reconsider 'in ten years'. Finally, SR was persuaded to give Alton another chance.

Track was relaid and half-derelict stations refurbished. At Herriard the old passing loop was craftily removed, ensuring that once any train departed from either end, no other could use the entire thirteen mile length until the first had completed its full course. Services could therefore never be improved; it seemed that SR was deliberately discouraging public reliance on the line, with another closure as its aim. Stationmasters were dispensed with, the line coming under the direction of one man stationed at Basingstoke, anticipating modern practice of one station-manager governing a nest of neighbouring points.

Reopening fell on August 18, 1924, with the first train in charge of the elderly E234, as ancient as the Basingstoke and Alton's original loco, dating from 1895. Three daily services were timetabled, no better than in 1901, again as if to dissuade passenger loyalty.

This line's claim to outside fame beyond its own bounds lies not in normal working but in two railway films shot there. The first was filmed on a Sunday in 1928, (a normal closure day) when for *The Wrecker* a spectacular crash was staged. A 4-4-0 express engine, No. 148, heading six carriages, was set to smash at speed into a steam lorry stalled on a level crossing. After its driver and fireman jumped clear, having opened up full throttle, the engine performed its 'lines' perfectly, disintegrating into a photogenic heap of dismembered parts amid clouds of steam. Her remains were recovered for scrap, and the track afterwards rehabilitated.

Film stardom was only a thin spread of jam to the light railway's life. Its daily bread and butter – passenger and freight journeys – became increasingly unpro-

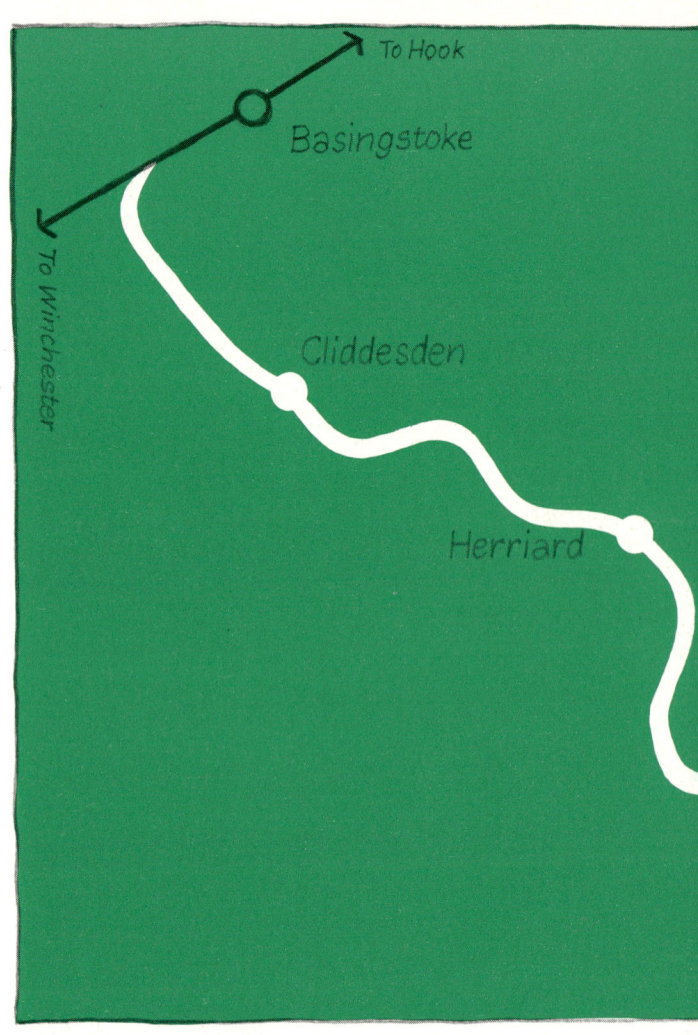

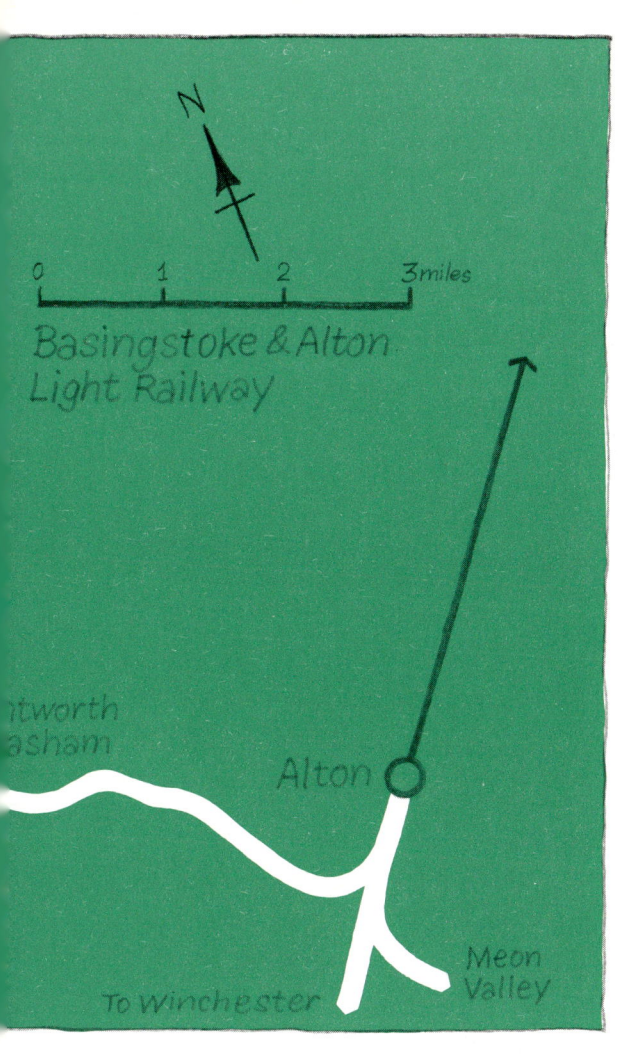

Butts Bridges, Alton, in 1978. Immediately to the right of this smaller of the two bridges, the Basingstoke and Alton line joined with two other now disused railways – the Alton to Winchester and Meon Valley lines – to run together into Alton.
M V Searle

Cliddesden station in June 1931, every inch the country halt of *Oh, Mr Porter!* Crews had time to dismount and face the camera of one travelling railway enthusiast. The locomotive is the former LSWR Adams 0-4-4T No. 234.
H C Casserley

The larger section of Butts Bridges, with their massive connecting earthworks, viewed in February 1978.
M V Searle

Rare shot of a mixed train on the B&A branch, showing well the intriguing hump of the leading covered wagon. Antiquated passenger stock at rear.
Lens of Sutton

Non-fuelling use of a tender shovel from the roof of carriage No. 226 in Will Hay's classic railway comedy, filmed after official closure of the Basingstoke & Alton Line.
(Still from Oh! Mr Porter by courtesy of The Rank Organisation)

Spontaneous comedy of the old school during station platform shooting of *Oh! Mr Porter* on the closed B&AR. A ramshackle carriage becomes a handy emergency milking shed.
(Still from Oh! Mr Porter by courtesy of The Rank Organisation)

ductive, as both took almost entirely to roads. Even on the actual day of closure September 12, 1932, a direct result of this desertion, public interest was almost nil. Exactly one passenger rode the final train, railway enthusiasts not as yet having adopted the somewhat depressing countrywide hobby of travelling by last trains, an interest created by the wholesale closures of the 1960s.

Goods traffic continued sporadically until final closure on June 1, 1936, after which track was lifted between Alton and Lasham. Lines remained awhile over the other part, making possible in 1937 shooting of Will Hay's immortal *Oh! Mr Porter!*, critically often considered in retrospect the best comedy of the Thirties.

One reason for Gainsborough Pictures choosing this location was its pastoral, quasi-Irish appearance. Stagecraft made it suitably ramshackle, with decrepit false fronting to Cliddesden station, renamed for the film 'Buggleskelly' in a whimsical fictitious Ireland. A false signal box was also added.

Kent and East Sussex locomotive *No. 2*, borrowed for filming, was similarly aged with a tall false funnel, serrated at its top *à la Rocket*, and nameplated *Gladstone*. Her co-star was an ex-LSWR express 4-4-0, No. 657, suitably mature with a birthday back in 1895.

Cinemagoers long recalled this film's exciting climax of a locomotive chase from 'Buggleskelly' towards Basingstoke, a combination of reality and trick photography, along with the logical illogic of Will Hay in his 'SRNI' stationmaster's uniform.

Soon after this, most of the surviving track was lifted. Two little-known fragments were left at the extreme ends; a quarter of a mile stretch from Alton for transporting coals to the outlying Treloars Hospital for Cripples (the line finally closed after many years' neglect, as late as July 1967); and a short works stretch.

After nearly fifty years' abandonment, evidence of a railway naturally diminishes yearly, but some landmarks are nevertheless identifiable. They include railway houses and some bridges, though many have vanished during modern road works. Level stretches of track have been absorbed back into the farming land from whence they came, but remains of cuttings and embankments survive, including a particularly impressive shorn-off embankment opposite Treloars Hospital. Cliddensden windpump lasted till 1947, and concrete platforms rather longer.

Today this is a district of three lost lines – the Basingstoke and Alton, the Meon Valley, and most of the Alton–Winchester route, only a small portion having been restored as the Watercress Line. All three met outside Alton. They still do, in desertion, at the double arches of Butts Bridges, which with their massive earthworks form the biggest joint reminder of this lost trinity. Within yards of the smaller round-arched bridge abutments the Basingstoke and Alton joined its two fellows, running with them almost immediately over the second and heavier girder bridge into the town.

Today all these bridges and embankments are silent. Alton, once hub of a four-spoked wheel (north west to Basingstoke, south into Meon, west to Winchester, and north east to London) keeps only its London connection, and two operational platforms. The third looks down onto rusted metals. Alton is the end, not the centre, of the line.

CHAPTER 10

The Hayling Billy

HAYLING ISLAND BRANCH

Hayling Island branch was a paradox when closures stalked the tracks in the 1960s. A line reasonably patronised, paying its way operationally, but doomed on two counts: passengers flocked in summer and the line became overcrowded, but no extra moneyspinning trains could ever be laid on, due to the line's layout; and instability of its most distinctive feature, the bridge joining island and mainland. £40,000 was the ransom price of the branch, the cost of restoring this bridge, when the usual committees of preservers and potential destroyers went into session.

Battling of a different variety had hit railway headlines at Havant, the branch's junction, whilst it was actually being planned, the notorious Battle of Havant of December 1858. At that time animosity between LSWR, LBSCR and SER (potential poachers of LSWR rights), over the new Direct Portsmouth approaches exploded into fighting worthier of a Western film than Hampshire. The LBSCR's reluctance to honour running powers to its rival for sharing the final run-in from Hilsea to Havant was countered by an LSWR attempt, backed by a Parliamentary committee, to force entry with a special morning freight train.

The LBSCR, proclaiming that any rival train touching its territory was in trespass, enlisted an army of loyal Brighton navvies to remove tracks and block the way with an old engine chained to a crossing. The arriving trainload of LSWR toughs, armed with sledgehammers in anticipation of such skulduggery, attempted slipping through near dawn, but were immediately ambushed by hordes of uncouthly yelling Brighton 'Indians'. Lineside fighting involving some 500 men apparently ended when the Brighton men retreated, ripping up more track as they went, though still under fire from LSWR cudgels and sledgehammers, whilst other LSWR 'Apaches' triumphantly drove off the captured locomotive.

Again as in a good exciting film, the tables were swiftly turned with a final shattering Brighton attack that herded the tired South Western men back into the goods wagons. In the more sober atmosphere of court the LBSCR continued fighting, accusing the LSWR of trespass, as they had threatened, but eventually the latter's rights were confirmed, and Portsmouth direct services began.

Initially the Hayling Island Railway Company, incorporated 18 months after the Battle, felt smugly independent of both squabbling parties, a self contained local enterprise committed to operating – peacably – nearly five single-track miles from Havant to a beach where ambitious railwaymen, following speculative builders, visualised a moneymaking new resort.

The site was uncompromising. Since acquiring a road bridge in 1824, Hayling had gained only one hotel and half an unfinished crescent. Horsedrawn visitors were discouraged by Chichester Harbour's creeks, amid which Hayling lay, thus described immediately before railway development: 'At low water . . . a vast area of many thousands of acres of mud, the effluvia from which in the summer season is far from conducive to health and renders this part of the country between Chichester and Portsmouth very insalubrious.'

Yet here was conceived a line aimed primarily at pleasureseekers, crossing by a subsequently famous spindly wooden bridge. Thereafter track hugged the island's western harbourside shore, just above shifting beach level, almost innocent of gradients or earthworks. Despite such easy terrain, opening was delayed until July 17, 1867, with trains being worked by the contractors themselves. Only eighteen months later it closed again, reopening in August 1869.

From January 1872 the still battling Brighton railway slipped its foot through the door, against a possible LSWR grab, with a temporary working agreement, formalised into a £2,000-a-year lease from 1874. A more ambitious LBSC scheme of 1886, to link Southsea, another *very* lost local branch, across to Langstone Harbour and a junction with Hayling, never materialised. Nor did early inter-island service experiments bring prosperity. The train ferry opened from Langstone to St Helens on the Isle of Wight, using the freighter *Carrier* (see Chapter 11) encountered so little support that services ended after only six years.

Passengers, increasingly attracted to Hayling for quiet beach pleasures, particularly with children (mud or no mud) were the branch's prime revenue. For them were built halts at Langstone (Langston on station nameboards, Langstone on most maps), and a more primitive North Hayling, to the end made identifiable to engine drivers after dark by a splendid old lamp nicknamed among crews as 'The North Star'. The terminus, South Hayling, was subsequently renamed Hayling Island. Almost throughout its entire life, any train on this branch was affectionately termed *The Hayling Billy*, or with less familiarity *The Havant Bill*. Station staff worked hard for what modern life calls little money in creating its spick and span image; the Havant porter of 1893 fetching and carrying on 16s. (80p) a week, rising to a dizzy 24s. (£1.20) on promotion in about 1900 to head porter.

As no passing place existed, services could never be increased, even during the inter-war and post-1945 booms. Twenty-four round trips daily were the absolute workable maximum. Once the train left Havant, crowds had to wait while it travelled the full route, unloaded and came back. At best a second train could be at the ready, cutting a few minutes off turn-round time. To the end, a half-hourly service was all the line's inbuilt peculiarities permitted.

Early trains, following the contractor period, were primitive, lit by oil lamps, trundling behind the Island's namesake engine, No. 96, *Hayling Island*. She lasted until about 1900. For the rest of the branch's long life Brighton or ex-Brighton 0-6-0T *Terriers* almost exclusively supplied motive power, the only class, at just over twenty-eight tons, suitable for the bridge's weight limitations. Accommodation allowance was a maximum of four carriages, plus two mixed wagons, or the 'perambulator van' peculiar to this route to a children's paradise.

The *Terrier* puffing-billies *were* Hayling Island; so much so that, at the end, a brewery purchased one example, No. 32646, restored her livery, and preserved her outside its Hayling Billy pub. For her it was a dignified end to a chequered career: working the LSWR's Axminster–Lyme Regis branch in Drummond livery; sale in 1913 to the Freshwater–Yarmouth and Newport Railway; a change to green and red from LSWR dress; renaming from her original title of *Newington* to *Freshwater* by Southern, still on the IOW; to final BR nameless numbering as 32646, a brief sojourn on a private steam line after the Hayling Line's closure, and her final resting place, where the Portsmouth Brickwood's brewery placed her in 1966.

People as well as engines underwent changes of occupation as the world spun into the twentieth century. The Great War, early in *Newington/Freshwater/Billy's* career, precipitated a previously unheard-of mass exodus of women from home or domestic service out to work, replacing men in men's jobs as they went to the Front. Thus many found themselves on the railways. Some, like the author's mother and aunt, worked in booking halls or season ticket offices; some actually on the platform. Havant boasted being the first provincial LBSCR station employing female porters and ticket collectors as a wartime measure.

When the 'boys' returned they were generally given back their old placcs and the women bidden appreciative but firm farewells. One such lady, Miss Amy Bright, a sprightly 81, loaned the present author a rare picture of Havant's uniformed quartette of two lady ticket collectors and two porters, nostalgically inscribed 'Happy days!', and painted a vivid portrait of wartime life aged twenty-one with the *Hayling Billy*. Before becoming a collector, Miss Bright 'did platform duties'. To quote: 'We had to sweep, clean the windows, and polish the brass handles with Globe Polish, and when it was finished it always looked very nice.' Such pride in cleaning the *Billy* was typical of branch railway staff before modernisation mechanised the pride out of polishing. When the ex-soldiers returned, the company's appreciation of good service was expressed in farewell presentations of 'a very nice lady's handbag for Miss Bright, and a travelling case for Miss King' (the other woman ticket collector), with the hope that they 'would always be as happy as when they were employed at the station'.

At day's end stock stayed overnight at Havant but the faithful *Terrier* usually ran on light to Fratton yard. Miss Bright the collector never forgot hitching a footplate lift – utterly out of the question for any woman before the war – back to Southsea, delight turning to trepidation as winds off Farlington Marshes buffeted the cab; 'and didn't the driver and fireman laugh!'

Another lady wartime porter, now Mrs Kite, confirmed to me the joys of riding the *Billy*'s footplate, when taken up to North Hayling halt for cleaning duty, from South Hayling. There the driver deposited her, with a bucket of steaming water from the engine, picking her up on his return run. Back at base she resumed porter's duty. Long before cries of 'Womens Lib!' went up, this woman was doing a man's job, entrusted with signalling in the afternoon train whilst the remaining male porter-signalman (whom she subsequently married) was absent with 'the goods' to Havant.

Between the two great wars men ran the branch, and tourism boomed. Never stereotyped, Hayling settled down to being a family pleasure place. Posterity may question Southern's assertion in 'South for Sunshine' that it ranked with 'The finest Resorts in the World'; but undeniably it was popular locally, and with numerous well-to-do London families seeking a Frinton atmosphere rather than the sophistication of a Torquay, coming down for long stays with toddlers, teenagers, nannies, nurses, governesses, and other staff, in a manner that is gone for ever.

Permanent residential development was delayed until the early 1930s and sited well off the line, making new householders dependent upon cars from the outset, hence wide fluctuations between seasonal and winter ticket sales. But even after another world war the public did not desert this area so markedly as it did most other branches to the sea. On one Whit Sunday, for example, 598 ticket holders jammed aboard three *Hayling Billy* coaches on one run, averaging nearly 200 per carriage. In 1961, long after many similar lines ended, over 32,000 alighted during August, more than balancing a mere 2,000 in unseasonal March. At this period one of the termini acquired its nickname of 'The Barracks', not from its forbidding appearance but because all its regular staff were then ex-Royal Marines.

Langstone Bridge, not staff or passenger revenue, was by then BR's worry. So parlous was the picturesque wooden structure that £40,000 of repairs were needed simply to make it capable of supporting future trains, more than the appointed enquiry panel cared to recommend. Instead, they chose closure before another summer overtaxed the bridge.

Hayling became BR's great irony; a line paying its way, open to still better income from those who would patronise additional summer services, if the

Last remaining LBSCR signal on Hayling Island, photographed in May 1961.
G Daniels

Terrier No. 32640 awaits arrival of her sister No. 32678, September 1962.
G Daniels

layout could but have accommodated them. The line in effect was destroyed by its own physical weaknesses, and closed in November 1963.

In addition to genuinely local farewells, there was a visit by the Locomotive Club of Great Britain, present at so many railway obsequies, packing a special *Billy* in a day of holiday junketing without the underlying sadness usually present on such occasions. *Billy* on that occasion comprised an AIX locomotive, plus a *Terrier* fore and another *Terrier* aft of five coaches.

On the very last run, *Auld Lang Syne* rang out from passengers in the guard's van as the *Billy* steamed off with a wreath on her firebox, continuously shrieking her whistle and blowing steam from her characteristic *Terrier* funnel with its local 'Hayling Island bird's nest' rim. Meanwhile another locomotive pushed from the rear against innumerable passengers jammed in with porters, ticket collectors, shunters, all breeds of railwayman. Six coaches were risked across the bridge on that final run, the heaviest load ever, and crossing the viaduct against luminescent moonlight on Guy Fawkes Eve, she looked unforgettable. Continuing to Havant, the *Billy* was greeted with cheers, bangs and crowds lining every fence to see her pass into the past, wheezily puffing.

'I am surprised that local people have not protested more vigorously' said the Havant station master. He echoed thoughts of such men everywhere, whose customers spoke too late, if at all. But a delightful Christmas card circulated widely in the area that year, showing *Billy* on the bridge, greatly treasured today all over Portsmouth.

Preservationists stepped hopefully in, with plans for services using lightweight electric trams. One was actually delivered from Blackpool Corporation, looking as incongruous stored at Havant away from its native Tower habitat as a London bus in Bahrein. Nothing came of the move, and the tram shamefacedly crept away to Lowestoft.

The *Hayling Billy* once more let off steam, figuratively but not physically, when the preserved engine outside the namesake public house celebrated her centenary, the old Stroudley *Terrier* having been built at Brighton in 1876. The Mayor of Havant, brewery directors, drum majorettes and Morris men joined with tourists and residents in doing her homage. Now even 'the biggest pub sign in England' has gone, after standing outside the tavern for thirteen years. She was taken by low loader to the docks, a smoke cannister working inside her funnel for effect, with the ash of her last fire still inside her firebox. Restored to SR livery, she was returned to the Isle of Wight.

Typical 'lost line' reminders are found on land; old trackbed, a deserted bay, sites of stations and halts. But at the harbour crossing massive piers poke up from mud or rising tides, the sides of the centre span through which ships once slipped whilst trains waited. They were deliberately retained to chart the safe deepwater course. They mark the grave of one of the south's most loved shorter branches.

Primitive little North Hayling Halt, with 32661 about to pull in. *W J Greer*

Great War women porters and ticket collectors, among the first on the LBSCR: Mrs Freckleton and Mrs Haynes (Porters), Miss King and Miss Bright (collectors). Original card inscribed 'Happy Days!'
Miss A Bright

↗
Terrier No. 32646, the engine now preserved as 'The Hayling Billy', at Fratton shed on Boxing Day 1949. Her Westinghouse braking system was a typical feature of Hayling locomotives.
Pamlin Prints

Guard Norris displays, in the branch's last days, the impressive lamp from North Hayling known to crews as 'The North Star'. It was the only distant indication after dark that a halt existed.
F J Norris

Christmas card issued in aid of Havant and District Railway Retirement Association. It shows AIX No. 32650 on Langston Bridge.

A fine photograph of No. 32646, the last 'Billy', showing her characteristic 'Hayling Bird's Nest' chimney rim. About 1959.
S J Stevens

A classic view of Langston Bridge with Terrier No. 32662 cut to diminutive proportions by the vastness of sky, harbour and bridge. 4.05 pm Havant–Hayling Island train seen on November 2, 1963.
G Daniels

Hayling Island station in 1907, with horse trap meeting the trains.
Miss P Williams

Demolition in progress at Hayling Island station in about 1953.
Portsmouth Evening News

The Hayling Billy, restored to her original name of *Newington*, preserved outside the namesake Hayling Billy public house.
Miss A Bright

Remaining stumps of Hayling Island railway bridge today.
P Jennings

CHAPTER 11

Vehicles of Vectis

THE ISLE OF WIGHT

The Isle of Wight, it has often been said, is a complete self-contained microcosm of British scenery, geography, geology and topography. Its railway history, likewise, is in compact miniature the history of our railways in general – their rise, heyday, and reasons for economic decline, embodied in no less than seven separate companies each serving its own little world. Even today, the Island's only remaining line is making history, by being the sole example of a London Underground system running neither in London nor under ground, but through the countryside and over deep sea water.

Prosperity through tourism was brought to the Island, the Romans' Vectis, by railways from London to Southampton or Portsmouth, whence ferries conveyed ever increasing numbers as workers became entitled to annual holidays. Once ashore, it was up to local interests to transport them onwards to Shanklin, Sandown and Ventnor.

Thus arose, in the middle nineteenth century, seven separate railway companies, operating a total of barely forty-six route miles, each battling in summer for vital income to tide them over winter months that bordered on stagnation. Islanders themselves were totally incapable of supporting their own communication system.

Even before railways, the seeds of touristic prosperity were sown in a small way, enough to warrant extension of Ryde's vital pier by another 1,000 feet. In itself the extension did little to attract custom away from Cowes, travellers lumbered with baggage being naturally reluctant to tramp nearly a mile from steamer to shore. The only answer was transport direct to the pier, in the form of primitive horse trams, immediate precursors of the electric trams and pier railways that made this pier famous and sealed the island's success as a steamer-and-train holiday retreat.

First on the scene was the Cowes and Newport company, authorised in August 1859, a laggardly 34 years after the mainland's earliest railway. It entered the passenger arena on June 16, 1862 with three small locomotives (under Isle of Wight Railway auspices designated the historic numbers 1, 2 and 3); *Pioneer*, *Precursor* and a small 0-4-2 saddle tank. Goods working did not begin for several more months.

This was followed on August 23, 1864, by another small company with a disproportionaly unwieldy title, the Isle of Wight Eastern Section Railway Company, allied to the LSWR, builder of the stretch destined to outlast all the local lines into the present; that from Ryde to Shanklin, continuing afterwards on to Ventnor, the southernmost seaside resort. A branch was opened to the useful Brading Quay on the same day.

Within one year this line was carrying about 165,000 passengers and 17,000 tons of freight annually, a promise that in the next century blossomed into millions of passenger journeys though, ironically, the profit from them when considered as total annual turnover would not be enough to stave off ultimate closure.

When powers were obtained for a branch towards Newport the line's misleading appellation 'Eastern Section' was dropped, though in practice the only branch constructed was to Bembridge on the east. Grandiose plans, too big for a little company's financial boots, included ferries across to Hayling Island connecting for London, but the sole ship, *Carrier*, lasted in service only to 1888.

Developments thenceforth moved fast, as yet more holidaymakers and trippers, encouraged by new facilities, flowed in through the ports of Ryde, Cowes and Yarmouth. In September 1866 St Boniface Down, the Island's loveliest but most forbidding natural barrier, was pierced by tunnel from the Shanklin side, leading through to Ventnor and the popular south. All three main resorts – Shanklin, Sandown and Ventnor – began expanding once served by train, guaranteeing additional patronage from the mainland.

The custom of naming locomotives almost exclusively after Island placenames, maintained to the last, was established at the turn of the 1860s and 1870s when the Isle of Wight Railway christened three of its 2-4-0 inside cylinder tanks *Ryde*, *Sandown* and *Shanklin*.

The Isle of Wight (Newport Junction) Railway of 1868 was created to link Newport and Sandown across the interior via Merstone, which proved from its beginnings to be a fiscally precarious little line, in monetary straits even before starting in 1875 on a Sandown to Shide route. Expenditure on a viaduct near the junction of the Ryde and Newport, involving a four year delay in fund raising, dealt the ailing railway its death blow. Passengers, however, suffered little, as the Cowes and Newport and the Ryde and Newport were permitted to take over services by arrangement with the Official Receiver.

Great prestige was brought to Vectis by Queen Victoria, with the building of Osborne House in Italianate style, and Prince Albert's fanciful Whippingham church, served by a local Whippingham station. The Royal Train customarily ran down from Windsor to Gosport by special loops built at Slough (GWR) and Staines (LSWR) to avoid reversing, and onwards by ferry and train or carriage.

Smallbrook Junction, near Ryde St John's Road (the latter a suburban station about a mile from the port) was opened up westwards on December 20, 1875, in agreement with the Cowes and Newport for joint working, an early instance of amalgamation far ahead of the great nationwide merger of 1923. Every important centre was linked by rail within the mid-century, including the thinly populated and therefore unprofitable area in the extreme west, not surprisingly the last line to open and the first to close in modern times.

The latter-day Freshwater and Yarmouth connection ended in bankruptcy largely due to disagreements with the more powerful Isle of Wight Central Railway, at whose junction the new line branched off. The two parties failing to agree on matters on property, the Freshwater company was forced to build its own ramshackle tin station, instead of sharing the Central's, and to purchase extra rolling stock it could ill afford, ensuring its demise.

Island prestige briefly broke international barriers in 1878 when a local locomotive won a major gold medal at the great Paris Exhibition. She was permitted to run back across France to Dieppe under her own steam – crewed by Negro stokers, an extraordinary novelty – amazing the French with her capabilities at speed.

Individual railways tended to appear, disappear and merge with greater regularity than on the mainland, hardly surprising in view of the very limited distances over which they were able to chase those all-important fares in the face of fierce local competition. Collectively, nonetheless their summer seasonal turnover was eminently satisfactory from the 1860s onwards for about a century. Nearly a million passenger journeys per annum in the early twentieth century rose to about one and three quarter million in the 1920s, heyday of train and steamer travel. Yet economics over the year posed headaches unknown to other lines with their reasonably stable year-round traffic of business as well as holiday travellers, due to the almost totally seasonable nature of their trade. For long winter months expensive stock lay idle and some stations, such as Smallbrook, closed altogether with signalling equipment removed; yet only by adequate maintenance of sufficient stock out of season could the summer demands on which revenue depended be met, to tide over another winter. An Island railway company was little different from a Sandown landlady, fevishly making monetary hay while the July sun shone, burdened with background thoughts of a profitless November always lurking in the back of her mind.

Local placenames continued to be the favourites for locomotives, with such examples as *Brading* (1879) and *Bonchurch*, built by Beyer and Peacock in 1883. The latter's considerable claim to local fame was the manner of her arrival on the Island. At St Helen's Harbour, Brading, *Bonchurch* toppled off the lighter ferrying her from the builders, spending the best part of a week lying immersed in salt seawater. Islanders, eager to impress visitors, never forgot to point out *Bonchurch* along the line, cheerfully chugging around for many years after her unplanned swim.

Further shades of amalgamation hung over the island and its unnecessarily haphazard services and cut-throat competition. The Cowes and Newport, the Ryde and Newport, and the Isle of Wight (Newport Junction) Railway, all in financial troubles due to rivalry over short distances that were unable to support even one of them in comfort, took the logical step of joining forces. As a result another new route was opened, through the glorious but unprofitable centre of the Island, via Merstone to a second Ventnor station, Ventnor West. Its final miles included the magnificent forests of St Lawrence, where a station was constructed seemingly half hidden by woods and hills, serving little more than the tiny historic church for which St Lawrence was touristically celebrated. Much of this section was begun by yet another local company with a tongue-twister for a name, the Newport, Godshill and St Lawrence Railway Company – the number of little companies with Newport in their titles is to this day confusing.

The bigger Isle of Wight Central Railway, born of all this amalgamation, acquired thereby the greatest mileage of any company, with just under thirty out of a total of about forty-six route miles on the island.

An embarrassment of railway riches, indeed, was the outcome of individual and collective activity. Comparatively slow though the Island initially was to adopt its first trains, once committed it made up for lost time by a network which, as any map indicates, was too extensive to be justified by largely seasonal traffic. 'The Island is at least sufficiently – some may think far too much – supplied by railways' declared a handbook sage of 1898.

The late 1890s saw the arrival of a locomotive class soon found almost indispensable for local short haul working, the 0-6-0T *Terrier* acquired from the London Brighton and South Coast by the Isle of Wight Central. 2-4-0 tanks proved equally ubiquitous in time, almost all of them adopting the practice of using local names as identification.

At Ventnor was excavated one of the system's most distinctive features, a series of coal merchants' caves cut deep into the chalky cutting where the line emerged from its St Boniface tunnel at the signal box. These caves supplied the locomotives for their next journeys. At one time the means of coaling was simply a series of discarded freight wagons stripped down to their underframes, floored with rough old sleepers, a primitive but effective means of coaling on a level, eliminating some of the backbreaking shovelling of a fireman's life.

Once into the new century, a rival arose whose future threat most railwaymen failed to appreciate; the Island's first boneshaker bus, laid on in 1905. That buses should steal the very lifeblood of trains was unimaginable. Tourists as yet stuck firmly to railways. 'New Attraction: Osborne House now open to the Public every Tuesday and Friday; Cheap Bookings from all Island Stations to Cowes and Whippingham Stations, from which Osborne is Easy of Access', crowed a typical guide of 1906.

Excursions were the passengers' delights and the railways' prime source of summer revenue apart from journeys to and from the ports, as witness this contemporary exhortation: 'During the Season cheap Railway Excursions to all Parts daily. Weekly Tickets covering use of ALL TRAINS AND ALL RAILWAYS IN THE ISLAND (except for Ryde Pier) for SEVEN DAYS are issued at EXCEPTIONALLY LOW PRICES'. It paid handsomely for the local companies to work together for their common good, pooling resources in all-Island tickets, instead of leading their former self-contained little lives.

Through tickets from London encouraged Island holidaymaking, mankind being instinctively averse to such supreme efforts as re-booking at each stage of a journey. 'Through Tickets to all Island Stations, from all Stations on the South Western and South Coast Railways', ran a representative advertisement much flaunted in guides of the early 1900s; 'During the Summer Season, May 1 to September 30, TOURIST TICKETS AVAILABLE FOR SIX MONTHS are issued from Waterloo, Victoria, London Bridge, Kensington, Clapham Junction etc. Also EIGHT AND FIFTEEN DAY TICKETS AT A FARE OF 11s. Third Class'. How much of the journey would eleven shillings, or 55p, cover today?

Not all could as yet afford a full week for their holidays, both because wages were low and because many employers still 'stood off' staff at slack periods nominated by themselves, without pay, expecting them to count such breaks as summer 'holidays'. A weekend was all these could manage, hence the popularity of weekend return fares, ranging from a luxurious 23s. 6d. return from London (£1.17½) First to 15s. (75p) Second and only 12s. (60p) return at spartan Third.

Complaints about the fares charged are no modern phenomenon. As far back as 1914, on the verge of world war, Isle of Wight holidaymakers considered local tariffs good reason for grumbling. A virtual monopoly of transport, over a system divorced from healthy mainland competition, enabled companies to charge as much as 3d. (just over 1p) a mile First Class, a stiff imposition when even gentry reckoned £6 a splendid weekly income and a top secretary earned £2.50. Second Class at 2d. a mile was far above what the average father could scrimp and save, and even Third, at Island rates, put a severe strain on his wallet. Worse still, the Island demanded exorbitant rates on arrival merely for the privilege of setting foot on its property, before even joining the train to one's destination, levying as much as 10d. (4½p) a head as Ryde Pier toll, Second Class. On the other hand, Holiday Runabout tickets offered outstanding value at only 7s. 6d. (37½p) weekly, Second Class, for unlimited exploration of the entire isle by all available routes.

War apart, the Island's main landmark date in the twentieth century was the same as that which divided old from new on every other British rail system, 1923; a date which is as significant in railway history as is 1066 in the wider context of British history. 1923 brought amalgamation into the giant new Southern Railway, and a long overdue overhaul of Island rolling stock, by then the laughing stock and despair of the general public, who found precious little sympathy for that minority of railway enthusiasts who considered the local stock a wonderful working museum of antiques. 'Antiquated' was the average holidaymaker's preferred word.

Altogether the Southern inherited, from one small island, the incredible total of 18 locomotives, 90 passenger coaches, and no less than 600 freight wagons. How the original gaggle of little lines coped with 600 wagons was never made really clear.

The faithful characteristic Island *Terriers* were retained, but most of the other creaking locomotives were replaced by such improvements as 02 class 0-4-4 tanks. Ex–LBSCR class E1 0-6-0Ts were ferried over, bigger and stronger than the small *Terriers*, particularly for goods working. The 02s operated at first in their old LSWR livery and numbers, most of the imports having LSWR origins. Even these were far from new, having seen anything up to thirty years' service. Most former Island engines were thereafter scrapped, except for *Wroxall* and *Ryde*, which puffed on to 1933.

Southern also replaced a great many antique coaches, a motley and haphazard collection of mainland cast-offs, among them ancient London Metropolitan eight-wheelers and a railmotor which had been new in 1906. Some better preserved specimens were rebuilt, with seating along the lines of the Twenties' popular road horse brakes with one long sideways bench on each side, flush with the walls, instead of normal seating. One little line managed to stand aside from the changes despite the gigantic take over, a case of mouse versus elephant almost unequalled elsewhere. Thus, the minor Freshwater line continued to be independant for about eight months after the 1 January, 1932 deadline.

Under SR ownership Island railways prospered, although it was an uneven prosperity confined to summer months. So greatly did the three main resorts expand that the Brading-Sandown section was re-laid as double track, and passing loops were added at strategic points on many single lines.

Motoring also was on the increase, though its longer term implications for railways were as yet unappreciated. Car ferries quickly became operative, cashing in on a growing trade from the mainland. In the 1920s local advertisers encouraged motorists to use cars for holiday-making, with such blandishments as 'Cars transferred to the Island without being slung'; a better boast than the rival Channel Islands could make until quite recently.

Electrification from Waterloo to Southampton and Portsmouth brought further holiday traffic after 1937, but within two years it was killed by another world war. Only localised traffic kept the lines going, with a minimal war-effort commuter service in Cowes shipyard workers and men drafted into the aircraft industry. A small unexpected additional export trade also grew up in wartime, in home grown tomatoes, encouraged to replace the more famous Guernsey and Jersey tomatoes which were lost to Britain when the Channel Isles fell in 1940, the only portion of the British Isles actually invaded and occupied by

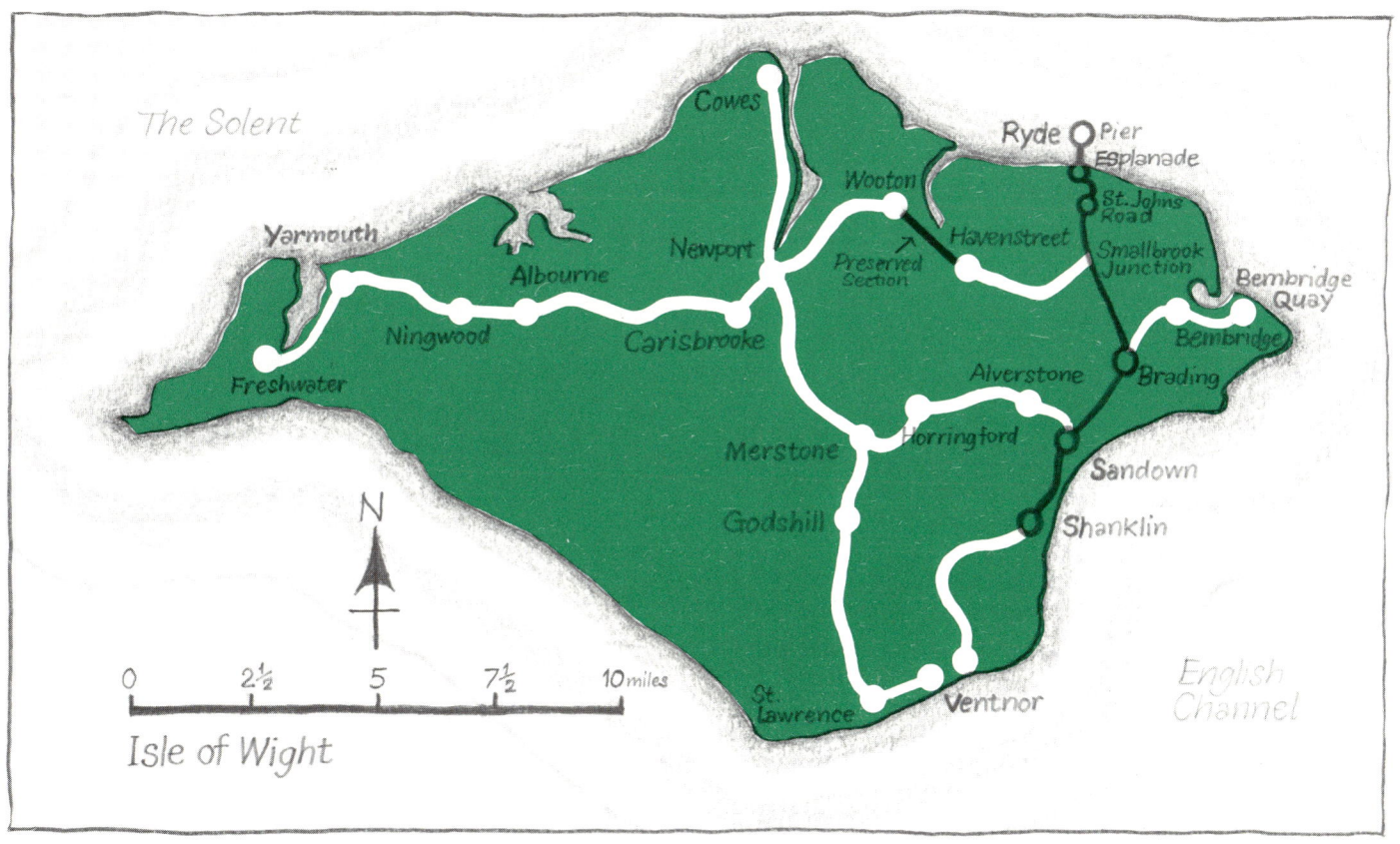

the Nazis.

Peacetime brought a resumption of holiday arrivals, a trickle in 1946 that became an ever increasing flood. Steam engines were still sent to the Island as late as 1949; one of the final imports was No. 35, *Freshwater*, (02 class 0-4-4T), keeping to the end the policy of local names. *Freshwater* in her smart livery was familiar to almost every post-war visitor landing at Ryde.

Definite trends towards increased private motoring and a local bus take-over became more and more apparent during the 1950s, steadily eroding rail ticket office sales. It was a national trend, spelling death to innumerable small lines in only one single decade.

Not a few holidaymakers were actually deterred from using trains by confusion as to which lines were open or closed, resulting in further missed revenue, as becomes clear from a Ventnor guide book of about 1955: 'Through bookings to Ventnor from all main line railway stations. Visitors are sometimes misinformed that through bookings cannot be obtained, due no doubt to some branch lines having been closed. There is, however, no question of closing the main Ryde to Ventnor line, which has a direct connection to the Portsmouth–Ryde ferry'. In practice, this line, too, was ultimately truncated, losing the lap from Sandown to Ventnor.

Among early closures was the scenically impressive stretch through St Lawrence to Ventnor West. When in about 1955 the author and her mother wandered onto the deserted platform, the former trackbed, minus rails, had already become thickly overgrown with grasses, and massive spikes of beautiful wild purple shrubs half engulfed the lineside, though the small station buildings were as yet intact and unvandalised. Nature quickly reclaims her own on the fertile and mild Isle of Wight.

The eternal problem remained unsolved – grossly overtaxed peak Saturdays in summer with serious overcrowding the rest of the week, against patronage reduced to the barest minimum off season. Such scant local traffic as existed was further diluted by the counter attractions of buses and cars. Though as many as five trains an hour ran in 1955 to Shanklin and Sandown, traffic on other lines, which even at their peak had never rivalled this busy route, steadily declined.

A special post-war feature was a huge traffic in PLA, or Passengers' Luggage in Advance, in which Wight of necessity was originally a pioneer. During June, July and August it often became necessary to operate complete trains composed entirely of box wagons for this purpose; a distinct improvement upon earlier operations when vans normally used for transporting baggage were also used for fish, and baggage arrived smelling strongly of its piscine contacts. Eventually 'Fish Traffic Only' vans were adapted to overcome this smelly problem.

Murderous queue conditions at Ryde among thousands of jostling people encouraged everybody who had once tried an Island holiday to in future get rid of any heavy cases by PLA. Thus they could travel free handed, ready for the Saturday quayside fray. The not inconsiderable worry of awaiting a boarding house confirmation of safe receipt was considered a lesser problem than hauling cases personally, knowing that two or even three ships would depart before one came anywhere near the head of the Portsmouth queue. Ryde was still worse, when train after train pulled out leaving people behind in the overheated

W14 running round at Ventnor; a superb back-lit shot of 1965.
G Daniels

Train from Ryde emerging from Ventnor tunnel in August 1965.
G Daniels

Cross-country Cowes–Ryde Pierhead train at Ashey, 1964.
G Daniels

A striking view from above of Ventnor station in 1965, showing full layout of station, shed and sidings. *G Daniels*

crowd; full or not, trains had perforce to leave exactly on time to coincide with their Up fellows at vital passing loops.

Far more entertaining, from a holiday visitor's viewpoint, was watching work in progress on another railway film, not quite so universally remembered as the immortal *Oh, Mr Porter*. Entitled *Chip off the Old Rock*, it was a travelogue shot on the Ventnor line with cameras mounted on a specially fitted engine and carriages. And there was an amusing outcome of a production by Ryde Repertory Company of that classic of all railway classics, *The Ghost Train*; among the props was a signal complete with moving arms and counterweight, looking and sounding so authentic that it was afterwards installed beside a real railway at Fishbourne to perform a genuine operative function, directing cars onto the Fishbourne–Portsmouth ferry.

To the end Wight railways wore a certain air of living in the past, which was not confined to rolling stock. It was only about ten years before the end of steam that the old lower quadrant signals were replaced – with almost as outdated upper quadrant types, when all around the colour-light revolution was in progress.

As always, these lines lost money in winter; and by now summer no longer virtually guaranteed a chance to recoup losses. Not only buses took trade from the trains; private motoring expanded, here as throughout the land, the greatest single factor in reducing former demands for trains. Some mainland lines with year round incomes, could survive; the seasonally fluctuating Isle of Wight lines could not, and closures began in earnest.

Merstone to Ventnor West went on September 15, 1952, followed by Newport–Freshwater and Brading–Bembridge (September 21, 1953) and Newport–Sandown (February 6, 1956). This in spite of howls of protest which at least persuaded the Transport Commission to delay closure of Cowes for five years and of Ventnor for seven, although this was repudiated in the light of the fatal Beeching Report.

Ryde–Cowes finally folded on February 21, 1966 and Shanklin to Ventnor on April 18, 1966, leaving only the brief but financially viable fragment between Ryde Pier and Shanklin still operative. The final steam trains, drawn by numbers 14, 16, 17, 22, 24, 27 and 31, ran on December 31, 1966, bringing a century of Island steam to an end. A factor bearing on closure of the line between Shanklin and Ventnor, despite the latter's attraction as a resort and its innumerable hotels and boarding houses, was the long tunnel beneath St Boniface Down, opening within sight of the station. The costs of making ageing tunnels safe for intensive modern working dictated the survival or closure of many a mainland line, and so it was here; modernising and strengthening Ventnor tunnel was considered excessively costly when set against expected revenue.

The remaining Shanklin stretch was deemed suitable for electrification, the motive power of a world in which steam was rapidly dying, almost dead. It was completely closed down for the purpose until March, 1967. In tune with Island tradition, the re-opened section's 'new' trains proved to be someone else's cast-offs, albeit good ones; old London Underground electric sets banished from Town in favour of improved stock but with many years of life in them yet. They were brought over car by car, the sets broken up for transporting, on vehicle ferries, and reassembled locally.

Underground trains, incongruous though they appeared in theory, proved highly satisfactory with their wide double sliding doors for quick transfer of large crowds, plentiful standing room, and capacious luggage dumps inside the vestibules. Today they maintain regular timetables all year round to Shanklin.

Re-use accounts for much of the abandoned mileage, from complete sections to a single building, as at Horringford where the station has been charmingly converted into a private house whose well stocked sunken flower garden and lawns are the former trackbed, the house opening onto a terrace that was the platform. Setting a trend for other authorities, the County Council purchased some stretches for redevelopment. The Merstone–Ventnor West and Brading–Bembridge lines were sold privately but Newport–Freshwater and Newport–Sandown went into council ownership in their entirety in 1962, as did Cowes–Smallbrook Junction at £40,000 in 1970, including a valuable Newport town centre station site. Much of this land has reverted back to agricultural usage, some as ready made farm tracks, but road works and industry also took their share. Between Alverstone and Horringford a local water undertaking took track for heavy ditching equipment. Track in the scenic Yarmouth and Freshwater area was retained for development into public long distance footpaths, and another bridleway was planned on the Newport to Cowes stretch. Additionally a company entitled Vectrail after the Romans' Vectis, was formed for possible limited rail revival.

Of greater appeal to railway lovers is the brief one and a quarter mile run between Havenstreet, or Haven Street, and Wootton, near Ryde, revived commercially for public pleasure as the Isle of Wight Steam Railway Centre. Like the more famous Bluebell Railway, it runs through woods and fields, a sentimental reminder of the sights and sounds of steam. Havenstreet station is maintained as a typical country station, but at Wootton a new station has been constructed to cope with increasing crowds. Six engines serve the line, the oldest dating from 1878, including the nostalgic little tank number 24. Like the Island's original companies, the Steam Railway relies on antique rolling stock, the 'youngest' carriage being half a century old; not for economic reasons but because the line is an operative steam museum as well as a pretty ride. At Havenstreet stationary relics are shown, such as some of the earliest Wight carriage bodies.

Two extremes of railway history thus keep flanged wheels turning today; traditional steam locomotives hauling traditional stock, and efficient utility Underground trains transported from across the sea.

No. 16 *Ventnor* running-round, 1965.
G Daniels

A small pull-and-push at Ventnor West, the 'other' Ventnor less well known to holidaymakers, 1951.
Pamlin Prints

W2 on freight train in Newport yards, 1953.
Pamlin Prints

Cowes–Ryde train passing the token at Smallbrook Junction
on a Bank Holiday in 1954.
Pamlin Prints

Wroxall, looking towards Ryde.
G Daniels

Freshwater Yarmouth & Newport Railway's 0-6-0ST No. 1 in
Newport station, June 1921.
H C Casserley

Holiday train on arrival at Ventnor in about 1955, showing part of old coal merchants' caves in chalk behind.
M V Searle

2 pm train leaving Ventnor for Ryde behind W14, 1965.
G Daniels

Southern No. 11 with Stroudley four-wheelers, ex LBSCR, at Newport. AIX class 0-6-0-T, 1930.
NCB

Rhapsodical IOW Central Railway advertising in 1906.
Ward Lock Ltd

Railway Routes

DECIDE TO SPEND YOUR HOLIDAYS IN
THE ISLE OF WIGHT
(THE GARDEN OF ENGLAND).

WARM IN WINTER. COOL IN SUMMER.

FASHIONABLE WATERING PLACES, COMBINED WITH QUIET SEASIDE RESORTS.

Unrivalled Golfing Facilities. Nine Golf Links within a radius of Nine Miles.

CHARMING & VARIED SCENERY.
BEAUTIFUL WALKS & DRIVES.

The Best and Safest Bathing in the British Isles.

BEAUTIFUL SANDS.

SAFE BOATING. YACHTING. GOLFING.

FISHING (FRESH AND SALT WATER).

Osborne Now Open to the Public every Tuesday & Friday.

Cheap Bookings from all Island Stations to Cowes and Whippingham Stations (from which Osborne is easy of access).

DURING THE SEASON

Cheap railway excursions to all parts daily. **Weekly Tickets**, covering use of **all trains** and all railways in the island (except Ryde Pier) for **seven days** are issued **at exceptionally low prices**.

Pleasant and cheap steamboat excursions almost daily, round the island and to Bournemouth, Weymouth, Swanage, Southampton, Southsea, and Portsmouth (the first naval yard in the world).

Good hotels, boarding and lodging houses, in all parts of the island at reasonable charges.

The principal towns and places of interest are Ryde, Cowes, Sandown, Shanklin, Ventnor, Freshwater, Totland Bay, Alum Bay, Newport, Carisbrooke, Osborne, Bonchurch, The Landslip, The Undercliff, Bembridge, St. Helen's, Brading.

Visitors can reach the island by frequent express trains from Waterloo, Victoria, London Bridge, Kensington, Clapham Junction, &c., either *via* Portsmouth and Ryde, Stokes Bay and Ryde, or Southampton and Cowes.

Well-appointed steamers connect at Ryde and Cowes with trains.

Free transfer of luggage between the boats and trains.

Through tickets to all island stations, 1st, 2nd, and 3rd class, from all stations on the South-Western and South Coast Railways. During the summer season, May 1st to September 30th, **Tourist Tickets**, available **for six months**, are issued from Waterloo, Victoria, London Bridge, Kensington, Clapham Junction, &c. Also **Eight** and **Fifteen Day Tickets** at a fare of **11/-** (3rd class).

Cheap Week-End Tickets are also issued all the year round, by all trains, on **Fridays**, **Saturdays**, and **Sundays**, available for return by any train on any day (except on Fridays and Saturdays) up to and including the following Tuesday, at the following fares—1st class return, **23/6**; 2nd class return, **15/-**; 3rd class return, **12/-**.

List of Apartments and accommodation at the various Island Watering Places, also Guide, on application to

H. K. DAY, MANAGER, I.W. Railway.
CHAS. L. CONACHER, MANAGER, I.W. Central Railway.

July, 1906.

Former IOWR loco *Ryde* with branch line train at Bembridge, in July 1928.
H C Casserley

Closed and falling into decay. Ventnor station in October 1969.
J H Appleton

Horringford station charmingly adapted as a house with sunken garden on the old trackbed.
J H Appleton

Disused track returned to agriculture, leaving part of the embankment. Godshill, 1969.
J H Appleton

The only operative IOW line today, Ryde–Shanklin, operated by cast-off London Underground electric units.
M V Searle

St Lawrence station abandoned in about 1955, half buried in luxuriant IOW foliage. Nevertheless, the buildings were intact enough to fascinate the author's mother.
M V Searle

CHAPTER 12

Across the Sea Bed

SOMERSET & DORSET JOINT RAILWAY

According to Somerset legend, after the crucifixion nearly two thousand years ago, Joseph of Arimathea, tin-merchant and uncle of Jesus Christ, sailed up the Bristol Channel into a shallow inland sea extending to Glastonbury, fourteen miles inland, otherwise known as Avalon. On landing there he planted his staff near the shore, which henceforth blossomed every Christmas as the Holy Thorn, as it still does today. Joseph knew Somerset well. Several times, legend continues, he had crossed the same lagoon, a vast counterpart of Poole Harbour, to his own tin-mine on the Mendip Hills, bringing his young nephew for His education during the 'lost' years between boyhood and the period of ministry.

The tradition that Christ visited the British Isles is enshrined in Blake's *Glastonbury Hymn*, better known as *Jerusalem*:

> And did those feet in ancient time
> Walk upon England's mountains green?
> And was the holy Lamb of God
> On England's pleasant pastures seen?

Those same geographical contrasts, mountainous hills and dead flat pastoral 'levels' where Joseph's inland sea formerly lay, ruled the deliberations of men born eighteen centuries on, pondering how to get from Here (the Bristol Channel proper) to There (Glastonbury or Avalon), and thence to the summit of Mendip and down again.

Joseph of Arimathea employed three forms of transport in negotiating a route from Channel to Mendip summit; boat of very shallow draught; duckboarding on lagoon-edge mire; and mule or foot uphill. Modern generations elected to follow almost exactly in his steps (off the Channel; across peaty moors which formed the old sea bed, prone in winter to become a sea again; thence to Glastonbury; and in later years to a Mendip summit) not in Roman fashion, but by train.

In the same year that Glastonbury acquired a first step towards transport improvement, its 1833 canal, a legend was created that was as up-to-date as the Holy Thorn was ancient. An industrial legend was born that was to have a direct bearing on railway development. James Clark of nearby Street entered partnership with his brother Cyrus, who had opened a fellmongering and sheepskin working factory; a partnership soon to split into two separate concerns with James graduating from woollen slippers to shoemaking and the forming of Clark's shoe empire, and Cyrus turning to the sheepskin trade that became equally famous as Morland's of Glastonbury.

Clark's encountered lean times in the 1840s, largely due to poor outlets before the creation of good road transport. The clue to expansion was through the railways which everywhere were contributing to industrial growth. It well behoved James Clark, despite heavy personal workloads, to ensure himself maximum influence in bringing trains to the area by becoming a founding director of the early Somerset Central Railway. The nearby Abbey Arms thus became the proposed SCR's headquarters, and Glastonbury its 'capital'.

A meeting in 1851 proposed a line from Highbridge, a reasonable anchorage and adjacent to existing railways, with possible southward extensions and a branch to the cathedral city of Wells. No cuttings or tunnels were needed over this dead flat seabed terrain, only embankments above winter flood level, helped by use of 'rhynes' or small canals alongside the track (into which on occasion derailed engines were later known to nose dive).

That year, 1851, one railway survey prematurely stated that 'there is a branch line in progress which is intended to pass close to (Glastonbury)', though the first sod was not actually cut until 1853. Probably it was of peat, of which most of the Somerset moors were composed, used as a sweet smelling fuel and in time a useful source of freight revenue to the railways.

Somerset Central Railway opened on August 17, 1854, when six First Class carriages covered the twelve miles from Highbridge in thirty-five minutes, about the same time as a century later.

Glastonbury, rejoicing, blended sacred and secular, as was its wont, with a huge procession assembling in the vast abbey ruins where King Arthur was buried, carrying banners very different from those borne by the monks of old. 'Railway and Civilisation!' one proclaimed; others 'Where ther's a Will ther's a Way!', Zummerzet spelling of a word pronounced 'thurr'.

Not for long was the early sneer that this line ran 'from nowhere to nowhere' true. Quickly proposals were raised for an extension north to Burnham-on-Sea, in order to open up that quiet sandy resort as a port for South Wales, as well as the Wells branch. Quick developments were largely due to Robert Reade, second company Secretary, who also urged progress towards the Dorset border, paving the way for Dorset railway interests to meet the SCR in a complete chain from the Bristol Channel to the English Channel, from Bath to Bournemouth.

Burnham was a difficult proposition as a port, cursed with extreme tides, which retreated literally to the horizon and reached the sea wall for only about two hours either side of each high water. Nonetheless a steamer slipway of 900 feet, and embedded with rails, was built in line with the station across the promenade. Alongside was dredged a narrow 'cut' for slim ships of shallow draught to berth. Freight could be taken by wagon to their sides, but passenger coaches probably never used the slipway; travellers normally walked across to embark.

Trains came through from Highbridge on May 3, 1858, initially worked by the Bristol and Exeter Railway on a rental basis. In came the Cardiff excursion steamer *Iron Duke*, followed by a train of 700 Bristolian excursionists bound for Cardiff after marching to the jetty behind a railway staff band. Regular services then connected with certain trains.

Glastonbury to Wells opened on March 3, 1859 (not until the 15th for public service). Later an additional halt, tiny Polsham, was added. This, again, was worked by the Bristol and Exeter.

In November 1856, the first sod was cut at Blandford, down in Dorset, for the other partner in an ultimately joint venture, the Dorset Central, to begin a single line off the LSWR at Wimborne reaching towards the SCR. Work on closing the resulting gap was frustrated for some time by a common stumbling block where two small companies worked in one area and were each linked to bigger railways: a battle between narrow and broad gauge. Mixed gauge (a third rail) brought compromise.

Dorset Central, smaller and weaker of the two companies, opened to Blandford via Spetisbury on November 1, 1860, under working agreement with the LSW for a percentage of receipts. Somerset Central, meanwhile, built itself a new Highbridge station, to end sharing the B&E building, and planned workshops which, once expanded, became the famous Highbridge works for repair of locomotives and rolling stock.

This was a crucial decade for both companies. Leases to the B&E were terminated, putting Somerset Central in charge of its own affairs; gauges were rationalised; and a single operative line came nearer reality. Geographically, theirs was the most logical of all mergers.

Thus in 1862 the combined concern became the Somerset and Dorset Railway (not yet Joint), 'linked to all parts of the narrow gauge system', comprising already some fifty track miles in two sections, still with that infuriating sixteen-mile gap. They were formally wedded at a Templecombe ceremony, roughly at the halfway mark, followed by a reception at Burnham.

In the same period the Cardiff–Burnham steamer crossing was reduced to only one and a quarter hours, and the line was extended south from Glastonbury as far as Evercreech.

Plans began to be shaped for the most important development yet, from Evercreech through the then flourishing Somerset coalfield of Radstock and thence to Bath; and the Templecombe–Blandford gap was at last closed, on August 31, 1863.

Two years on a complete service was advertised to France, leaving Burnham at 8.05 am, with only twenty-five minutes allowed between arrival at Poole and sailing at 12.30 for Cherbourg by the *Albion*, docking in France at 6 pm. Total journey time was therefore a commendable ten hours.

Last memories of the gauge battle faded in about 1870, with removal of the unsatisfactory third rail of mixed gauge, but popular nicknames bestowed on the Somerset and Dorset lingered longer, in fact to the very end. For those in a hurry, and slightly anti-train, S&D always stood, unfairly, for 'Slow and Dirty'; but for 'Swift and Delightful' if one enjoyed watching the greatly contrasted passing scenery at leisure. A third group, consignors of china, Clark's shoes, live pigeons and other freight labelled FRAGILE: WITH CARE: THIS SIDE UP, preferred the appelation 'The Smash and Dash'. That epithet seemed not entirely inappropriate to myself in childhood, during the latter days, with porters happily swinging heaps of FRAGILE boxes into guards' vans.

Work finally began in 1864 on the long new route north east from Evercreech to Bath, thus raising the former's title to Evercreech Junction; a through link to the money spinning Midlands and north. No two routes could have been more contrasted than this and the original Burnham line across a former sea bed. To reach Bath the line actually climbed the Mendip massif, blasting through rock at the hands of 3,000 men, twisting and reversing to find negotiable gradients, ever upwards to the summit called Masbury, 811 feet above sea level. Trains, such as the famous *Pines Express* to the pines of Bournemouth, hauling up Masbury, usually double-headed, were always an impressive sight.

In July 1866 the first train left Bath too early for many rejoicers to be about; but at Evercreech (eternally Ever*screech* in local parlance) crowds appeared, and at Wincanton their enthusiasm so delayed the train as to miss an all-important Templecombe connection. The gaffe was not allowed to be forgotten by those who called the S&D the 'Slow and Dirty'. Thereafter Bath–Evercreech–Bournemouth was termed the Main Line, and the older Evercreech–Highbridge–Burnham as The Branch.

The Bath Extension was an engineering triumph, but the costs of two years' blasting, and of building seven viaducts, four tunnels, and many cuttings and embankments, as well as costly new Fowler 0-6-0s and other 0-6-0Ts, grossly overstrained the company's financial resources, precipitating its end as a separate entity. Crushed by their own expansive schemes, the directors could but sell out.

Combined Midland and LSW terms, better than the GWR's offer, were accepted in 1875, after long legal wranglings, The Somerset and Dorset lost its old name, henceforth to be the Somerset and Dorset *Joint* Railway.

Early Joint days were memorable for the worst local crash in history. On August Bank Holiday in 1876, near midnight, a return Bath Regatta excursion ploughed head-on, on a single line, into an up train from Wimborne. The impact was heard in the still summer air five miles away. Nearer, the non-stop whistling of both engines (0-6-0Ts Nos. 5 and 7), the shriek of escaping steam, and cries of the injured were horrifying. Twelve passengers and a guard died. Joint Company compensation was generous, and some child orphans of the disaster were offered employment, safeguarding their future maintenance.

This was a great age for excursions, as railways opened the world to parochial mankind in a manner the like of which their grandparents had never dreamed. Such concerns as Clarks of Street, original advocates of railways in Somerset, regularly chartered specials leaving at dawn and returning long after midnight, kept awake by the oom-pahing of their factory band. A typical outing of 1885 cost employees 4s. 3d. (21p) for a ten-hour return trip to Plymouth over adjoining companies' lines. Cardiff to Burnham steamers did well, aiming at associated railway custom as far afield as the Channel Islands: 'Passengers, parcels and goods are conveyed at Through Rates between Cardiff and all Stations on the Somerset & Dorset Joint Railway, London, Portsmouth, Gosport, Southampton, Guernsey, Jersey, Lymington, Weymouth, and all Principal Stations on the London and South Western Railway'. Timetables were issued for each day of the month, allowing for tidal differences at Burnham's often tideless slipway. Typically, sailings from Cardiff might be on Monday at 8 am; Tuesday 8.30 am; Wednesday 9 am; or in the afternoon at 4, 5 or 6 pm.

At the other end of the run, through travel was improved in 1885 when a short cut-off from Corfe Mullen to Broadstone, near Poole, was opened, overcoming the delaying practice of reversing trains bound for Bournemouth.

Bridgwater branch did not open until July 21, 1890, turning Edington Road into Edington Junction and bringing total mileage to over a hundred.

Life on this railway settled into a certain routine, suffering more from climatic vagaries than material disasters. Somerset, it has been pointed out, is an area of unusually sharp contrasts, where twenty or so miles of completely flat moors, without even hedges as windbreaks, meet hills rising to nearly 1,000 feet. When it rains, it rains, catching the full quota of Westerly precipitation. When winds howl, they moan with great ferocity, carrying waves of snow.

March, 1891, provided just such an example of weather battering a local railway. A three-day blizzard buried an entire engine near Shepton Mallet to the top rim of its funnel for twenty hours; only that funnel and the black cab roof indicated that a train lay under the snow. One drift, fifteen feet deep, was estimated at nearly a mile long.

Flooding was a peculiarly local problem, remembering that much of the line crossed an old sea bed, drained by hundreds of criss-crossing 'rhynes' that overflowed in wet winters to merge with swollen rivers and high tides and restore something of the wide shallow landlocked sea the Romans knew. In a scene that Joseph of Arimathea, looking towards Glastonbury might well have recognised, only one thing intruded modernity: a train hissing and splashing along its raised embankment above the flood. Glastonbury station, fourteen miles inland, was sometimes flooded between platforms. On one occasion at least, floods and tides met at Burnham to embed a complete train to the hubs in wet sand, whilst seawater put out the locomotive's fire.

Only in the last two decades have elaborate flood works reduced this annual transformation, too late to save the Somerset and Dorset its worst floundering.

As if consciously celebrating a new century, the railway adopted in about 1900 the brilliant and famous livery of its middle years. Trains sported one of Britain's smartest colour schemes, with engines and carriages alike painted a bright Prussian blue, lined out in gold, contrasting with polished brass and a scarlet buffer block. These blue trains are today recalled with deepest nostalgia.

Fine crests added to the effect, changed from the former Somerset and Dorset badge of a divided circle picturing the arms of Dorchester against Glastonbury Tor and Abbey together with a primitive passing train, into a Joint railway symbol: again, the Dorchester arms, with those of Bath replacing Glastonbury, as if emphasising superiority of the Main Line over the older Branch. New engines were ordered at about this time; five 0-6-0s and three 4-4-0s.

Burnham slipway's future came under much debate, as by then it was used mainly by excursion steamers paying only 5s. (25p) each to berth, though admittedly they brought paying passengers across the road onto waiting trains. To demolish, or adequately maintain in hope of increasing traffic; that was the question.

Transfer of the slipway from railway ownership to Burnham council solved the issue in 1905, and pleasure sailings continued, but Highbridge, two miles up the local river and with adequate wharves, was overtaking Burnham as a port.

More engines were purchased just before the Great War, the more powerful Fowler 2-8-0s which became the line's mainstay.

Pleasure traffic naturally dropped in wartime, but the SDJR was compensated by heavy increases in freight and military specials: hospital trains for the convalescent homes of Bath; loads of tanks from Dorset (still a tank training centre today); troop trains for Southampton embarkation. Special rails were laid to a German POW camp in Dorset, and a link to the short military railway to Blandford Camp, well used by personnel and civilian cooks, cleaners and mechanics. The SDJR gave men as well as services to the war effort. Over a hundred from Highbridge alone went overseas. Thirteen never returned.

The last SDJR stock acquired before the big 1923 grouping was a motley collection: Midland Class 4 0-6-0s, replacing old *Scotties*; Class 2 4-4-0s; LMS 0-6-0Ts and others, bringing the stable to 80 engines crewed by 92 drivers and 93 firemen.

Like women at the sales, the SDJR had got somewhat carried away with all these purchases and found itself in such financial straits that an offshoot to Wimborne (in any case carrying only one train a day) was axed as an economy. It was perhaps just as well that amalgamation lay ahead.

The landmark day, January 1, 1923, saw the SDJR vested partly in the LMS and partly in the Southern, standing geographically astride both regions. Meanwhile the GWR entered the Cheddar Valley – subject of the next chapter – bringing three of the Big Four into one compact area.

For a time during 1923–5 the famous Prussian blue livery, and the smart green corduroy staff uniform, continued in use.

Excursion traffic boomed in the travelling Twenties, but against increasing competition from motor charabancs and a few private cars. The sad nationwide story of railway passengers gradually deserting for the roads has been recounted in earlier chapters. Losses mounted, forcing such economies as staff reductions and abandonment of the old SDJR blue livery, for undistinguished unlined black for locomotives and standard Southern green for stock. Trains never looked the same again in Wessex.

Freight also took partly to roads, but railway carriage of heavy goods held up, particularly in Mendip quarry stone and crates of shoes and sheepskins. Into the 1940s, the crates of Clark's shoes on Glastonbury platform, labelled for South Africa, could give passengers unlikely ever to travel abroad a certain thrill. However, coal movements on the rails likewise declined, as the once important Radstock collieries lost ground, taking away more revenue.

Highbridge works finally closed in May 1930, after nearly seven decades' service, putting three hundred men out of work, disastrous to this small brick-making town that was so dependent on the big engine shops for a living. Some men, determined to remain in engine repair work and knowing no other, were compelled to move as far away as Derby and Swindon.

Local usage of trains continued to dwindle, redeemed by heavy through excursion traffic and highlighted by the Daily *Pines Express* roaring magnificently over Masbury, usually double headed. SDJR/SR shipping interests wound up, giving over Highbridge warves to private berthing, and two platforms at the important Templecombe interchange station were taken out of use; all early symptoms of an ultimately fatal illness whose eventual outcome could only be compulsory euthanasia on the orders of Dr Beeching.

Locomotives of these contradictory Thirties included some fine 'Black Staniers' from the LMS, which disappeared within a decade as another war broke out, in favour of less distinguished ex-LSW 4-4-0s.

Passenger services were drastically curtailed during the 1939 Phoney War (three a day, morning, noon and night, on the Glastonbury–Burnham and Wells branches), but other traffic remained steady and even, indeed, increased. Freight rumbled day and night over these useful cross country lines, reasonably free of bomb damage except at the Bath/Bristol and Poole extremities. Millions of tons of weapons and ammunition came through (part of Clark's shoe factory at Street itself produced torpedo heads), with long lines of tanks on flat trucks.

For wartime passengers, waiting at Glastonbury for the morning or noon 'London' train (no more than the connection for Evercreech, changing again at Templecombe for the true London express), the clanking couplings of goods trains at the opposite platform are still one of war's most abiding memories. The nearby yard was always busy, as was Snow's timber yard, next door and virtually integral with the wooden station.

Peaceable goods, too, usually were in transit, not least crates of live pigeons and poultry, and wagons of fresh turves of peat. Peat from Ashcott or Shapwick, always a favourite West Country fuel, did much business as a substitute for rationed coal. The largest peat company ran its own two-foot gauge tramway.

Troops came through: Australians, Canadians and New Zealanders, to camps outside Glastonbury and Street. The Glastonbury railway engineer's department became a transit camp for gum chewing Americans, who in onward lorry convoys threw handfuls of sweets to rationed children. In reverse, prisoners of war came to Dorset and Somerset camps. On one occasion, an evacuated mother with her child found themselves alone at dusk at a blacked-out Evercreech Junction with a dozen fierce looking Italians and only one seemingly ineffective warder. Fortunately, the connection arrived on time.

At least one mixed train – goods wagons, milk tankers and mail vans – operated on Sundays. Colloquially known as the Milk Train, it was a godsend to London Police and Service fathers on short leaves to their evacuated families in safe Somerset. Their official passes allowed them aboard and thus gave them a precious extra day of sanity away from the Blitz.

Such fathers sometimes took elaborate care never to mention the horrors of bombing before the children. Yet for an evacuee, taken for the ride as far as Templecombe by parents anxious to delay for an hour the final farewell, there was nothing but pleasurable excitement in seeing his or her first bomb damage, when that station and some lineside houses were hit. Such is the ghoulishness of childhood.

Most other stations escaped, though as a precaution against raiders jettisoning bombs while on the run from burning Bristol, windows were crisscrossed with anti-shatter black paper. Posters appeared in waiting rooms warning that 'Careless Talk Costs Lives' or that 'Coughs and Sneezes spread Diseases' – but country porters nevertheless still remembered to put bowls of local primroses on the table in spring. Despite wartime rigours, both postal and rail freight services allowed evacuees to send fresh primroses, packed with wet rags and moss in old Clark's shoe boxes, to relatives enduring city bombings, arriving fast and therefore fresh.

Some semblances of peace were maintained, not so much on the Main Line with its links to bombed Bristol, Bath and Southampton, as on the Branch. Seaside trips continued throughout the war to

Burnham, and the increase of the return fare from Glastonbury to 2s. 1d. (10½p) from only 1s. 11d. (9½p) raised more resentment in some mothers' breasts than the activities of Hitler.

Annual treats were still highlights, when specials groaned in from Evercreech, each coach booked for the Sunday Schools of a different village. Hundreds of children poured out at Burnham, happily scuttling across the line directly in front of the engine to a white wicket gate and thence straight across the road onto the beach and the disused slipway of Cardiff steamer days. Cruising through miles of long waving grasses and drying 'ruckles' of peat bricks, it was difficult to remember there was a war going on, until one noticed lineside tank traps or, on returning at dusk, barrage balloons silently rising on thin guyropes from fields of cowslips and mauve cuckoo-pint.

Passenger traffic briefly revived after the war, while petrol rationing lasted, as war-weary Bristolians and visitors from farther afield came down to refresh themselves among Dorset's thatched villages or on Burnham sands.

Relaxation of petrol coupons, however, began again the slide towards car superiority. Railways lost custom as hundreds of cheap cars became hundreds of thousands. Those who drove down also used the car for touring, robbing both trains and pleasure steamers of patronage, sometimes precipitating a staggeringly swift end to them both.

Nationalisation into British Railways in 1948, which assigned the ex-SDJR first into Southern Region and later into Western further hastened the end, as committees of accountants looked into takings rather than the value of rural railways as a public service.

Railwaymen were to accuse British Railways outright of deliberately running down each component section to create an opportunity of closing it as a 'rationalisation' measure, and of being indifferent to alternative ideas. Much bitterness developed, though in fact some, at least, of the ensuing closures were not entirely unjustified.

The Wells branch, for instance (closed on October 29, 1951) had run for several years carrying an average of only six people, largely because reliable buses duplicated the route, almost parallel to it, and ran hourly instead of three times daily. 0-4-4T No. 58086, last of a type familiar hereabouts since the 1870s, had the gloomy honour of pulling the last train through the familiar level crossing gates of Glastonbury towards the towers of exquisite Wells. The author, at some distance, was surely not alone in sparing a tear for childhood days of pleading with ruddy faced Somerset drivers for a short, half frightening, moment on their fiery footplates at the termini.

On the same day the Highbridge-to-Burnham closed to normal passenger traffic, although special excursions were accepted in summer for another eleven years, a maddening sight to residents forced to wait for buses to Highbridge. In 1963, Burnham station closed altogether.

Bridgwater branch also ended, reasonable enough in that it received four trains from Edington Junction, each carrying only about six people. The rest had taken to cars, or rattle-trap vans with attached pig-trailers. It remained open for freight-only, one train a day, until October 1, 1954.

Contrast: that word continually crops up in writing of the variations between hills, heaths and lowlands in Somerset and Dorset. It applied, too, to their railways. The SDJR, as it was called long after acquisition by SR and then BR, was obviously dying by 1954; yet few railways celebrated their centenaries more enthusiastically than this one, in that year, ignoring future omens.

Clark's of Street, of course, organised jollifications for the railway they had helped create, and which in return had helped give their shoe empire its early impetus. A hundred descendants of James Clark, many in crinolines and top hats, were among seven hundred guests aboard a special train to Burnham. Celebrations hereabouts, whether for a single child's birthday, a whole Sunday School, or a complete area, invariably meant a trip to Burnham across the flat moors. It was an instinctive choice, one of local life's 'of courses'. For this occasion No. 4320 (class 3F 0-6-0), draped with bunting and with an inscribed smokebox, assumed her old number and the familiar SDJR initials.

Accusations of deliberate running down mounted after this heady interlude, as the nationalised owners redirected freight over other routes, not necessarily shorter or better, and truncated excursions.

Anger turned to fatalism after the railway's most prestigious train, the noble *Pines Express*, was also taken away. The last local run of the *Pines* on September 8, 1962, was an occasion of mingled splendour and sadness, with crowds gathered for miles along the route to see it roar out of their daily lives behind No. 92220, the massive 2-10-0 *Evening Star*.

Soon after this the fatal Beeching Report announced the intention to entirely rob much of Wessex of all trains, earmarking both Main Line and Branch. Freight, formerly so heavy, was forthwith curtailed, and in June 1965 the Wincanton-to-Blandford section closed. Others followed, among them Bournemouth West station in October 1965. The entire Highbridge–Evercreech line finished on January 3, 1966, as did Radstock–Wincanton. The whole SDJR system was finished by the appointed date, March 7, 1966, but for a few fragmentary remainders attached to reprieved alternative lines: Bath Junction to a Co-op coal siding; a track near Radstock, again for coal; Basonbridge to Highbridge (milk); Poole to West Moors (general freight); and Blandford to Broadstone, for milk and goods.

The last weeks were busy with numerous specials bringing enthusiasts and returning exiles from miles around. Among them came 4F 0-6-0 No. 60, the last genuine ex-SDJR locomotive to pass Glastonbury, and two fine green Southern Pacifics hauling for the last time over high Masbury summit.

Final regular trains were followed along parallel

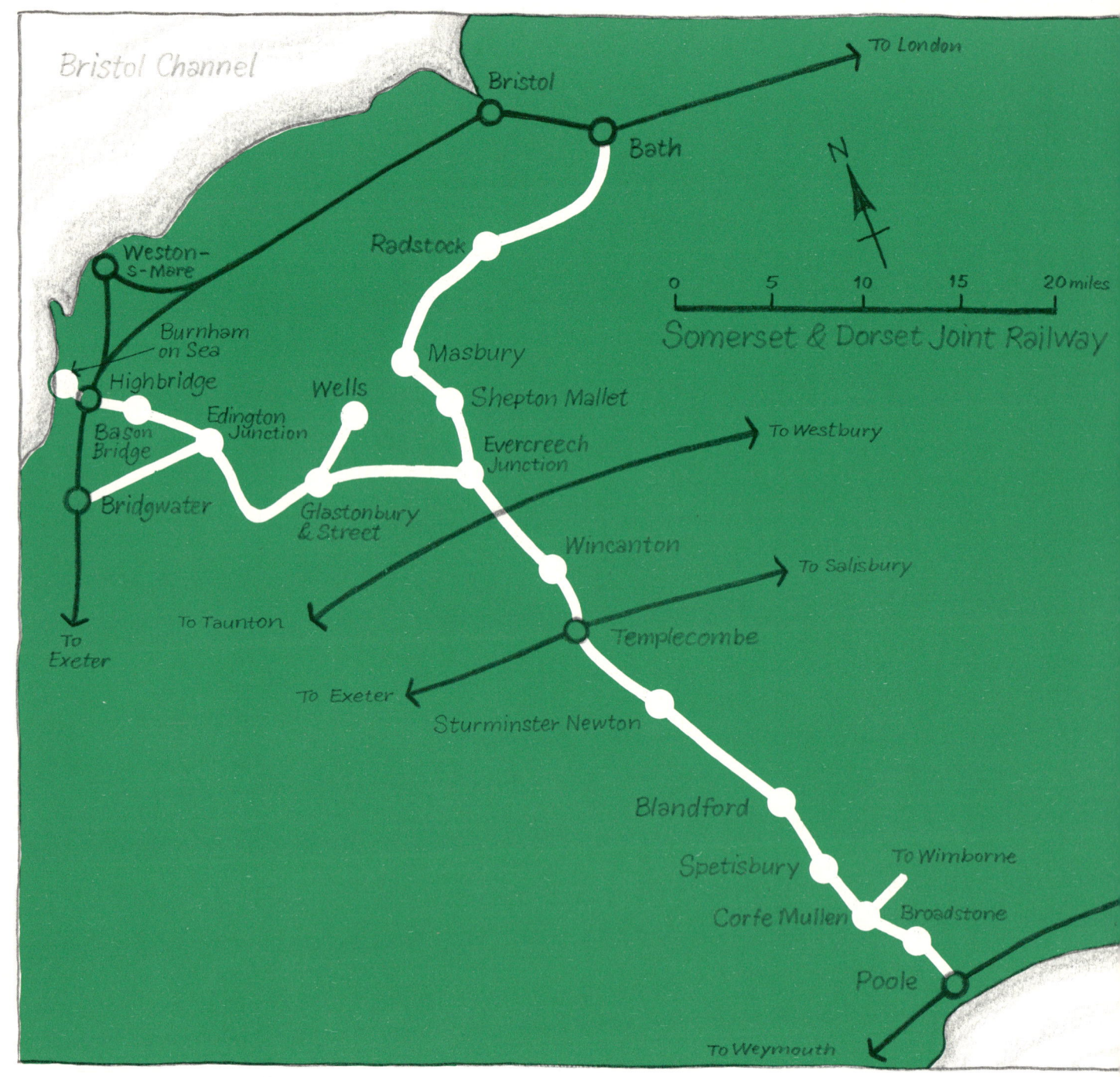

open moorland roads by processions of cars filled with local people unable to believe they were seeing their last trains, and more hard headed enthusiasts draped with cameras. The final timetabled train out of Evercreech carried a coffin, symbolising the end of two lives: the demise of the Somerset and Dorset, and the end of all steam in the West Country.

I missed the harrowing Ides of March, 1966, but returned later to The Branch on a lone Glastonbury Pilgrimage devoted to trains.

The station stood silent but intact, with rusted metals. Already nature had taken the 'Glastonbury and Street' name board, and draped it with pink roses. As I stood dolefully on the empty platform, reliving innumerable journeys, an anxious figure came over the line by the usual wooden crossing (habit dies hard) and marched up the ramp. 'Be 'ee waiting for Lunnon train, Miss?' he asked. Reassuringly, I said I knew the last had gone without me.

Over at Burnham, all of what had been a cosy red brick station lay sprawled across the trackbeds, a shattered rubble heap burying more happy memories.

All over the two counties remains are still to be found, from the weed-grown viaduct into Bournemouth West to complete stretches of embankment. At Shepton Mallet a fine disused viaduct forms an impressive background to the landscaped gardens of the Babycham factory, while Bridgwater's former SDJR station is a road freight depot.

Burnham slipway still has its old embedded rails, mournfully running into the sea at high water. Many holidaymakers speculate as to their use; few realise that goods trains once used them, and afterwards Burnham lifeboat.

At various points plans have been mooted, as on other disused railways, for returning level trackbed to the fields whence it came. At Evercreech, one more enterprising farmer is said to have considered building

Clark's shoe factory, Street; a major reason for bringing trains to nearby Glastonbury, an influential Clark being also a railway director. *M V Searle*

Today, Somerset winter flooding is largely controlled. Up to the 1940s the flat moors often returned to their former nature as a lagoon bed. Here, in about 1920, the track and train are the only features above water, which sometimes swirled across the line itself; hence the embankments.

Glastonbury station about a year after abandonment. Rusty permanent way still in position, and buildings as yet unvandalised. *M V Searle*

Heartbreaking scene for we who associated Burnham-on-Sea with Sunday School specials; destruction in progress, 1966. *M V Searle*

two dams across a cutting, lining the resultant hollow with plastic, and creating a reservoir for his cattle.

The Somerset and Dorset officially died on March 6, 1966. But did it? Strictly speaking, its obituary could not be written for another eleven years, for one final short fragment between Poole and West Moors remained open until May 2, 1977, having survived all those years for occasional freight. Thus, like King Charles and many other doomed railways, this was 'an unconscionable time a-dying'.

Even now, it is not entirely dead. So long as one person exists to repeat anecdotes of riding to a Burnham Sunday School treat across the peaty Branch moors, and returning from homeward station to village in a deliciously smelly pig-trailer behind a neighbour's delivery van, the Somerset and Dorset will periodically return to life in the telling.

Dereliction in the heart of busy Radstock, March 1978.
M V Searle

Wintery dreariness accentuates the pathos of a once prosperous railway, climbing over the height of Mendip-top, 1978.
M V Searle

The fine Kilver Viaduct near Shepton Mallet, seen around 1900. *Showerings Ltd (Babycham)*

Coming off the viaduct, No. 75073 coasts down into Shepton
Mallet on the 1.10 pm Bath–Bournemouth West.
G Daniels

Part of the disused viaduct today, incorporated into landscaped
gardens of the Babycham factory at Shepton Mallet.
Showerings Ltd (Babycham)

Midford Halt, near Evercreech in 1965. The stone walls at right are highly characteristic of central Somerset. *G Daniels*

Binegar station, looking towards Evercreech in 1965. *G Daniels*

Sturminster Newton station and signal box, facing towards Bath. *G Daniels*

40634 waits at Broadstone, Dorset, while working a Templecombe–Bournemouth West train in 1962.
G Daniels

An ex-SDJR fire-bucket notice crudely adapted to read 'SR' after amalgamation, still in existence at Sturminster Newton in 1962.
G Daniels

Through-train from Birmingham to the south at Shepton Mallet behind 2P No. 40509.
G Daniels

Whittaker's tablet apparatus 'at the ready' with tablet and pouch positioned. Broadstone, 1959.
G Daniels

The physical climax of the main-line Somerset and Dorset run, climbing over the top of the Mendips at nearly 1,000ft a.s.l. 73065 hauls a relief to the famous Bath–Bournemouth *Pines Express* in June 1962. *G Daniels*

CHAPTER 13

Lost Lines of Avon

SOMERSET & AVON BRANCHES

When new boundaries were recently defined, large areas were taken from both Gloucestershire and Somerset to form another county, Avon, named after the rivers watering its two great cities of Bath and Bristol. The several disused railways immediately west of Bristol's Avon Gorge thus now belong to both Avon and what remains of the original Somerset. They followed the Bristol Channel coast to Weston-super-Mare, last outpost of Avon; behind the Mendips towards Blagdon, the anglers' Mecca; and from Clevedon through Yatton along the glorious scarp face of the Mendips past the Somerset tourist traps of Axbridge Lake, Cheddar gorge and caves, Wookey Hole, and Wells of the most exquisite cathedral in English Christendom. Why, serving such attractions, should such branches ever have declined?

Each of these three railways had reasons for opening, working, declining and closing. Historically their saga opens in 1847 with the shortest stretch, a shuttle off the main line at Yatton (later junction for the two other branches) to the quiet grey stone resort of Clevedon, facing Wales across the Channel; modest nowadays, but then increasingly popular among Bristolians content with one day out near home, allowing maximum beach time.

This one-station extension of about three pretty miles on broad gauge was inaugurated on July 28, 1847 and reduced to standard in 1879. For over a century Clevedon branch did about fifteen daily return journeys in summer. Into the earlier 1950s crowds still packed in. Not until the end of that decade did the motoring conversion seriously menace it, when replacement of trains by diesel railcars was a first sign of decline and change. For a while they appealed as a novelty compared with the over-familiar picturesque little steam trains that rumbled away past a pond thickly covered with brilliant waterlilies and, at journey's end, stood gently panting like overheated spaniels, exhausted by three miles' puffing. For we to whom changing at Yatton for Clevedon was a way of life, the hard announcement that the final service would run on October 3, 1966 seemed unbelievable. But it was true enough.

So was the death of the next (chronologically) in this Avon and Somerset group, the scenically impressive and touristically useful Cheddar Valley route, continuing southwards from the same interchange station of Yatton.

'Is such an individual as (a lady) fit to travel by railway . . . to risk a rapid journey in one of the locomotives of the Western or the South Western trains, to rattle on at the rate of thirty miles an hour?', a physician wrote with genuine concern in 1839 of the effect on any 'person endowed with such exquisite sensibility of the nervous system that the . . . tumbling down of a set of fireirons produces a headache for the day'.

Ladies thirty years on, when the Cheddar Valley line became reality, had toughened, so long as First Class was provided. Mere women, the bulk of female travelling citizenry, and made of sterner stuff, piled cheerily into Third with children and heavy baskets to create a very evenly balanced Up and Down trade; tourists from everywhere to the magnificence of Wells and the subterranean mysteries of Cheddar and Wookey; countrywomen in reverse to shops and markets at Bristol and Weston. Agricultural produce formed an important third source of income. Crate upon crate of tomato-sized 'Cheddar' strawberries (actually from Draycott, the next station) were stacked on platforms, with sacks of fine potatoes. Until those industries declined locally in face of less flavourful factory imitations, Cheddar cheeses and Somerset cider also travelled in fair bulk.

On August 3, 1869, the Cheddar Valley and Yatton Railway flagged out its first service, as far as Cheddar. By next Easter it reached Wells, where from the opposite direction the East Somerset Railway had already arrived, on March 1, 1862, coming in from Witham and its earlier terminus of Shepton Mallet. Both CV&YR and ESR being broad gauge they linked amicably enough, but less happy was the coupling with the Somerset and Dorset, coming in narrow from Glastonbury and intruding into their trackway. Tussles ensued between them and the Board of Trade over rents and safety rules, ending in standardisation of all three and practicable interchange of goods and passengers at Wells.

A mere nine chains of SDJR track still sat between the ex-ESR and CVYR halves of what was effectively a through run. However not until 1878, after absorption by the GWR, did trains cross the gap, leading to closure of the old ESR station and elevation of Tucker Street as the GWR's Wells station. The SDJR kept its own Priory Road, through which GWR trains rather ridiculously slipped without stopping, forcing passengers to walk to Tucker Street for connections, so near yet so far when loaded with luggage. Only carless railway monopoly could have sustained such a system for so long. Not until 1934, in the upsurge of motoring, was Priory Road jointly adopted, to last until the closure in 1951 of the Wells–Glastonbury branch which had originally caused the confusion. After this Wells was reduced to one station, Tucker Street, for a few more years. Like the last green bottle of the song, that too is gone, and now there are none.

The two parts of the main route were always unevenly patronised. Tourist interest, a prime revenue source, was concentrated between Wells and Yatton. The section averaged a creditable £20 a mile daily takings, improved still more when regular Bristol excursions came through to Cheddar and, later, Wookey, both popular despite the fact that Cheddar station lay a half hour's tramp from the beginning of the Gorge and caves, and Wookey some two miles from Wookey Hole. Trippers tolerated such distances, allowing railways to build stations frequently two miles from the villages they purported to serve. Such sitings of stations were to be in many cases, including the Cheddar Valley line, a direct cause of decline and demise once buses and cars became universal and carried people where they wished to go, instead of to the 'nearest point' which in fact was nowhere near.

Riding the line was a trip in itself, for glorious Mendip and moorland views, soft scents of hay through open windows, and delightful villages. Cheddar was surely one of the GWR's brightest and cleanest stations, smart to the end in chocolate and cream, pampering passengers with drinking water taps, icy cold, and country sights of strawberry boxes and clanking of milk churns. The dairy farms of pastoral Somerset in this quarter supplied up to ten large milk vans to London on Sundays alone, apart from weekday yield. For any Somerset exile returning from London stepping onto Cheddar platform meant stepping directly into the sanity of tradition on the land.

Roads destroyed what the railways built, here as throughout the land, luring tourists into cars and cheap coaches and freight into lorries. Most visitors came by road by the early 1950s, though holidaymakers with luggage (the author included) often found trains easier, with one change at Yatton, right to the last days. Strawberries, vulnerable to excessive handling, naturally went more and more by road, needing only one loading from farm to destination instead of manhandling at goods yards, arriving quicker and fresher. With both these sources of income truncated, and local users deserting for buses which ran through instead of 'near' their villages, no alternative remained but to close the entire Yatton–Cheddar–Wells–Witham route to passengers from September 9, 1963.

Life twitched a little longer, in the form of freight to the formerly famous paper mills hereabouts, notably at Wookey Hole. When this, too ceased, only a little loop near the Witham extremity continued, serving an important quarry. Here, railway history comes full circle, and moves on a tiny scale into another revolution: so greatly does Somerset limestone quarrying still flourish today, as it has for centuries, that instead of closing at Witham, BR have actually opened a new one and a half mile service branch to Merehead, and expanded sidings at Witham itself.

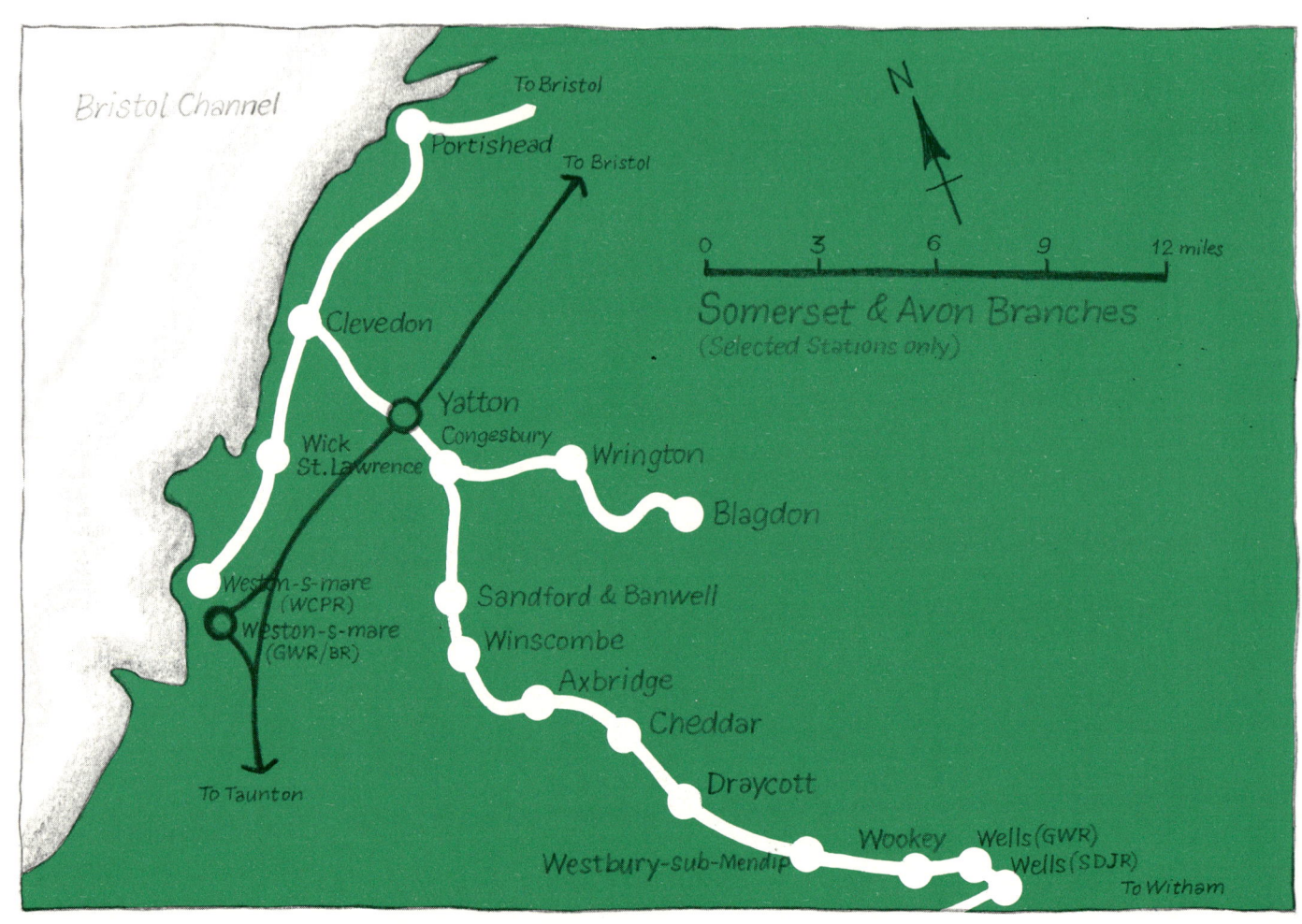

A different kind of beauty lies north of the Mendips, less sharply defined than where the Cheddar cliffs and dead-flat moors (former sea bed) come within walking distance of each other. Only recently has it become tourist conscious, through the wonderful fishing of the Blagdon and Chew Valley artificial lakes. Snoozing gently while the tripper coaches pass it by, it lives a quiet but organised agricultural life. Trains here are difficult to imagine, though the last were reality only twenty years ago.

Appropriately, it was farmers and big landowners instead of city businessmen who dreamed up the Wrington Vale Light Railway, branching off at Congresbury – pronounced 'Coomsbury' – on the Cheddar line, primarily for moving milk, butter, live stock and market-garden produce. Bristol Waterworks, providentially in the act of beginning Blagdon Lake as a giant reservoir, saw the benefits which would accrue to themselves in backing the line, which the GWR agreed to work.

Their combined resources made the WVLR ready for opening on December 4, 1901. Once the reservoir was completed, constructional materials dried up, leaving the line to the slightly ruminative life of pastoral fetching and carrying; goods to Bristol, and villagers to towns and other villages.

The old familiar story of buses destroying trains duly repeated itself here in the 1920s. Axing half-empty trains only made bus timetables more attractive, beginning the vicious circle that nearly always ended with closure. On September 14, 1931, passenger carriage ceased, though produce was taken to Blagdon until November 1950. A little freight kept the Wrington–Congresbury section going as late as June 10, 1963. Now this pretty branch is but a dotted line captioned 'Track of old railway' on the map.

Yatton, once so busy with the Cheddar, Wrington and Clevedon branches all joining the main line that in 1921 tracks were quadrupled each side of the station to alleviate a notorious bottleneck, thus lost its place as a junction.

Last in this district to open, but early to close, was the coastal Weston Clevedon and Portishead Railway. This formed part of the 'old iron empire' of the so-called Colonel Stephens Railways, named after that extraordinary shoestring rescuer of light railways which were usually acquired cheaply when they were financially tottering.

On December 1, 1897, the first part opened, but the full length to Portishead did not function until August 7, 1907. Transformed from a proposed tramway into a full light railway, this line of great charm served some seventeen 'stations', most of them request stop level crossings, between growing Weston-super-Mare and its two northerly sisters. Rolling stock was noted for its infinite variety, from two or three truly superb saloons to an old LSWR set, a fine railcar and its little brother, a glorified truck. Engines similarly ran the full gamut, from the handsome burnished and polished 2-2-2T *Weston* of early days, through an ex-Jersey Railway purchase of almost comic profile to conventional *Terriers*. Clevedon was unusual among resorts in that trains rumbled along the middle of one of its main shopping streets.

Disentangling the fortunes of the WC&PR is no easy matter. The Excess Insurance Company, as its long-lasting and final creditor, withdrew its claim in about 1939, but the line's rightful owner was untraceable. Nobody wanted the once so useful little line, linking strings of enchanting spots off the tourist track. Services therefore ended on May 13, 1940 (this was local railways', as well as England's, 'darkest hour'). The GWR, buyers of the track but not the stock, rescinded their plan for using part as sidings for coal wagons from Bristol and South Wales, then prolific features of this area, on discovering that not one GWR locomotive was light enough for the Light Railway. Track was lifted, and the line lapsed into such limbo that today younger local residents have often never heard of it, regarding it simply as a walking or cycling trackway without consciously recognising its original purpose. Its only major engineering work, a bridge across the Yeo River, lies forlorn and broken.

Clevedon to Yatton was lifted after closure on October 3, 1966. Right through to Cheddar, Wells and beyond the railway-scape is the same: abandoned, grassy embankments, and empty cuttings under old stone bridges. Around Polsham, on the little Wells-Glastonbury branch the scene looks deceptively like it always did, with low ruler-straight embankments that ought to carry rails. However, on closer inspection they are found to carry only one's childhood memories.

The East Somerset Railway project at Cranmore, beyond our maps in the Frome direction, has restored a short stretch to stream pleasure traction, based on restoration of Cranmore station. Hopes of running steam trains towards Shepton Mallet are as yet unfulfilled. For years plans have been discussed for turning the main Cheddar Valley line into the desperately needed road bypass for Axbridge, now that tourism lasts almost the whole year, and all goods travel by narrow roads through ancient towns whose beauty and peace they destroy. But still no road appears over the disused trackbed.

Station Road, Cheddar, leads to overgrown trackbed used only as an unofficial local footpath, in some parts considerably obstructed. It is a heartbreaking sight to those who recall this as one of our sprucest country branches, immaculately weeded, passing through neat, clean stations proudly polished by polite and friendly platform staff with soft Somerset accents.

Thousands – yea, millions – visit Cheddar yearly to tread where our dimmest ancestors walked, or descend Wookey Hole into the bowels of pre-history. Pathetically few, beyond ex-Somerset exiles returning in sadness, bother to walk down Station Road and ponder how history belongs to only fifteen years ago, as well as to infinities of time.

The end of the line – literally. Near Dulcote quarry, Wells, in 1974. *C G Maggs*

Wick Wharf. View upstream. Fragments of bridge behind. *C G Maggs*

Weston Clevedon & Portishead Railway carriage sheds in an advanced state of decay in 1963, used for housing tractors and farm sundries. *C G Maggs*

Opening day at Cheddar in 1869. Note the banners (left) and greenery as platform decoration.
Locomotive & General

← Scanty remains of WC&PR bridge at Wick St Lawrence in 1963.
C G Maggs

Weston 2-2-2WT (ex-Furness Railway No. 35) on opening day of WC&PR.
Locomotive & General

Portishead, with train, in 1938.
Locomotive & General

Wookey from adjacent road bridge in 1947.
Locomotive & General

Wells (GWR) in 1948.
Locomotive & General

Wrington station, seen in April 1957.
E Course

CHAPTER 14

To the Twin Villages

LYNTON & BARNSTAPLE RAILWAY

Asked to name Britain's most loved lost line, in retrospect if not in working life, many in the southern half of England would surely nominate the Lynton and Barnstaple Railway, which maintained full public and goods services over nearly twenty miles of North Devon and the Exmoor foothills. It was one of the few narrow gauge lines, apart from the Vale of Rheidol in Wales, coming under working control of the Big Four at the 1923 grouping, and operated through its final decade or so by the Southern.

Lynton and Barnstaple traversed some of the finest scenery anywhere in the British Isles, a magnet to travellers ever since it was opened up, first by improved roads with stagecoaches, and later by railways. Holiday travel was made practicable; not least to the poet Shelley. Few quarters of this kingdom so enchanted beholders as Lynton, perched nearly 800 feet above a spectacular coastline, and its twin Lynmouth, at the foot of the long forested hill, where two glorious rivers rushed from narrow gorges into the Bristol Channel.

Local scenery more closely resembled the mountainous terrain of Wales or Europe than anything English. Not surprisingly, therefore, when a railway did finally appear it, too, bore a closer resemblance to a mountain than to a mainline system; narrow gauge, picturesque, and following a tortuous hilly route. Its technical origin was, indeed, a mountain railway; the Festiniog of North Wales.

For additional interest, the leading light behind the Lynton and Barnstaple's opening was the man who first published *Sherlock Holmes* and gave us the still extant *Titbits*. George Newnes, the great Victorian magazine magnate, first saw the Twin Villages as a tourist, travelling with his wife around Devon by carriage. Falling in love with the district, Newnes resolved to adopt it first for holidays every summer and Christmas, in a new mansion of his own building, Hollerday House, and later for permanent retirement residence. He could well afford to maintain Hollerday, built after establishing his first major success, *Titbits*, and the publication in his *Strand Magazine* of the *Sherlock Holmes* stories, following *A Study In Scarlet* of 1882.

Newnes enthusiastically and generously busied himself about local affairs, donating Lynton's whimsical mock-Tudor town hall to celebrate his son's coming of age, and sponsoring a hydro-electric scheme making this one of the earliest towns connected to electric light. In 1890 he added to his gifts the cliff railway which alone of Lynton railways remains in use today, an invention actually introduced to Britain by the magnate. It was to prove the cart before the railroad horse, the vital final link in a transport chain once the Lynton and Barnstaple materialised some years later.

The cliff railway was unique in being powered by water and gravity, its two cars – one up and one down – each having a large water tank beneath. Filling of the top tank with simultaneous emptying of the lower car enabled the top train, on release of its brakes to descend and pull up the other lightened car at the same time. It remains the only alternative, accomplished in minutes, to one of the longest and hardest uphill drags in British seasidedom, from Lynmouth promenade to the nearest year-round bus service terminating at Lynton.

Forty years before the first conventional train appeared, local interests began lobbying for a railway, conscious that the embryonic hotel trade was exposed to stalemate as other resorts became more accessible. It was true that coaches had encouraged the opening of three good Lynton hotels, one alone stabling a hundred horses and many carriages, and a number of wealthy men had begun a trend towards lavish country homes well before Newnes built Hollerday, but this was the total of the Twin Villages' development, whilst their rivals visibly swelled.

Not until 1895, late in railway history, was a scheme finally adopted, based on local money and requirements. Newnes, as in most things, took a leading role in planning as well as financing this scheme. His persuasiveness weighed the balance in favour of a narrow, rather than standard, gauge of only 1ft. $11\frac{1}{2}$ins., chiefly a mountain railway gauge, ideal for such hilly country, enabling construction of tighter curves, reducing expensive engineering works and costing scarcely a third of a standard gauge line over the same route.

From the start it was realised that patronage would be local, the district as a whole lacking industry and relying for profit mainly on summer visitors, plus the regular traffic of housewives to Barnstaple market and businessmen on the move. There would also be coal. Lynton and Lynmouth, though housing barely two thousand in the late nineteenth century, were extravagant coal burners, getting through several complete ship loads annually. It was expected that coal prices would fall dramatically with quicker and cheaper transport than horses and carts. (Incidentally, this point was later proved in a very definite rise when the line closed.)

In the summer of 1895 Lady Newnes was invited to 'honour the Directors by cutting the first sod' where Lynton station was to arise, in a most inappropriate position high above that town in the suburb of Shambleway, far from the beach even with the extension of the cliff railway, and nearly two miles by extremely steep road down the sides of a gorge. Lynton itself was not near, 200 feet below the station.

Other stations were planned for Woody Bay (again, a long, long tramp from the bay it pretended to serve), gorgeous Parracombe and Blackmoor, and thence inland via the curiously named Bratton Fleming and Snapper to Barnstaple Town, ending at a bay alongside the main line station. Engineering work was demanding, as the line twisted and turned through the hills, often high above deep valleys through hanging woods in a manner distinctly reminiscent of the Festiniog Railway on which it was partly modelled. At Chelfham, nearer Barnstaple, the line crossed a river by a 75ft. high viaduct.

Early in 1898, with opening day on the horizon, a stationmaster was appointed for Lynton at the lavish salary of 25s. (£1.25) a week, plus free housing, coal, light and uniform. Further stationmasters were appointed along the line, for whom were built lineside cottages costing £200 apiece. The driver of the last Lynton stagecoach, displaced by trains, was made Chelfham stationmaster, a resiliant illustration of the maxim 'If you can't beat 'em, join 'em'. The company, by opening day, owned a respectable four locomotives, sixteen coaches, plentiful coal wagons, and a total staff of about seventy.

Official opening was fixed for May 11, 1898, with Lady Newnes – of course – cutting a ceremonial red, white and blue ribbon to let the first train into Lynton, behind the 2-6-2T *Yeo* (all locomotives bore snappy three-letter names) before distributing medals to Lynton schoolchildren. Not until May 16 did public services begin.

The cliff water railway slipped into place as an extension between Lynton station and the beach, 750 feet below. Without it, itself a reasonable walk from the station, many holidaymakers would surely never have reached the strand and would have resolved, quite understandably, never to patronise Lynton and its railway again.

Placidly the L&BR settled into a predictable existence, barely keeping above the waters of solvency in winter, but recouping to a certain extent between May and September when excursionists and hotel guests poured in to enjoy the splendour of the Twin Villages, with the scenic approach as part of their pleasure. For local people, up to two hours for a nineteen mile run was a matter of discontent; for outsiders unfettered by time, the line's leisurely pace was part of its charm, and would be to the end.

At least once a regal accolade was granted, when in 1905 one engine driver was solemnly paid 'Royalty Money' for safely conveying Queen Victoria's daughters, Princess Christian and Princess Victoria, during a West Country tour.

As the nineteenth and twentieth centuries merged, campaigning for a Lynton station that actually served Lynton intensified, but nothing was ever accomplished. Lack of such an elementary amenity in the long run effectively sealed the L&BR's fate, once cars and buses gave more direct access.

Early in the 1900s larger hotels began bridging the gap between station and town with special buses, for those guests who might be discouraged from another stay by a long walk at journey's end. In 1903 Newnes, too, turned to combined bus and rail operation to entice more Ilfracombe passengers onto his line at their nearest station. His solution was a spartan open boneshaker, minus even a windscreen and with wooden seats tiered up behind the driver like theatre stalls. It was a shortlived experiment, partly owing to the zealous activity of a Devon policeman in stopping this disturbing vehicle careering along country lanes at all of 8 mph. Magistrates took a poor view of the interloper, concerned with preserving the quiet dignity of rural Devon. Sold off to the GWR, Newnes' buses entered service between Helston and the Lizard, but in later years the GWR revived similar services for Lynton and Lynmouth, as is seen in a typical hotel advertisement as late as 1933: 'G W Rly motor coaches call at hotel'. Newnes' venture was an historic landmark, as the earliest railway feeder coach service.

Passenger traffic naturally fell off during World War I, holidaymaking coming more or less to an end. Barnstaple's trade and market nonetheless justified a skeleton service for residents, backed up by an unexpected rise in demand for pit-props, much carried by the L&BR. So good was this trade that application was made to the sister Festiniog Railway for loan of extra wagons, a request that the FR refused.

Summer weekends became busier than ever after peace was declared, with numerous excursions in conjunction with standard gauge operations through Barnstaple. The 1920s brought the peak of rail excursion traffic, but all the same this was inadequate compensation for a reduction to barest minimum working off season, a problem also experienced by the equally tourist dependent Isle of Wight railways.

Absorption into the Southern at the 1923 amalgamation brought no further prosperity, though the Southern did tackle essential track renewal, beyond the old company's current resources. In 1925 a new 2-6-2T (No. E188), *Lew* was acquired, and overdue modernisation carried out on the elderly *Lyn* of 1909.

Southern renumbered the engines (*Yeo* as No. 759, *Exe* 760, *Taw* 761 and *Lyn* as 762), and gave them a new livery that considerably smartened appearances but did little to fill ticket office coffers on their former scale. The Southern certainly did its best, including Lynton in its widespread 'South for Sunshine' advertising as among 'The Finest Resorts in the World' which it certainly was, and is. But no line apart from those serving the most heavily patronised areas was proof against the debilitating Depression, and it became clear that a line which through most of its life had run in and out of debt was likely to continue in that unsatisfactory state. Such departures as steam heating in carriages, instead of ancient footwarmers, to encourage winter travel, were unlikely to increase revenue more than marginally.

The run had become too slow for local taste once buses gained a foothold, serving villages previously reliant on trains at up to two miles distance. Holidaymakers minded the snail's pace travel less than the

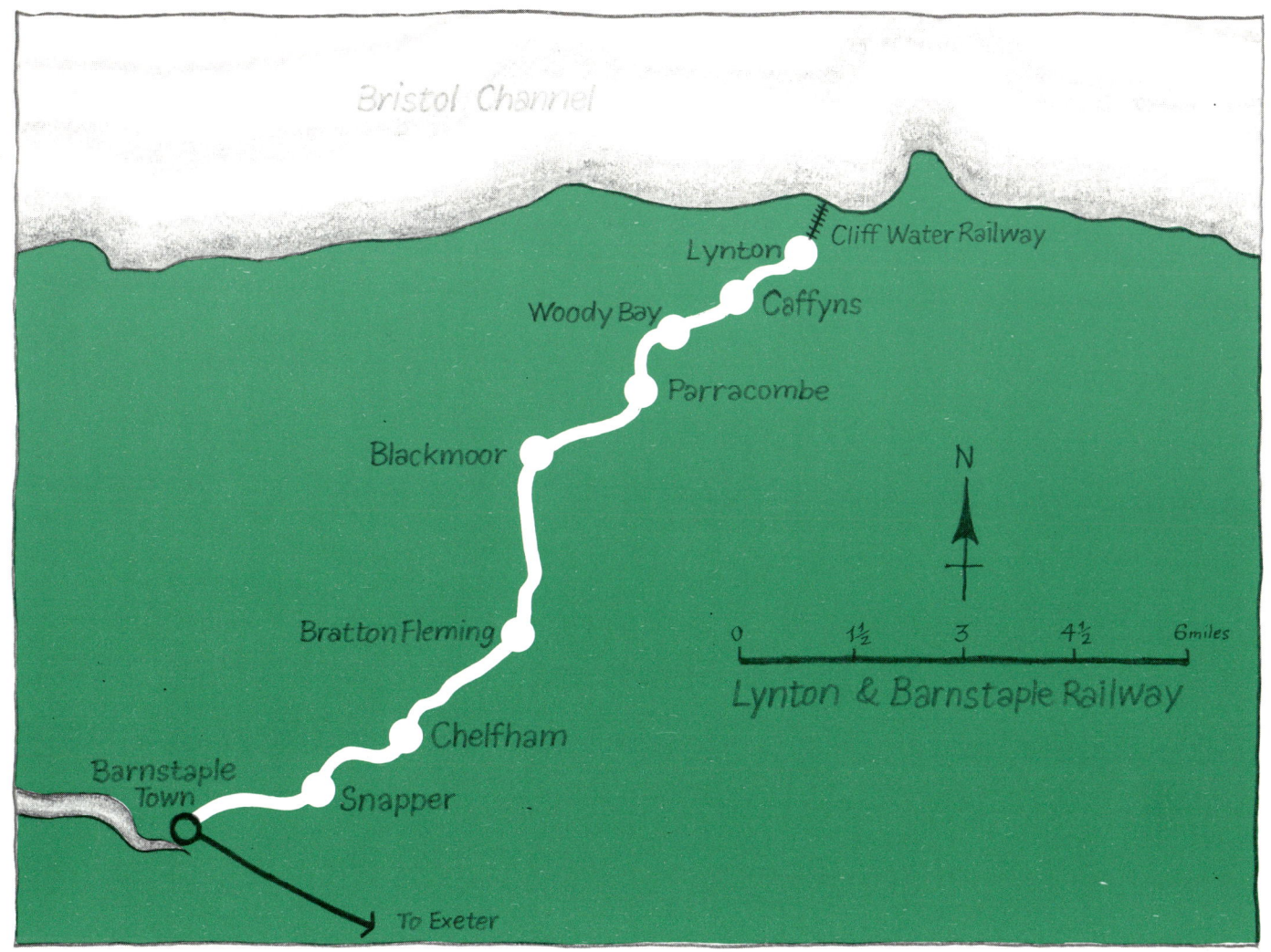

ill-planned timetable by which one train left whilst they were still confined to boarding house breakfast tables, and the next did not leave until about noon, too late for sightseeing beyond Barnstaple.

As a final blow, in 1935 the Southern discovered that there was such acute deterioration in the permanent way that only two courses were open: expenditure of larger sums of money than such a line warranted, or closure. Southern, with almost no hesitation, opted for closure. The Lynton and Barnstaple Railway had then existed for only thirty-seven short years.

The final train ran on the evening of September 29, 1935, pulling out of Lynton to *Auld Lang Syne*, cheers, detonators on the track, and a few moist eyes. The stage coach driver who became a stationmaster saw it pass.

In November, Southern auctioned in the former carriage shed almost every movable asset from lamp posts to complete cranes and signal boxes. The turntable, ideally suited to some other narrow gauge line, went to the Romney, Hythe and Dymchurch Railway.

The old picturesque 2-6-2Ts and 2-4-2Ts *Lyn*, *Taw*, *Exe* and *Yeo*, with the SR brake-compo coach 6993 and saloon brake 6994 were all disposed of, and the engines broken up; but the newer *Lew* was reprieved for service on a coffee plantation in Brazil. Stations were sold off for private use. Quiet Bratton Fleming fetched only £100, but Woody Bay made about £400 and Lynton £475.

Chelfham, Bratton Fleming and Woody Bay all survive today as solid private houses, as does the Lynton terminus, still named Station House, while Blackmoor works as a cafe. Chelfham Viaduct stands gaunt in disuse, as do several lesser bridges, spanning grass that was a railway. Much of the track is walkable, often through magnificent scenery.

At Barnstaple Town the Lynton and Barnstaple bay was recognisable, as was the swing past the quay through a car park, when the author last passed through a few years ago.

Newnes' remarkable water railway works on, the first part of the total railway route from Barnstaple to Lynmouth and sea level to be built, and the last to survive. It is still a genuine godsend – a necessity – in uniting Lynton and Lynmouth, physically so close yet, thanks to their massive hills, so far apart. Tourists patronise it well for its novelty as well as its convenience.

Could the Lynton and Barnstaple itself have held out for but two more decades it, too, might have survived. But who in the 1930s would have dreamt that such locomotives would so soon vanish?

An association, formed in 1981, has been studying the feasibility of partial tourist-trade re-use, a committee member having acquired a brief half-mile stretch, and of bringing back *Lew* from South America. But whatever happens this will surely remain over its greater length a lost line.

2-6-2T *Yeo* at Lynton in May 1935.
H C Casserley

Lynton station as a cafe in 1964. Now a private house.
Real Photographs Ltd

E 762 *Lyn* on shed.
Real Photographs Ltd

← Earliest part of the total system to open, but outliving it all. The cliff water-railway at Lynton is still in operation today, worked by filling (at the top) and emptying (at the bottom) of the water tanks under the cars.
M V Searle

E 188 on train at Lynton, bunker first.
Real Photographs Ltd

Chelfham station after track lifting, but still recognisably a charming rural station.
Real Photographs Ltd

E 769 *Yeo*; ex-L&BR engine in post-amalgamation Southern livery.
Real Photographs Ltd

Caffyns Halt with abandoned coach after track lifting, well on the way to becoming a lost line.
Real Photographs Ltd

Hurricane (RHDR) on the ex-Lynton & Barnstable turntable at New Romney, Kent.
M V Searle

Blackmore station converted into an inn. Despite extension at rear, and obscuring tree, the characteristic roof formation of stations on the L&BR can be discerned.
M V Searle

CHAPTER 15

Farthest West

LISKEARD & CARADON RAILWAY, CORNWALL

The intricate railroad network into and around the formerly immensely rich Caradon mines, which also operated one of Britain's more curious passenger ticket systems, was never a victim of Beeching's Axe. They sank into disuse so long before Beeching's time that on maps lines now continually peter out into blankness.

Mining has been Cornwall's wealth from Roman days. Tin, copper, lead and kaolin were dragged to waterways by horses until canals brought promised expansion. But when the Looe Canal opened to near Liskeard in 1827 it was for farm commodities; Caradon copper was yet undiscovered. Within a decade this canal's freight changed completely, decline in farm patronage chancing fortunately to coincide with discovery on bleak Caradon Hill of mineral seams of extraordinary richness.

Providentially, railway mania was contemporary with these developments, probing into every new excavation till lines entirely encircled Caradon Hill, bringing down copper and tin as well as quarry granite, and connecting miners' communities with each other, their workplaces, and Liskeard, representing civilisation. The resulting Liskeard and Caradon Railway could hardly be expected to fail – unless the mighty mines themselves, unthinkably, faltered.

Mine after mine opened during the 1840s, the largest among about twenty-five concerns being the giant South and West Caradon workings, employing 500 hard-swearing, hard-labouring men, for whose families cottage colonies rose in recently desolate territory. Lesser mines, like Gonamena, used 200 men in their heydays.

Initially loads were dragged down primitive tracks, impassable in rain, a slow method holding back profits. Rails were an obvious solution, horse powered at first, and in 1843 the L&CR was duly formed, aiming north from the canalhead basin at Moorswater near Liskeard to South Caradon, with branches to granite quarries at Cheesewring and the newer Tokenbury tin and copper mine. Over 1 in 60 gradients, loaded wagons ran down under gravity alone, controlled by brakemen, hauled up empty by horses from the company's own Moorswater stables. Cheesewring provided sleepers of granite instead of conventional wood, and the canal company, doubtless anticipating increased cargo income, ferried rails free.

On November 28, 1844, the main line through St Cleers and Crows Nest to South Caradon opened. In March 1846 came the 3-mile Cheesewring branch, but seriously underestimated costs – £3,000 a mile – almost milked the promoters dry.

During one good year, 1851, the L&CR conveyed some 40,000 tons of ore and granite to the canal, plus coal, bricks and farm goods at upwards of 2d. (1p) per ton a mile. Canalside yards expanded as more mines opened.

In 1857 a further mineral railway was proposed, continuing southwards to Looe, relieving freight of expensive delays at locks; this eventually became the present passenger Looe line.

Enthusiastic after their Looe opening celebration in 1860, the directors began looking beyond upward horsepower and downward gravity for Caradon, planning for steam with corresponding realignment of tracks and other improvements. In 1862 the Looe Line came under the L&CR's operative wing, and their first locomotive was hired, *Liskeard*. The first of three new engines was ordered, the 0-6-0 ST *Caradon*. Through forty ensuing years the district had but three locomotives of its own, this and two close sisters, *Cheesewring* of 1864, again 0-6-0 ST, and *Kilmar*.

Copper prices temporarily fell, but soon South Caradon, the largest mine, boomed again. Nearly 700 laboured there, dwelling in simple stone cottages. Wives and children customarily walked along the rails from village to village on their otherwise roadless heights, and with their menfolk hitched lifts by leaping aboard crawling wagons and sneaking off short of any manned point where they might be questioned. These were the first illegitimate passengers of a railway which in its heyday carried thousands, yet never issued normal tickets or had any formal right to carry people.

Mines continued flourishing and folding, and shortlived Gonamena of the stone sleepers declined, but in 1880 came the richest copper strike ever, at East Caradon. Soon 250 men were labouring, some 650 feet down, and profits over a decade averaged £9,000 a year. In all these enterprises the railway played its integral part, shunting ore and granite from sidings to main line, and linking workers' communities. Wisely, however, the L&CR set about fully acquiring the Looe mineral continuation, as far-sighted insurance against recession; there, passenger adaptation could be a paying alternative.

Discussions during the 1880s ranged over the sensible merger of the Caradon, Looe and canal companies, and less realistic possibilities of an extension northwards right across to Launceston.

Caradon and Looe branches were promoted as mineral lines, without passengers. But up to 600 people worked at some mines, and many thousands lived nearby on the lonely hills, their only roads the poorest tracks, hence their habit of hitching unpaid rides by the passing trains to Moorswater, or even through to Looe and back. At first the authorities ignored this risking of necks, but in time they became more aware of potential income from these regular uninvited guests. Lacking any formal passenger powers, they ingeniously overcame requirements by selling travellers 'free' passes for a few pence, supposedly a carriage charge for their cases, bags, parcels or umbrellas. The umbrella, not its owner, was the commodity theoretically carried. Only heartier fighters achieved the covered brake van, instead of rattling unsprung trucks, fitted only with running boards, coupled behind the mineral trains. The L&CR began openly advertising pleasure services to the popular Cheesewring country, though fully aware that they were not entitled to transport human beings anywhere at all. Hundreds of Sunday School children enjoyed jolting up in open tracks, smothered in smuts, singing hymns all the way, on 'Special Pleasure Party' terms, evading rules by travelling on passes instead of real tickets. Thirty or forty four-wheelers sometimes took part, behind the company's total motive power of three 0-6-0 tanks. How the children must have yelled on the return trip, when they went down in smaller groups under gravity with only a brakeman, blaring a horn at each approaching gate, followed by the engines running light.

So popular was the Cheesewring trip with other locals that another clever ticket scheme was devised, again bypassing the law, whereby a Caradon line passenger purchased a genuine ticket to Looe, where he had no intention of going, with which came his 'free' Caradon section pass. Booking First entitled him to a wheeled chicken coop, otherwise it was the usual trucks with running boards, hitched to goods trains for this immensely popular summer outing run.

Ambitious extensions twisting over 1,000ft hills towards the GWR and LSWR at Launceston were begun in May 1864, through three intermediate stations; but only one-and-a-half miles ever emerged.

Caradon people and Caradon railways both relied on Caradon minerals for existence. Mighty South Caradon therefore reflected a whole area's destiny when it declined from an employer of 500, when copper prices fell in face of newer, cheaper overseas sources, to merely keeping operational. Freight receipts correspondingly tumbled in a few years by 50 per cent and creditors, led by a Receiver and the Canal Company, fell on the L&CR.

A minor revival at South Caradon in 1883 temporarily staved off full disaster for 350 remaining employees; then prices crashed again. The vast mine closed in 1885, followed by the briefly reopened West and East Caradon, Glasgow Caradon Consols, and the rest. Mine closures depopulated whole villages, and the few inhabitants left reverted to old ways, hitching ticketless rides on occasional stone trains, jumping off before contact with Moorswater officialdom. In about 1900 railmotors were considered for these cut-off villages' benefit, but never actually tried.

Copper price rises in about 1900 inspired the last twitch of life but another slump quickly dealt the final blow. Caradon Hill of the twenty-five mines became a graveyard of half deserted villages, abandoned workings, and unused railways. The only labourers left clung to the Phoenix United tin mines until they, too, were liquidated.

Villages like Pensilva, St Cleer or Darite (Railway Terrace) became ghost settlements. Only rare granite trains reminded anyone of the L&CR's gasping continuation, a millstone liability to its sister Looe line, on which full passenger services flourished, as an alternative income to freight, using a new engine, *Looe*, and the old Caradon rolling stock. Moorswater shut down and the Looe line leased the old mineral line. With only tin and granite for revenue it was a poor asset on which Looe spent little and cared less.

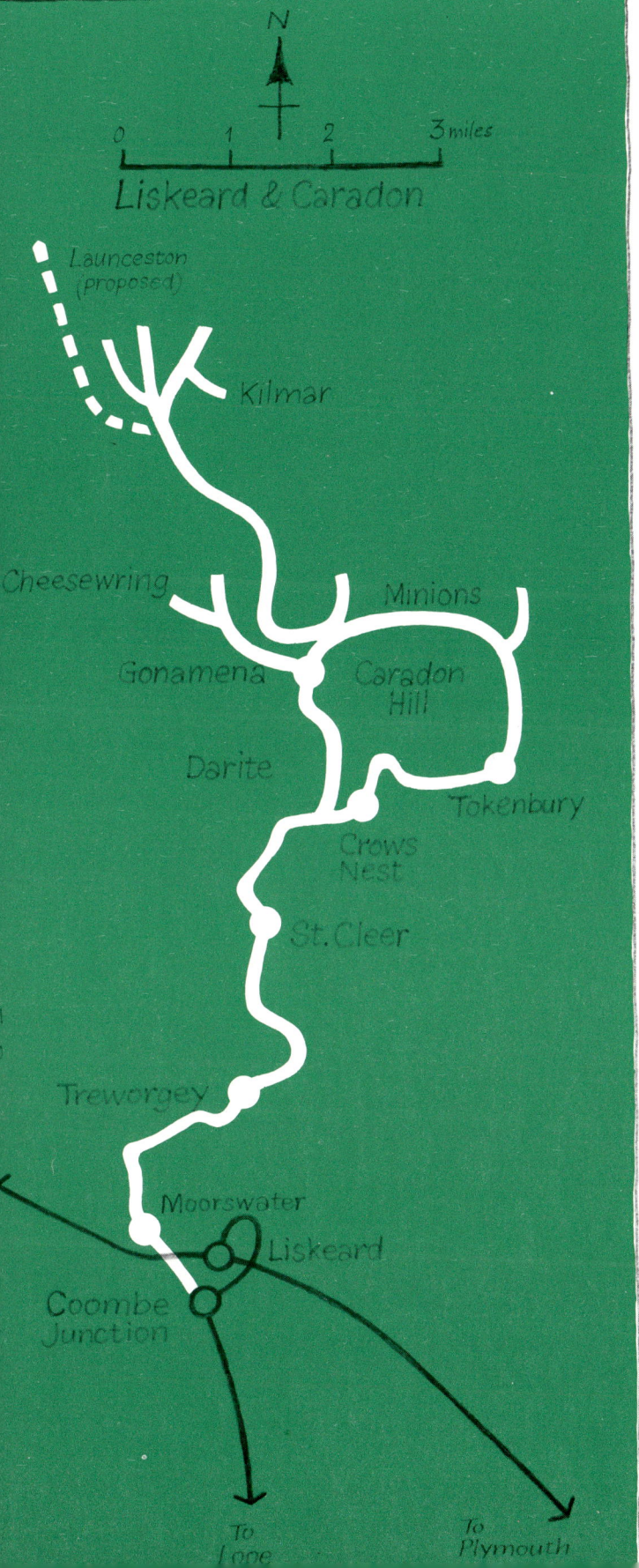

Finally the Liskeard and Looe Railway successfully offloaded the Liskeard and Caradon onto the GWR in 1909, but itself kept independent of that giant until 1921. Granite ceased at Cheesewring and on 1 January 1917 lines north of Moorswater permanently closed; they were lifted by the GWR and shipped to Flanders for restoring track worn out by heavy Great War usage.

L&CR remains were substantial into the 1930s, and some features lasted considerably longer. Moorswater shed served the Looe section until 1961, and sidings to a Liskeard clayworks were only lifted in 1973. At Moorswater and over the hills trackbeds are still traceable, though metals were lifted half a century ago, so deeply do sleepers bite outlines into the ballast which retards natural growth. Twenty years ago a long untruthful old signpost still read 'To the Cheesewring Railway'.

Railway Terrace, where trains picked up men and wives while the guard stopped to brew tea, keeps its name, though the village reverted to its former name, Darite. Derelict mine buildings litter gaunt hills, desolate reminders that men and trains once moved over the landscape.

In a Bodmin transport collection is a more curious relic; the firebox sheet of little six-coupled *Caradon* which, after two rebuilds, was broken up in 1917. Thirty years later it was put across a running stream as a rough-and-ready 'gents' for Moorswater shed men working Looe trains. Colloquially it is sometimes called the Looe Loo, a flippant end to a serious tale of exciting discovery, backbreaking labour, and village development, that all slid from disillusion to dissolution before many of us were born.

Caradon mines and site of original Goonamena track with stone sleepers. *Locomotive & General*

0-6-0ST *Caradon*.
Locomotive & General

The other half of the mines-to-harbour system, the Liskeard and Looe extension, continuing through Looe town to the quays. GWR 2-6-2T No. 4568 running light, past shoppers who fail to stand and stare; obviously, trains in the streets were a not-unfamiliar sight in 1958. *NCB*

Moorswater station, looking north. *Locomotive & General*

Clearly identifiable traces of Liskeard & Caradon line near Cheesewring in 1966, many decades after closure. *E Course*

Site of dismantled track, looking towards Cheesewring. *Locomotive & General*

Stone bridge over Minions–Upton Cross road, after line closure. *Locomotive & General*

117

CHAPTER 16

Kings and Bloaters

THE NORFOLK COAST

Railway mania in a large coastal county such as Norfolk did not necessarily lead to a rational line following the sea. On the contrary, a combination of numerous small companies each too absorbed in its local kingdom to consider onward running on either side; stipulations of rich landowner backers; and such geographical impedimenta as wide marshes and crumbling cliffs, caused its final coastal chain to display inordinately sharp quirks: now along the seaboard, now diving well inland, then back almost to the beach.

To negotiate all Norfolk resorts in sequence by train from King's Lynn to Lowestoft, just across the Suffolk border, would have involved seven or eight changes, and taken one from the vicinity of the favourite home station of five British monarchs at one extremity to the home station of kings among bloaters and herrings at the other.

King's Lynn, unlike most already existent ports, did not particularly welcome railways, alleging that its port trade in fact declined instead of expanded as its coast-wide contacts with all eastern England changed into a one-way traffic from Lynn to London.

'The calamity of rail roads', in Sir James MacAdam's words, indeed reduced King's Lynn's port monopoly, running fish and produce direct to cities instead of around the coast. On the other hand, they opened up the same district for pleasure to millions, from London shopkeepers and their boisterous broods to Midlanders saturating themselves in Bank Holiday freedom. On this line a third pleasuring category could be added, infinitely better bred but with the same addiction to personal gratification; kings and princes with their regal shooting parties.

The Lynn and Hunstanton Railway, on which stood the royal Wolferton station, serving Sandringham, began services on October 3, 1862. It merged with the West Norfolk Junction Railway in 1874, under the combined title of Hunstanton and West Norfolk, until it was swallowed by the Great Eastern in July 1890. Its course, after the pretty heaths around Sandringham, was chiefly natural or reclaimed marshland, proclaiming the ocean's nearness.

Wolferton became nationally known after the brilliant wedding of the future Edward VII, through pictures and descriptions of the marvellous 2-2-2 engine painted pale cream (the nearest thing to bridal white on iron) and rose-garlanded, drawing the wedding special.

Settling down as a genial country squire, Edward also adopted Wolferton, with its private drive right down to the line, as an estate shooting box for lively luncheon parties out with the guns. Conscious of this regal patronage, the owners later rebuilt Wolferton station in the popular sham-Tudor manner, around the core of the king's sumptuous private waiting rooms. Special sidings were installed for royal coaches.

A complete circus arrived in 1866 for a young prince's 21st birthday entertainment. Villagers, accustomed now to royalty, gossiped less about the guests than the elephant who deprived the station of a lamp-post by yanking it from the platform, wherewith to batter off the yard gates.

Some of the most lavish and beautiful trains ever seen in Britain travelled the Lynn and Hunstanton section in those heady decades, including the Great Eastern's sumptuous, blue-upholstered, clerestory palace on wheels for Queen Alexandra; the magnificent *Claud Hamilton* 4-4-0 engines; and the early oil burning monster *Petrolea*.

Commoners as well as princes quickly adopted the Norfolk coast, once opened by railways, particularly Hunstanton. This was among Britain's most convenient of all seaside stations, virtually beside the promenade and pier. A thousand trippers at once poured from excursion trains at Hunstanton's lengthy island platforms on Sundays (most still worked Saturdays). One special every ten minutes was not uncommon. Big factory outings rolled in from the hard-working Midlands, already worked into an ale-hued haze of merriment en route before painting Hunstanton the shade of red they considered its due. Six trainloads, each of 1,000 workers, might arrive within one hour.

Hunstanton's phenomenal adoption by holidaymakers encouraged continuation to the next extant seaport, Wells-next-the-Sea, operated by the West Norfolk Junction Railway from August 17, 1866. Wells became a remarkably active little railhead for its size. Excursions apart, a commendable twelve trains daily served its own populace, plus considerable freight in fish boxes. Building costs were low, based on easy terrain and backing from a landowning speculator bent on creating a New Hunstanton resort on his own estate. The route had undeniable charm in its contrasts between open downland, marshes, dunes, and a glorious run almost level with the waves near Holkham.

Travel from King's Lynn to Wells normally required changing at Heacham Junction, but outing specials went straight through. Everyday rolling stock, incidentally, made this line a moving museum to the end in 1952, when a set of fine ancient clerestory coaches, gas lit, was still in use.

Instead of continuing coastwise, the railway next looped far inland through undulating countryside to Fakenham. It passed England's nearest equivalent to Lourdes en route, the shrines to Our Lady of Walsingham, over trackbed opened by the local Wells and Fakenham Railway, backed by Lord Leicester, on December 1, 1857. Initially worked by the Eastern Counties, the company kept nominally independent for five years before becoming fodder for the property-hungry Great Eastern.

Fakenham station was for some reason built with platforms almost at track level, French style. This was to prove such a handicap to all but the young and vigorous that to keep its custom, the company perforce raised them later, submerging the floor levels of the central public buildings. Waiting rooms and ticket offices were thereafter approached downwards by flights of steps.

For many centuries Walsingham, with Glastonbury and Canterbury, was among England's major religious pilgrimage objectives, attracting royalty and devout peasant alike. Many piously negotiated the final mile barefoot. Revived some 300 years after its suppression during the reformation, the cult became more active still with the New Shrines in the 1930s. Pilgrims returned, now mostly by train.

Anglican and Roman Catholic shrines being in different quarters of the town, local railways adapted themselves to organising devout crowds. Roman Catholic specials often were halted about a mile short of Walsingham itself, nearer their shrine than the official station. On major festivals, notably Easter and Whitsuntide, pilgrimage specials were a moving sight, as thousands alighted to form into singing processions.

Straight across inland and due east, another section of now disused track, part of a longer east-west route, headed straight towards Melton Constable from January 19, 1882, turning that town into an important junction for Cromer, Norwich, Yarmouth, Lowestoft, and Mundesley-on-Sea. Its population increased ten-fold in thirty years thereafter.

Like the Hunstanton route, this too had its lineside nobility, able to afford the full range of Victorian ostentation. Lord Hastings kept his personal waiting room, approached by a private drive and left by a special entrance onto a special platform. Kings occasionally mixed with commoners, at Sandringham charity events; but lords, even though generous benefactors, preserved their lordliness.

Returning coastwards was the topographically more interesting Melton Constable-Sheringham line, opened as far as intermediate Holt on October 1, 1884 and through Sheringham to Cromer on June 16, 1887. However, after only six operative years the line was taken into the Midland and Great Northern fold. Gradients up to 1 in 80, unusual in East Anglia, taxed local railway navvies across the pretty hills to Holt, but, as compensation, materials were readily to hand; quarries from whence came the track ballast and building stone are still identifiable.

Enthused by railways and talk of their beneficial action on resorts elsewhere, planners visualised new resorts that would make rich businessmen still richer. Like Selsey, Seabrook, Minster and countless other speculative developments, they usually disappointed their backers by refusing to grow. Overstrand and Trimingham in Norfolk developed very little under railway blessing. Factory working Everyman, on holiday, felt uneasy without the familiarity of crowds, yelping happily in similar urban accents, all around him. He obstinately went on with the masses to Great Yarmouth, or to a lesser degree to Cromer.

Early twentieth-century popularity of the bigger resorts spawned such crowded holiday specials as the *Norfolk Coast Express*, running in three sections behind one engine for final transit to Sheringham, Cromer, and the increasingly patronised Mundesley-on-Sea, though this was about the limit of the latter's growth. Great Yarmouth would always outshine the rest of Norfolk, as surely as Blackpool dominated Lancashire for a similar type of holidaymaker.

Looking cartographically erratic, the shorter coastal stretch between Cromer Beach station and North Walsham via Mundesley, reached Mundesley on 20 June 1898 for freight, and for passengers only ten days later, in time for the peak summer rush. However the Cromer end was not completed until August 1906, operated by the MGNJR and Great Eastern. It was said to be the making of Mundesley. Hotels sprang up, and wealthier families took houses for entire summers, while their breadwinners continued sweating in City banks, coming down each weekend to join them. Some of these still preferred travelling by steamer, to such an extent that certain Thames ships and Yarmouth's Friday 'London Boat' earned their nicknames of 'Husbands' Boat' or 'Fathers' Boat'.

Excursions proliferated in the early 1900s, as legislation gave workers weekly half-days, minimal paid holidays, and that most joyous invention ever of officialdom, Bank Holidays: a whole extra Monday at Easter, Whitsun and August for escape from long hours on poor pay, roaring to the seaside in happy sardine discomfort to breathe Yarmouth ozone for ten hours or more on a four-bob fare; a mere 20p decimalised.

Of course, it often rained on Bank Holiday; scorching August might turn unseasonably cold. But weather rarely dampened a hard worked mechanic's spirits; he was free, and that was what mattered, except perhaps on such occasions at the Great Storm of August 26, 1912, when eight inches of rain in twenty-four hours washed away the means of return to his livelihood. Trains stood idle, marooned by burst banks, landslips, and tracks washed right off their beds. Superhuman navvying reconnected Cromer and Mundesley to civilisation within a week, but local legend still speaks of an unluckier train trapped inland near Aylesham for over a month.

North Walsham, junction for lines radiating to Melton Constable, Mundesley and Cromer, also carried the longest continuous stretch in this area of over forty miles to Great Yarmouth, creating a Mecca for holiday campers and caravanners, centred on Caister and California. When the line opened, in no less than six sections, between 1877 and 1881, most of this lovely clifftop land was yet virginal. Facing the exhilarating North Sea, with fine beaches and nearness to popular Great Yarmouth, it was a developers' dream.

Authorised independently and finally entitled the Yarmouth and North Norfolk Railway, this line kept

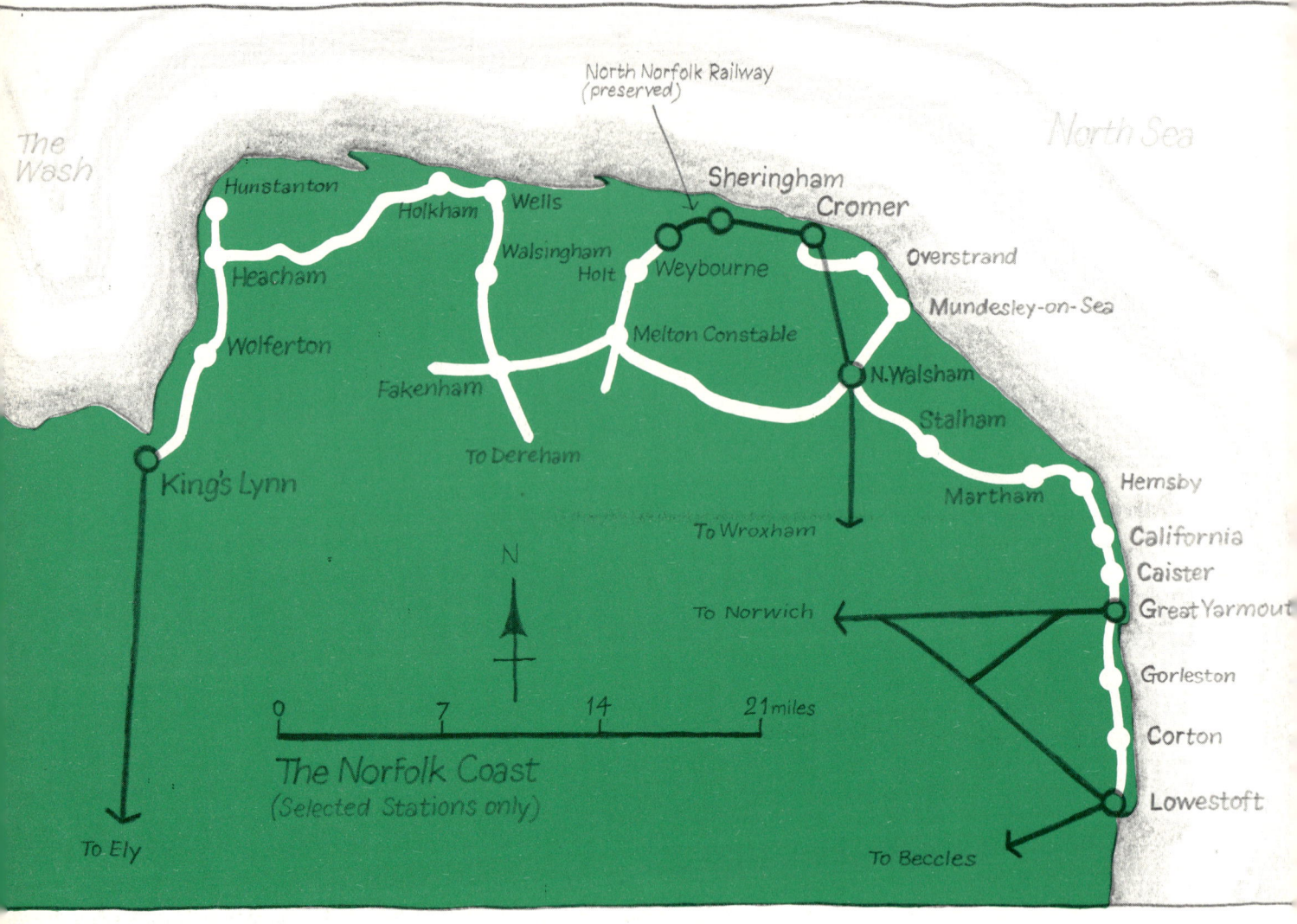

the monopolising Great Eastern at bay for some time, relying on backing from land and factory magnates anxious to improve the marketing of their products or bring coal to small new industries. Like the Lynn and Fakenham, this was a contractor's railway, built as a speculative venture by a London company on mortgaged and bonded funds, in the hopes of selling it at a handsome profit to some local concern desirous of acquiring a railway without actually having to construct it.

Near Caister trains ran alongside the sea in a manner rarely encountered today except at Dawlish, Leigh-on-Sea, and some Welsh resorts. Passengers need only let down windows on long, studded, leather straps to smell and hear the waves. 'If only we could get out here!' wailed children impatient of the few remaining miles to Yarmouth. Eventually they *could* get out, when both this run and the final stretch after Yarmouth to Lowestoft became Norfolk's holiday camp land. This development of camps in the Twenties and Thirties was born as an antidote to the Depression, which put hotels beyond many folks' means. In any case, tastes were altering towards informality, reflected in unfettered female fashions and the de-vulgarising of a healthy tan.

New halts opened to serve spreading camps, notably California and Caister Camp. A special *Holiday Camps Express* was devised for this uninhibited travelling breed, crowded to capacity from 1934 to 1939, and after the war until 1958, serving Mundesley, Caister and Corton areas by ingenious reversals.

From about 1933 frequent railcars also plied the holiday camp coast to Yarmouth Beach station making up to some extent for the decline in the district's older traditional fish traffic.

'Gorleston . . . is remarkable for nothing but the ruins of an ancient building, supposed by Camden to have been a religious house.' So an unusually painstaking topographer dismissed that place, devoid of even one bathing machine, in 1811. Could he have returned in 1911 he would have been astonished that the barren cliffs and bare beaches now housed a charming bathing resort, of very different character from extrovert Yarmouth; green, relaxing to London-torn spirits, slightly sedate but happy, where children romped with balls or yelled at Punch and Judy. They came by the railed coaches dismissed by the same unperceptive Georgian scribe as 'unlikely ever to come into general use'.

Gorleston gained a three-mile branch from Yarmouth in 1903, over a very splendid iron viaduct across the placid intervening Breydon Water. On the

Sidestrand Halt (Norfolk & Suffolk Joint Rly route from Mundesley to North Walsham). One of several hopefully opened halts expected to encourage growth of new resorts and camps. *R S Joby*

California Halt, another holiday camp addition to Norfolk's list of stations, seen when new in 1933. Set up for M&GNR railcar services. *R S Joby*

Railway Routes

Eastward Ho! for Holidays

SKEGNESS, SUTTON-ON-SEA, MABLETHORPE, SHERINGHAM, CROMER, GORLESTON-ON-SEA, YARMOUTH & LOWESTOFT.

For an invigorating and health-giving Holiday the East Coast Resorts are unrivalled.

These Resorts offer exceptional facilities. Golf, Boating, Bathing, numerous Beach Attractions, &c.

The Sands are firm and extensive, and afford excellent opportunities for Cricket, Tennis, &c., while for the children they are an ideal playground.

Send a post-card to Superintendent of the Line, G.N.R., Dept. W.L., 3, York Road, London, N., for ILLUSTRATED HOLIDAY BOOKLET, gratis.

Making for the coast from inland Dereham in 1936. *Pamlin Prints*

'Eastward Ho for Holidays!' Great Northern advertisement of about 1916. *Ward Lock Ltd*

same day, July 13, the Norfolk & Suffolk Joint Committee opened its clifftop route onwards to Lowestoft through Gorleston, serving the new retreats of Hopton and Corton. Again, the line's capacity expanded considerably when this coast broke into a string of holiday camps and bungaloid pleasure developments, spawned as a result of the railway's convenient presence. Corton, the early nineteenth century's 'undeveloped village about a mile to the north of Lowestoft, situated on a high cliff commanding an extensive prospect of the sea', became the twentieth century's communal playground.

Great Yarmouth and Lowestoft both expanded their old established fisheries when trains came to rush their crates of cured herrings, kippers and bloaters to London. 'The principal part of the commerce of Lowestoft is derived from the herring industry' it was written in Georgian times. It remained true a century later when workers' specials annually arrived in droves, bringing salters and curers from London and the Midlands to earn good money for a short season. Several daily freight trains took local herrings, bloaters and other cured products to city markets. From the north as well as south came workers by train; Scottish fishwives and fishermen, eager to pick up additional money during a season luckily not coinciding with their own. Not until the 1930s did this heavy fish freight fall, and with it the workers' specials, as the familiar story of rail goods being transferred to lorries able to enter the very gates of fisheries and factories became universal.

Holiday camp expresses continued, but milked of their former overcrowded monopoly by cheap motor-coaches, followed by the family car revolution. Who relished manhandling prams and cases when everything for everybody could be stuffed into a small Ford's boot? Local travellers in Norfolk, likewise, naturally took to using buses from their own village high streets instead of stations up to two miles distant. The car inspired spiral towards the final Axe had begun.

Working across the map in the same order as our survey of the Norfolk lines' births and lives, the catalogue of their obituaries begins with the Lynn and Hunstanton (May 5, 1969; goods five years previously); continues with Heacham–Wells (June 12, 1952; goods to 1964); Wells–Fakenham (October 31, 1964); Fakenham–Melton Constable on March 2, 1959, but with some goods working for another decade; Melton Constable–Sheringham, during 1964 (though a fragment has been restored at the preserved North Norfolk Railway). The Mundesley–Cromer section was specially unfortunate in that post-war clearance was too long delayed. Beaches stayed closed, as they were still mined, and who wanted a beach resort without the beach? Its fate was sealed on April 17, 1953.

The long route from North Walsham to Yarmouth via Stalham, past a whole string of small seasides like Caister, closed entirely on March 2, 1959, though track was not lifted for eight years. An earlier casualty was the brief Yarmouth Beach–Gorleston line, abandoned from September 21, 1953; but the lengthier ex-LNER route through to Corton and Lowestoft lasted until May 4, 1970, the most recent closure date encountered anywhere during the compilation of this book.

If one seeks to make one pilgrimage which will epitomise the decline and fall of these railways, one might well single out Yarmouth Beach station and its environs. Its long island platforms, adjoining sidings and yards are all flattened and asphalted into one seemingly vast parking area, the Beach Coach Station. There, the motor coaches which helped undemine the train's supremacy have total possession from Easter to autumn, line upon line of them. But against the outer wall one platform is kept, complete with original canopy and a cathedral-like vista of fine iron columns, with all its waiting rooms and offices, to serve as refreshment rooms and administrative centre. But for the expanse of emptiness below, one might be waiting for a train there. Trackbed outside has largely vanished beneath new roads, but the local authority has acknowledged the old days by naming three roads Great Northern, Midland and Stephenson Closes. Hunstanton's similar station, again once catering for thousands with lengthy island platforms, is also flattened, as combined coach park and fun fair.

More curiously, two disused stations became chapels: North Walsham, occupied by Jehovah's Witnesses until demolition during sewage workings; and, at the other devotional extreme, Walsingham, where Anglican and Roman Catholic pilgrims to Our Lady came in by train. This station became a miniature monastery of devout Russian Orthodox monks, who added the customary if slightly incongruous golden onion-dome of their faith.

Station houses survive everywhere, some decayed, some occupied, such as Dersingham, Snettisham, Ormesby and many more. Royal Wolferton, on the Queen's estate, is now Wolferton Station Museum. The Downside, with goods yards, was acquired by an enthusiast, including Edward VII's retiring rooms with panelled oak and gold plated door knobs intact, and the accessory still labelled 'Closet of the Century'. Much local opposition, on grounds of tourist crowds, was quashed by West Norfolk District Council in 1981. Its latest acquisition, at time of writing is the collapsible travelling bed of the young Victoria, before she was Queen. Currently (mid-1982) a £3,000,000 scheme is under discussion for privately reopening fifteen miles out of King's Lynn, including a section across the Sandringham estate, under the revived title of Great Eastern. A two and a half mile fragment between Great Rysburgh and Fakenham has been acquired as another prospective steam centre, whilst on a stretch between Wells and Walsingham a narrow gauge tourist line over SG trackbed was proposed in 1982. As yet neither of these have materialised. The rest of the trackbed can be divided into three classes; deserted; reclaimed for agriculture; and re-used for housing or roads, notably a major bypass near Stalham. Level track has often reverted to grazing and cropping, whilst 15 miles between Stalham and Hickling is now a ramblers' route, the Weavers' Way.

North Walsham with Yarmouth train in 1958.
NCB

43095 about to leave with slow morning train for Yarmouth Beach. Alongside is 61621 with London train.
NCB

LNER's Holiday Barometer for 1937, set fair on Lowestoft, Great Yarmouth, Mundesley, Cromer and Sheringham.
Ward Lock Ltd

Of routes still open, under British Rail, that into Sheringham is most attractive to railway enthusiasts, a border post between diesel present and steam-hauled past. Here begins the preserved North Norfolk Railway, utilising the original route to the next station of Weybourne for nostalgic steam pleasure runs. A fine collection of locomotives, rolling stock and memorabilia is on show at the Sheringham end. Holt station signalbox, from disused track farther along the line, is being restored at the NNR.

Everyday steam in Norfolk is sadly very dead. But long live even a few miles of steam in preservation.

M&GNR Class D 0-6-0 No. 72 at Yarmouth Beach, the station which is now a coach park.
Pamlin Prints

Days of dereliction where expresses formerly roared to the coast. Trackbed of M&GNR line from Yarmouth at deserted North Walsham. *R S Joby*

Masses of sycamore saplings rapidly engulfing an East Anglian halt in 1977.
S Levy

A grand old Great Eastern 2-2-2 (No. 1006) seen in about 1896 with a Cromer express. *NCB*

Crumbling and becoming grass-grown: once busy North Walsham as it appeared in 1964. *NCB*

Melton Constable. Its old nickname 'The Crewe of Norfolk' is now but an ironical echo.
R S Joby

Old locomotive shop at Melton Constable, filmed in 1972. *NCB*

Cromer Beach shed with 61540, in 1954.
Real Photograph Ltd

Lost and found; a fragment abandoned by BR, between Sheringham and Weybourne, in its new guise as the North Norfolk Railway. *North Norfolk Railway*

Frontage of Mundesley on Sea station in 1956.
Real Photographs Ltd

Mundesley on Sea station with N7 No. 69690 on North Walsham train, in 1956.
Real Photographs Ltd

CHAPTER 17

Oxford Accent

BLENHEIM & WOODSTOCK BRANCH

'She was the fayre daughter of Walter, Lord Clifford, concubine of Henry II, and poisoned by Queen Elianor, 1177 AD. Henry made for her a house of wonderfull working so that no man or woman might come to her. This house was named Labyrinthus, and was wrought like unto a knot in a garden call'd a maze. But the Queen came to her by a clue of a thredde, and so dealt with her that she lived not long after.'

So runs national history's legend of Fair Rosamund, as recounted in 1350. In the nineteenth century it was made popular again by Scott in *Woodstock* and *The Talisman*. The upsurge of tourism created by trains and improved roads brought thousands to Blenheim Palace at Woodstock, and the spot in the park known as Rosamond's bower.

In the more localised history of Oxfordshire, and in railway lore, the lady's story runs rather differently: born at Wolverhampton in 1883, vital statistics 0-4-2T, Class 517, number 1473; father, William Dean; godmother, Queen Victoria, during whose 1896 visit to Blenheim Palace (by the railway) she was publicly christened *Fair Rosamund*. *Fair Rosamund* the locomotive will always be synonymous with the Woodstock branch she worked.

Like almost everything else around beautiful and ancient Woodstock, some six miles north of Oxford, the branch was closely associated with the vast and magnificent Blenheim Palace, given to the first Duke of Marlborough by a nation full of gratitude for his victory at Blenheim. It was almost to be expected that the house and estate, completely self contained with every amenity from a full sized organ to its own roads, should ultimately acquire a railway. Not, of course, running actually into the grounds – 'not quite The Thing' in a still partly carriage-orientated society – but coming within minutes of the estate's main gates. It therefore served also the lovely old town, from whence came most of the ducal servants, farm workers and coachmen, and opened up for them and their old established glove making industry all the life of Oxford, and beyond.

Though within GWR territory, this aristocratic little railway was not built by that company, but by the current Duke of Marlborough, largely from His Grace's personal funds, for the 'public and local advantage' of Woodstock and the Palace. Its origin was a Local Act of 1886.

Nominally the branch was an independent company, and remained so for its first seven years of working, but actual staffing and operation was in agreement with the GWR, off whose main line out of Oxford it branched as a spur near Kidlington. Just over four miles long, it was of single track, with an intermediate station at Shipton on Cherwell and a neat little terminus at the far end of Woodstock town. Much of its final course lay over land owned by the Duke, as lord of the surrounding countryside as well as Blenheim, freeing the builders of financial necessity to buy land but, on the other hand, involving certain excavations which could have been avoided by straying beyond Marlborough bounds. The Woodstock terminus allowed for sidings and a small engine shed. This was probably one of England's loveliest platform scenes, with overhanging trees, immaculate topiary hedging, and well kept gardens, welcoming thousands of tourists as time went on.

On May 19, 1890, the branch was opened, initially with four trains each way, increased to a maximum of nine by about 1908, including two mixed trains. In 1897 the line formally amalgamated with its working partner, the GWR.

The Duke of Marlborough himself regularly patronised his 'own' railway in its earlier days, travelling with his starchily formal secretary in a private First-Class carriage, followed by a Second Class business mens' and upper class snobs' vehicle, with the usual gaggle of spartan Thirds for mere human beings. Even a ducal train might well be mixed, with goods wagons tagging on behind, taking estate produce and Woodstock's famous gloves down to the main line.

Life was generally uneventful, even in wartime, settling to a very stereotyped routine as the Twenties dawned. Excitement was limited to a weekly Saturday service, equivalent to other branches' market day trains, locally dubbed the *Woolworth's Special* from the coincidence of a return fare of only sixpence (2½p) for a trip to the nearest Woolworth's, universally advertised as 'The 3d. and 6d. Store' from its pricing policy of 'nothing over 6d.'. Usually the locomotive was the ubiquitous *Fair Rosamund*, affectionately known to everyone from the Big House to the smallest cottage as *Rosie*. Stock at this period included a steam-railmotor converted into an ordinary carriage. *Rosie*, originally open cabbed, had by then been given the comfort of a covered cab.

Rosie enjoyed a long, virtually incident-free life, almost entirely on her native Woodstock branch. The sturdy, handsome little tank was not withdrawn until 1935, when she was replaced by No. 4850. Not a few Oxonians, to whom she was part of everyday life for over half a century, expressed disbelief that such an institution could suffer the mundane fate of breaking-up.

Timetabled services fell slightly, immediately prior to World War II, down to nine a day. It was the first tangible acknowledgement of a tendency affecting almost every smaller railway in the country; that buses and, to some extent, cars, were beginning a serious intrusion into a monopoly in mass transport of both people and goods formerly held by the train.

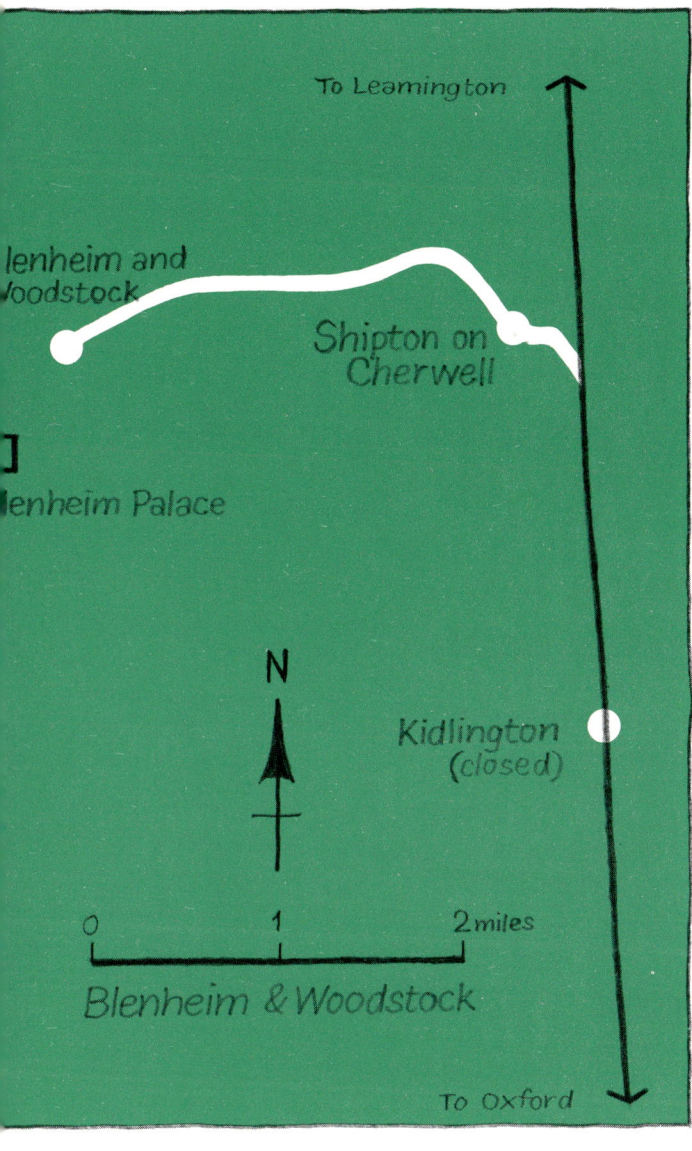

1952 was notable for two events, one hilarious, the other melancholy. Laughter and disbelief mingled at the curious spectacle of a steam engine (made from nothing but wood, though exuding convincing trails of steam) rattling around the streets of Woodstock. This was a property engine built for shooting of the railway comedy film classic, *The Titchfield Thunderbolt*. The apparently spontaneous escape of 'No. 1462' off the rails and into the streets required several days of repetitious filming.

Less amusing was the sad recognition of impending doom, represented in 1952 by yet another cut in services, to a mere six daily trains. Good connections suddenly became bad disconnections, with long waits at Kidlington for so short a run in to Oxford, spinning the familiar vicious circle of declining trains and still further declining patronage, as buses and cars milked more and more custom. Freight fell to one daily train, and Sundays became trainless. The heyday of *Fair Rosamund* and her efficient sisters already seemed a long way back in the past.

54XX class No. 5413 bore the brunt of latter day working, with three or four regular 0-4-2Ts. No. 1420 of these worked the last day's trains.

Closure in September, 1953, was announced but postponed, as more and more passengers gave up the impossible two-hour wait at Kidlington for a few miles' journey and, forgivably, took permanently to buses. The usual protests were made, and the usual quota of alternatives put forward for saving an uneconomic line including railbuses – literally, buses on rails – citing a 1930s conversion in provincial Ireland as prototype. Not surprisingly, the suggestion fell on unenthusiastic official ears.

On February 27, 1954, the last trains shuttled in and out of Woodstock and the little Shipton on Cherwell halt, behind 0-4-2T No. 1420. So anxious were the authorities, it seemed, to rid themselves of the branch, that already the old notice 'Change Here for Blenheim and Woodstock' had vanished from the local bay at Kidlington. With little ballyhoo outside its own locality, the ducal branch shut down. The final train was adorned with a wreath, signifying death to the line, plus a defiant Union Jack.

Track was lifted by about 1959, but most of the actual bed is intact, and walked for pleasure or short-cutting. Some bridges have gone, but three at least remain. A telephone exchange occupies much of the Woodstock goods yard, but the station itself is still easily identifiable, despite fitting of large glass windows, and is now a garage. Virtually nothing remains of the Shipton on Cherwell halt. Kidlington has been converted into offices for small local concerns, as have the goods shed and parcels room. An industrial estate takes over the former station yard.

Would Queen Victoria, who graced the line with her presence on the naming day of *Fair Rosamund*, or her ducal host who built this once useful line, have been amused?

Following the war, two more daily trains were axed, again reflecting national trends in a move away from railways towards handy small cars, available instantly at one's own behest instead of departing at inconviently long intervals. One autocar type carriage usually sufficed, increased to two on occasion. Freight continued to consist mainly of two commodities for which rural Oxfordshire was famous: agricultural supplies and fatstock to market in Oxford; or hampers of the celebrated Woodstock gloves, once a cottage industry and in modern times maintained by a local factory. Over a dozen glove hampers left Blenheim and Woodstock station daily, even to the last.

Specials brought in fluctuating revenue: visitors to a large annual agricultural show; swarms of tourists to Blenheim Palace; and, for a time during the Forties, a regular Saturday morning train at a good old fashioned fare of 6d. (2½p), the 'Tanner Special', ferrying local children to morning matinees at a Kidlington cinema, two stops down the line.

129

GWR 0-4-2T No. 1473 *Fair Rosamund*, at the terminus in May 1930 with train from Oxford.
H C Casserley

Rush hour commuters to the city – all four of them! – at the sole intermediate halt. *Lens of Sutton*

Blenheim and Woodstock station after closure in about 1955. Rails inside already lifted.
Lens of Sutton

← *Fair Rosamund* at Oxford.
Lens of Sutton

Blenheim and Woodstock station in April 1978, converted into a commercial garage yet still recognisable. Railings at right were part of original railway installations. *P Forbes*

Remains of branch line course, looking towards Kidlington from Woodstock in April 1978. *P Forbes*

Telephone exchange on site of terminus goods yard in 1978. *P Forbes*

Bridge support remaining near Woodstock, the only indication of the track's course. A housing estate is build across the nearby trackbed. *P Forbes*

Long view of Blenheim & Woodstock station showing an attractive background of flower beds and trees.
Locomotive & General

CHAPTER 18

'Mid Stations and Palaces

DERBYSHIRE

'Derby is emerging all at once from an almost sepulchral lethargy, or indeed impending sepulture, thanks to the intersecting lines of railroad which will bring hither people from all the quarters of England. The bustle has already begun, after years of deathlike stillness, and the consequences of it are immediately visible in the constructions that are everywhere going on – in the new houses that have started into existence as if by magic.'

So a traveller through the county-town observed in about 1839, as Derby jerked awake to the alarm clock of steam engine whistles. Though only one line as yet actually crossed right through the difficult Peak country itself, its perimeters were well served and Derby was in the throes of becoming what that age commonly termed a railway-town. As our observer continued: 'The head stations of the three railroads are near to each other on an open space of ground called The Old Meadows, contiguous to the London road . . . and it is calculated that the offices and buildings would occupy an area of twenty-five acres, with a continuous line of frontage to the principal edifice of upwards of a thousand feet. What a chance for an architect of genius and imagination!'

As a footnote, so fast did railway building in Derby progress between completion and typesetting of this book, that the author added: 'This expectation has since been fulfilled, and the front elevation of this general "embarcadero" is as magnificent as I had anticipated.'

Much had happened since a less perceptive brother scribe took a glance at the pioneer Grand Surrey Iron Rail Road in about 1811 and dismissed it in one sentence: 'This road does not appear to be much used; nor is it probable that it will *ever* come into general use'.

First across the Peak, rather than round it, was the unconventional Cromford and High Peak Railway of 1830, running diagonally through the bleak hills from Cromford Wharf on the Derby side to Whaley Bridge, east of Buxton. Its passenger days were brief, but its total lifespan was to be long.

Passengers were a low priority in the C&HPR's plans, this being a thinly populated countryside, wildly beautiful and undeveloped, whose fortune was mainly in minerals; Derbyshire limestone, local fluorspar, and lead. As a through freight route from the industrial Midlands, the thirty-three-mile long line would have value for transit of manufactured goods and coal. Its head and tail were the Cromford and the Peak Forest canals, themselves built for freight transit immediately before the railway age overtook them. Canal and railway served without despoiling the valleys; in the words of our previously quoted topographer: 'At Whaley Bridge the surrounding landscape is more striking than upon the summit of a very elevated ground . . . the Peak Forest Canal comes in as a very pretty feature of the landscape.'

Six years' work went into constructing the C&HPR, through tough rocky hill country. It opened from Cromford Wharf as far as Hurdlow on May 29, 1830, and thence to Whaley Bridge, the more difficult section, on July 6, 1831. Josias Jessop, the engineer, planned the course on the principles of a waterless canal, with lengthy straight and level stretches lifted one to the next by inclined planes, the equivalent on land of locks, up which wagons were hauled at the end of the section on ropes, by stationary steam engine. Wagons were at first drawn to the next plane by horses. Thus three ages of transport overlapped in practical use: canal, steam power, and horse haulage.

The railway became more conventional with the modification of Hopton incline for the use of locomotives. At 1 in 14 it remained for a long time Britain's steepest climb negotiated without such assistance as rack or pinion. Double heading was usual against the gradient; trains formed a splendid picture, billowing smoke and audibly straining like those described at the Great Exhibition by Thackeray as 'Like whales at sport, or elephants a-grazing'.

Other problems, once normal locomotion came, were tunnels excavated originally for horses standing only hands instead of wheels high. Hopton in particular – low, flat-roofed inside – barely accommodated the smallest engines; and the dripping everlasting dampness of its unlined walls made choking by smoke and fumes even more intolerable than to drivers on normal steam engines when plunged underground.

Only for a short time did passengers have use of this earliest Peak line, trundling comfortlessly aboard one single 'fly-coach' hooked on like an afterthought behind a goods train. Their thirty mile journey took nearly six weary hours, during which even the splendour of local scenery became tedious and boring.

Passenger carrying ended abruptly as early as 1877, after only twenty-two years' service, following a disastrous accident. Thereafter the line reverted to freight-only working, right to the end nearly a century later. Among its more unusual cargoes was water in quantity, conveyed in old loco tenders converted into simple tankers, supplying the isolated farms, small industries, quarries and cottagers of these excessively dry limestone uplands; the public regularly converged on prearranged siding calls to collect their water in jars, jugs and churns, trundled home by small wooden cart.

The LNWR leased the C&HPR in 1862, and absorbed it fully from July 19, 1887. The unproductive sections Ladmanlow–Shallcross and Whaley Bridge–Shallcross were closed soon after. LNWR steam engines were phased in, a motley band ranging over the years from small sturdy 2-4-0 *Chopper* tanks, through cast-off 0-6-0Ts from North London Railway, to latter-day ex-War Department utility 0-6-0 tanks, all necessarily of dumpy dimensions to cope with heavy gradients and tight curves. The final years up to the early 1960s found elderly ex-LNWR tanks and the old North London engines still going strong; 58850, 58860 and 58862 were as familiar as the scenery itself.

Early abandonment of passenger carrying proved a wise move, to be emphasised by the antics of runaway stock on steep inclines, scenes with more than a touch of the later Will Hay railway-film about them. The climax, worthy of the best in silent cinema, came in 1888 when two derailed wagons leaped right across Cromford canal, *and* across the adjoining MR line, to become heaps of picturesque scrap in a field beyond. Catch-pits were built afterwards, into which such runaways could be harmlessly diverted to commit suicide without damaging more track than was necessary; the wreckage of one of the last is said to be still visible.

True passenger travel through the Peak, in a normal sense, began with the throwing out of a line north-westwards through Matlock, towards Buxton and Manchester, following that instinctive doctrine of most early companies – that the shorter and more rural a line, the more pompously cumbersome should be its title; in this case, the Manchester, Buxton, Matlock and Midland Junction Railway. Behind it was a name associated by posterity with gigantic glasshouses in Derbyshire and London (The Great Conservatory of Chatsworth, and the Crystal Palace) rather than with trains; the inventive Joseph Paxton, one-time head gardener of the Duke of Devonshire's Derbyshire palace, Chatsworth.

Paxton's railway work was wide ranging, from administration and directorship to architecture. To paraphrase one of the most popular ballads of his time, though 'mid the pleasures of crystal palaces Paxton did roam, when it came to relieving the monotony of glass with brick, stone, and iron, there was no place like a railway station on a line that was virtually his own.

As early as 1835 Paxton was investing in railways, long before any Dalesman beyond the Cromford area had yet seen a train. He counted Stephenson, the railway king, among his close friends. Derbyshire, indeed, submitted early to locomotion partly because Stephenson had, allegedly, surveyed much of the county in person with Paxton, from a distinctive hired yellow horse chaise.

In about 1846, Paxton became a director of the powerful Midland Railway and, predictably, began planning communication farther into non-industrial Derbyshire from Ambergate towards Matlock and Buxton (as yet reached only by coach). This would also conveniently serve Chatsworth en route.

As a start he laid a twelve-mile section from Ambergate to Rowsley, a suitable railhead for Chatsworth. This was the meandering little line with the big name always shortened to MBM&MJR, of which he duly became chairman. 'Paxton has command of every railway influence in England', Dickens remarked with some truth.

People in many parts had demonstrated bitterly against invasion by snorting iron horses and probing surveyors. Not so in the Dales, where folk took an appreciative view of release from old limitations. When Paxton's scheme was announced places which in practice would benefit little from this first line rejoiced with those more directly involved. Hathersage and Chapel-en-le-Frith ran out of flags; Castleton and Hope danced; church bells rang from morning to midnight; bands boomed oom-pah in patriotic airs; inns were packed with celebrators; and school parties paraded the possible site of one station.

The necessary Parliamentary powers were obtained in 1846, work began three years later, and the line was completed as far as Rowsley by June 1849.

Paxton was quite literally head cook and bottlewasher of the MBM&MJR: chairman, architect, estate agent (he acquired land at Darley Dale far in advance of its actual use), employment officer, disciplinarian and staff officer.

Several stations were partly or wholly designed by him. Chief of these was Rowsley's original terminus, built before the later MR extension to Buxton; a charming little building where the future designer of the Crystal Palace showed his skill in a smaller medium, like a painter of giant canvases demonstrating his versatility in a miniature. Into this, the station for his ducal patron's Chatsworth, he put perhaps his best architectural work in Derbyshire. Rowsley station clearly reflected certain features found in the far greater Crystal Palace: curved roof brackets suggestive of the Palace's gigantic iron nave supports; round-arched window and door frames, in direct contrast to the prevailing Victorian pointed Gothic, and clean-cut simple lines instead of ornamented flamboyance.

When, on eventual continuation of the route, a new Rowsley station was required, Paxton's original structure was retained as offices. His hand also created many adjuncts of railway operation. Among these are said to be further offices at Rowsley and a stationmaster's house, some workers' cottages, station houses for Beeley and Matlock, and another staff house at Darley Dale. Cromford station was probably Paxton's work, at least in part; the alternative theory that it was built by G. H. Stokes makes Paxton's participation (or, at least, his advice) more rather than less likely, Stokes being in fact his son-in-law.

Matlock station was completed at about the same time together with Matlock Bridge, but the station's completion was no occasion for immediate rejoicing; on the final Saturday night builders downed tools, leaving behind them a smart new station; next day it was as incomplete as several weeks before, thieves having stripped every scrap of lead from its new roof overnight.

Meanwhile, every attempt to find a suitable design for the Great Exhibition had failed. In our chapter on the railways of Crystal Palace it has already been told how Paxton's blotting paper doodle, scrawled during a Midland Railway company meeting, produced the germ of the winning design; a sketch astonishingly close to the finished conception. During its development stage, Palace and railway interests again interwove, as a Midland colleague whose speciality was calculating the stresses and capabilities of iron girders and pillars, worked closely with Paxton. From his own Rowsley station Paxton took the plans down to Derby where, by happy chance, Stephenson was also waiting for the London connection. Munching pre-dining car lunches, the pair discussed the plan. Before journey's end, the much impressed Stephenson had agreed to try every possible means of getting this new design before the Exhibition committee at this late stage.

The outcome history knows well. The Crystal Palace was transformed from a sketch to reality. Derby city duly honoured Paxton with a banquet to make any modern Bunter gasp, its courses interspersed by a stream of adulatory speeches. Replying, Paxton recounted the story of the station board meeting doodle (now, incidentally, in the Victoria and Albert Museum). He attributed much of his success to the 'Bachelor Duke' at Chatsworth who 'by his liberality (gave) ample means for various experiments', alluding to the Great Conservatory designed for Chatsworth's precious Victoria Regia lily, on whose construction methods the Palace was based. Without that practical experience, Paxton held, 'there never would have been a Crystal Palace'.

For any normal mortal all this railway and Exhibition activity should have been enough. But not for a Paxton. He conceived his most gradiosely fantastic scheme yet, combining both his areas of activity, and was in deadly earnest when planning to girdle the whole of London with the Great Victorian Way, an extraordinary railroad encased within a 12-mile long glass and iron tube above ground, like an endlessly elongated Palace, constructed similarly of glass and iron. Nor would this tube have accommodated only trains, but also houses, shops and streets in a gargantuan glass case, above which eight lines of railway track would run, anticipating modern two tier motorway junctions. The enclosed space would have been 72 feet wide and 100 feet high.

Though the Queen and leading politicians looked seriously at the Great Victorian Way, its size and impracticability defeated it; the glass overground lost in favour of the more prosaic tunnelled Underground. Nevertheless Paxton's plan is worth recording, if only to illustrate the interweaving of his interests in glass palaces and in railways.

The Way was relegated to a dream in a file, but Paxton was still a director of the very real Midland Railway, and chairman of his own pet MBM&MJR. A complete through route from Manchester was not yet accomplished, but events were moving towards extension through Millers Dale to Buxton. When finished this would be counted one of Britain's most wonderfully scenic of all train rides.

The MR and LNWR had both taken shares in the line up to Rowsley, hopeful stakes in future developments, and in 1852 took it over on joint lease. In 1871 Paxton's own company, the Midland, finally got the whole line for itself, and began the constructionally difficult second stage through to Buxton. This task was made the more demanding still by the all-powerful Duke of Devonshire refusing to allow trains across Chatsworth park, forcing the engineers away from an easy riverside stretch into intractable hard, rocky hills.

Work was an almost exact repetition of the Midland's travails near Belper in the same county, as recounted in 1840: 'The Midland Railway was contending with no trifling difficulties about here, excavating a tunnel deep into the rocky bank of the Derwent and crossing the latter over a rudely constructed bridge raised on single piles, and again cutting down into limestone rock beyond it to complete a profound excavation.' The Midland, of course, won through, admitting the public for the first time in Derbyshire to 'the free use of so convenient a line of communication, which not only brings so many places and towns together at once, but also brings the south nearer to the north'.

North and south, embodied more locally in Buxton and Matlock, came nearer to joining hands when on August 1, 1862, the first trains steamed onwards from the previous terminus of Rowsley, as far as Hassop. In another year the line entered Buxton itself.

It was not long before Manchester-London expresses began thundering through this shorter and magnificent route, roaring over the grand stone viaduct of Monsal Dale and the high, iron one spanning Millers Dale. Far from despoiling the landscape, the viaducts became integral and focal features, pictured in scenes of 'Beautiful Britain' from the dawn of photographic picture books. They showed how nobility in architecture and splendour of nature could harmoniously live together, yet serve a purely utilitarian purpose – that of getting trains from town to town. Best of all was the sight in Midland days of that company's expresses in their rich deep crimson livery, moving against wide sweeps of natural green.

North to south, in a more or less straight line, was the aim of the Peak's third railway, again opening up superb countryside to all, as well as serving everyday transport purposes. The line ran down from Buxton towards Uttoxeter and followed part of the early Cromford venture to Parsley Hay. Local passengers were not the LNWR's main concern in promoting another route through Buxton, for the inner Peak was thinly populated. The main prize was to cut route miles and speed up mainline services between such cities as Stockport, via Buxton, and the south. Also in the LNWR's plans were tourists, for this line would pass close to one of the most celebrated beauty spots in Britain, glorious Dovedale, just behind the curious pyramidal miniature mountain of Thorpe Cloud, whose name made its own station nameboard a two-word poem.

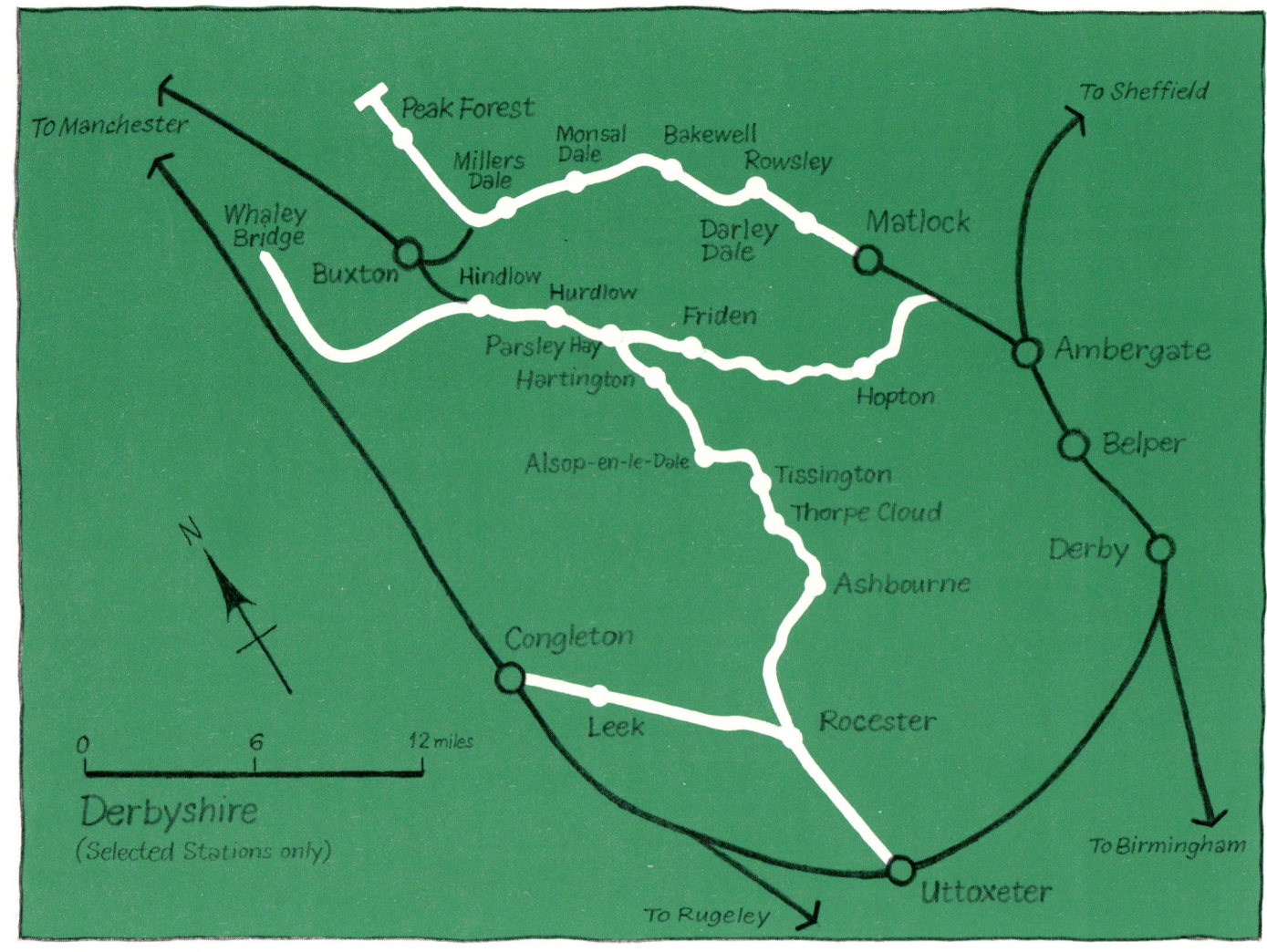

Construction, as elsewhere in rocky Derbyshire, was arduous, spread over nine full years at a cost of £1,500,000, an astronomical sum when companies elsewhere were building branches on £60,000.

Single track was considered sufficient, with regular passing loops, but prudently the builders allowed for future doubling when designing the many bridges and tunnels. Starting from Buxton, the line reached Parsley Hay – another poetic station name – in June 1892 for goods, and for passengers about two years later. It partly utilised sections of the Cromford and High Peak line, whose northern section had been early abandoned.

The rest of the new artery, from Parsley Hay down to Ashbourne, was not completed until August 4, 1899, so slow was progress in this difficult limestone terrain. Tunnelling was laborious, and one cutting through rock is said to have needed the services of 200 sweating railway navvies with many heavy steam cranes.

Unlike the Rowsley route, Tissington-line stations were generally primitive plank and wood affairs, but they served magnificent country; notably Thorpe Cloud (for Dovedale); Tissington; and such stations as Hartington and Hindlow, giving passengers superb views before even leaving the platform.

Despite the established presence of trains in other parts of Derbyshire, so isolated was some of this newer territory that large numbers of villagers had still never set eyes upon a train. To allay their natural suspicions of these hellish machines which seemed driven by the Devil himself, black with smuts and grinning through ruddy sweat, the company laid on, before official opening day, special free excursions to Ashbourne for villagers down from Hartington, thus craftily initiating them as potential paying customers.

Most were thrilled and delighted. When the first really hard Derbyshire winter occurred after the railway had been built, and all the roads were blocked with snow and villages were cut off for many days, they blessed the railway still more, as the game little tank engines forced their way in with vital supplies unobtainable by road. Trains would perform this vital winter task right through to the last days in the supposedly sophisticated 1950s and 1960s.

Buxton's civic pride insisted that both companies now serving the great spa should preserve its elegant tone by concentrating their termini on adjoining sites and giving them architectural homogeniety instead of conflicting designs. The symmetry of the resulting dual station was emphasised by a long unifying façade generally attributed to Paxton, or at least to his advice and influence; an impressive screen of glass and iron whose tracery and curvilinear ironwork visibly acknowledged the Crystal Palace as its sire.

Given the addition of the subsequently famous Leek and Manifold railway, running off westwards and geographically belonging mainly to adjoining

Staffordshire, the Peak was remarkably well served by lines both across and all around its perimeter, despite the fact that its interior had few settlements above the status of a large village, Buxton, Matlock, Derby and Ashbourne being nearer its outside edges. The only real operational mistake was the northern part of the early Cromford and High Peak, whose section from Whaley Bridge to Ladmanlow was discontinued as early as 1892, while other lines were still being built; in any case, this was almost exclusively a freight venture, but for its brief passenger experiment lasting only between 1855 and 1877.

The rest of the Peak lines blossomed and flourished to greater or lesser extent until the early 1920s, when the repetitious theme song of country buses intruding conveniently into village centres, nearer than trains could go, began to be sung ever louder. The second verse of the song – family cars – told of now certain decline, as trade was milked further from trains, though none as yet dreamed what the final sad verse would bring.

First to open, and first to fall, was not surprisingly the Cromford and High Peak. Solely based on freight, various sections were shut down erratically according to their current degree of remaining profitability between April 1952 and September 1967.

Typifying the larger process of decline on a fine goods and passenger railway was the beautiful route via Tissington, reduced by the earlier 1950s from six to four daily trains, usually consisting of only two antiquated non-corridor coaches behind a dispirited old ex-LMS 2-6-4T. One local factor which mitigated heavily against the now very real threat of closure was that which had led villagers so to rejoice when the line opened; Derbyshire's notoriously severe winters. Even in modern times villages were often cut off completely by snow bound roads for days on end, reliant only on the sturdy little trains to get food and fuel. So deep was the concern about future harsh winters that petitioning for retention of emergency winter service won a long reprieve, from November 1, 1954, when all local passenger trains ceased, right through to October 7, 1963 when the last emergency, freight, and through-excursions all ended. Thus Tissington, Thorpe Cloud and their neighbours were left at the mercy of the less effective winter road clearance services. One track fragment, from Hindlow up to Buxton, was kept for conveyance of quarry stone, an important item of local economy.

More than mere local services were lost after 1963. Visitors from as far away as London had poured in for Tissington's celebrated well-dressing ceremonies and colourful traditional celebrations. Walkers in legions always descended on Thorpe Cloud and the Dovedale area, to walk alongside the placid, tree-lined Dove, gaze up at the mysterious Cloud, indulge in scree-running, or negotiate the famous, un-nerving stepping stones over the river. If ever trains served Paradise, it was here. Today the walkers and climbers still come, by the coaches and cars that killed the trains, to enjoy the line in its new guise of the Tissington Trail.

On the Buxton–Matlock route decay was first manifest in closures of single stations: Hassop in August 1942; Monsal Dale (August 1959); Great Longstone (September 10, 1962). Not until March 6, 1967 were all the local trains which stopped at the remaining stations withdrawn, leaving residents with the maddening spectacle of unattainable Manchester to London expresses roaring through in swirls of mocking steam.

About a year later, these, too, disappeared, diverted from April 1, 1968, along with through freighters, leaving the whole line, cut at such expense and heavy manual labour by the Victorians, lying silent, its magnificent viaducts reduced to focal points on calendars instead of serving pieces of a living railway system. Only a fraction kept a twitch of life, a goods-only section from near Millers Dale into Buxton.

Decay and dereliction were not to be the fate of so many of Derbyshire's lost lines as had occurred elsewhere. Miles of track were destined to be spared and converted to public pleasure because of the glorious scenery they opened up, first by rail and now as long distance footpaths and bridleways. Stations were convenient for conversion into resting points, refreshments places, car parks and access points, as has also been done on a similarly scenic disused railway system in Durham, the Blaydon and Consett, now the Derwent Walk.

Best known of Derbyshire's rail trails is the Tissington Trail over many miles of the old Ashbourne-Buxton line, for which the Peak Planning Board began negotiations in 1965. Two years later the trackbed and appurtenances were formally acquired. Grants were obtained for soiling over the trackbeds and making them readily walkable – though extremely good feet, boots and ankles are still needed to tackle even half this lengthy walk – and for installation of public amenities between Ashbourne and Hartington. The walk was to be named 'The Tissington Trail' after the great tourist attraction village of the well-dressings. It was claimed as the first converted railway of its kind in England.

Access being mainly by private car, car parks were opened at such strategic points as Tissington itself, Ashbourne, Hartington, and Alsop-en-le-Dale. In time it became possible to tramp all the way to Parsley Hay through the finest scenery in the Midlands.

Hartington signal box, standing high and strategically placed, became a park warden's office, and the former weigh-hut of Alsop-en-le-Dale was made into a useful public resting place and shelter. Other visible remains include Ashbourne tunnel; Thorpe Cloud station house, Tissington station cottages, and some fine bridges and viaducts.

Cromford and High Peak line, the old mineral line touching on similar ground to the Tissington at one end, likewise became after closure in 1967 a public pleasure way, the High Peak Trail, about thirteen miles of splendid hiking pathway from Cromford through to Parsley Hay. Here again, the Peak Planning Board was the instigator, acquiring the first few miles which make a very delightful walk. Above Hindlow, abandoned since 1869, is tougher going, but well booted explorers penetrate it for its wild beauty

44129 leaving lay-by at Darley Dale with Up freight in June 1958. *Daniels*

Hopton Incline on the Cromford & High Peak Railway in 1934. LMS No. 7527.
H C Casserley

Monsal Dale with Manchester express running through in 1958. *G Daniels*

← Millers Dale with DMU at left-hand platform, bound for Buxton, 1967. *NCB*

44902 at Darley Dale with Down freight. *G Daniels*

The almost mountainous nature of Peak District scenery is conveyed in this shot of Millers Dale in 1967. Buxton-bound DMU. *NCB*

Buxton–Millers Dale train filmed in 1963. *NCB*

Splendid geological study in a Peak Forest cutting. St Pancras–Manchester express in June 1933 behind No. 1061.
H C Casserley

Millers Dale in June 1933. Johnson 0-4-4T No. 1421 with Buxton branch train.
H C Casserley

and industrial archaeological interest. Plans also included acquisition of a further seven miles of trackbed outside the official Peak National Park, for extension of the Trail.

Industrial archaeology is a very special feature of the High Peak Trail, remembering the line's original unconventional construction of level stretches raised through ascending country by inclined planes and haulage. At Longcliffe stables are to be seen, reminders that horses worked the flat sections; at Middleton incline is an original winding engine over 150 years old; this and its impressive stone housing, visible from afar, has been restored as a heritage of the working past. Burbage tunnel, on the longest abandoned northerly stretch, is still traceable by roughshod hikers, and several other inclines can be seen elsewhere. As late as 1952 Whaley Bridge incline was operated by a local mill, where a horse continued to be used for lifting up wagons in the original manner, harnessed to a pulley, beam and spindle.

On a third trail, walkers can plod out of Derbyshire towards Staffordshire along the disused Leek and Manifold branch. This, too, has become a properly maintained footpath with official vehicle access and comprises eight miles of old trackbed with many scenic attractions.

On the deserted Buxton–Matlock section, much remains to be seen, including the dominant Monsal Dale Viaduct, scheduled as of architectural and historic value; stations at Darley Dale (occupied by an engineering concern at time of writing), New Rowsley (packing cases store), Hassop (a farm implements firm), and Great Longstone, now a private home. A new Peak Rail society occupies part of Matlock station as a centre for a proposed preservation scheme for the Matlock–Buxton section. As yet (1982) Peak Rail is still raising share capital and acquiring rolling stock; but even if it does come to fruition, the situation for the rest of Derbyshire will remain the same.

The earlier section, out to Rowsley old station, the original MBM&MJR, is still rich in mementoes of Joseph Paxton as both architect and railwayman. Edensor, the model village so charmingly laid out under his direction, is a living memorial to his work as an early town planner. His first Rowsley station continued as goods offices until recently, has been kept in good order. Scattered around the district are former railway houses attributed to him, in continued occupation. The line's trackbed is well used by walkers, out towards Rowsley, from which station his historic Crystal Palace designs were taken London.

The classic epitaph, 'If you would see his monument, look around you' means nothing now on Sydenham Hill, where only a vast open space shows where Paxton's Crystal Palace stood and glittered for over eighty years. But in Derbyshire it seems highly appropriate to anyone who explores charming Edensor after walking his lost railway line.

The Tissington Trail today at Hartington, on the former Buxton–Ashbourne line, seen in pale December mist. *J H Appleton*

Old signal box and a limestone cutting on the Tissington Trail, adapted for walking from the Ashbourne–Buxton railway. *J H Appleton*

Dramatic shot of a deep cutting with the Tissington Trail clearly showing as a narrow footpath worn into white limestone. *M V Searle*

Walking the track, virtually unrecognisable as such in its modest footpath form, through the beautiful Manifold Valley.
Countryside Commission

NL 0-6-0T No. 58860 at Middleton Top, 1950.
Real Photographs Ltd

CHAPTER 19

Wye Wanderings

THE WYE VALLEY & FOREST OF DEAN

Two kinds of natural riches have been exploited by mankind in the Wye Valley and Forest of Dean from commerce's dawn: riches from underground – coal, iron and other minerals – and quality shipbuilding timber from the hills. Roman miners littered these woodlands with workings and trackways, still traceable today.

Passage into the wider world was by the navigable Wye to Chepstow. Many inland villages sustained small shipbuilding industries utilising local timber, whilst at Chepstow, approaching the sea, ships up to 650 tons were constructed. Ninety ton ships were navigable upstream as far as Brockweir, and shallow lighters to Ross, or even right through to Hereford. The river was much more reliable than very rough tracks through deep untamed gorges. Few villages look less like a port now than lovely inland Llandogo; yet once it maintained a thriving sail passage for goods and passengers as far as Bristol, through Chepstow. Barges carried down heavy grindstones and millstones, exported as far afield as Ireland. Wire works opened at Tintern before 1600.

Eighteenth-century iron furnaces abounded, fed on Wyedean trees, and water powered lathes kept local turneries turning. This period also added a new industry, which in time would commercially supplant the old: tourism, born of improved roads. As yet it was confined mainly to the carriage classes, or wandering horseback poets and painters, enchanted with glorious Wye and Dean.

Railways, final development in this thousand year old sequence of industrial and transport progress, and centred like existing tracks and roads on the border town of Monmouth, killed Wye navigation, but gave remote romantic Tintern Abbey to Everyman.

Anticipating steam, railed tramways operated intensively carrying coal, iron and timber. In May 1810 an Act authorised building by the Monmouth Railway of one across Dean from Coleford and Redbrook to May Hill, a Monmouth suburb, with provision for passenger wagons, possibly for the first time anywhere. By about 1817 that line was open.

In 1853 steam was planned from Dean into South Wales, crossing the Wye at Monmouth but not as yet entering its valley; the Coleford, Monmouth, Usk and Pontypool Railway. The section to Monmouth's main station at Troy, named after the nearby River Trothy, opened on October 12, 1857, worked by locomotives borrowed from another sister, the Newport, Abergavenny and Hereford Railway, off whose junction the CMUPR sprouted. Both were acquired by the larger West Midland Railway after about a year, and were merged again into the GWR by about 1887.

At right angles to these routes from Monmouth, single tracks were driven into the Wye Valley itself, both up and downstream, beginning with the glorious stretch from May Hill up to Ross-on-Wye, opened by the Ross and Monmouth Railway on August 4, 1873. From the start it was GWR-worked, though the GWR did not acquire it outright until 1922. In 1874 the GWR bridged an awkward gap into Troy with a one-mile spur.

Wriggling and twisting like a Wye salmon, beneath towering rocks, following the river's contortions, the trains passed hundreds of feet below the landmark of magnificent Symonds Yat. A long uphill slog awaited those who alighted here for one of England's most celebrated of all panoramas. Beyond the tunnel where it dived underneath the Yat Rock, towards Lydbrook, the Wye Valley line passed touristic Goodrich Castle before leaving the riverside to join the Hereford–Gloucester route at Ross.

Also from Lydbrook, the Severn and Wye Joint Railway ran off into the Forest with a junction for Cinderford; a route of quite remarkable natural beauty. However, this beauty was denied to passengers as early as July 8, 1929, when the unviable branch closed.

A delightful and lesser known railway which made its way by looping curves from Wye to mid-Dean, was built over Monmouth Railway territory in 1875, utilising a route proposed under a stillborn Coleford Railway Act of 1872. Opened on September 1, 1883, it was worked by the GWR, who soon absorbed it and made most of this glorious region GWR dominated. This line possessed only one intermediate halt before its complex junction at Coleford with the Severn and Wye Railway.

The longest and finest route through the Wye Valley, from Monmouth down to Chepstow, opened on November 1, 1876. It enjoyed the fullest life of all this group, taking latter-day sustenance from tourism to Tintern Abbey and to many superb viewpoints accessible from lineside halts. River transport vanished almost immediately after its coming, but a concession was made to keeping at least one older local industry alive. A standard-gauge tramway near Tintern branched off to Britain's oldest water powered wire works (dated 1566), replacing an earlier tramway from works to riverside made under the 1875 Wye Valley Railway Amendment Act. In 1901, about twenty years after going over to tinplate as the Abbey Wire and Tinplate Company, the works closed, but the tramway continued until 1935, serving a sawmill, and was lifted only because by then its hopelessly buckled metals were too costly to replace.

The Wye Valley Line, as the total Monmouth–Chepstow route was usually known, cost its founders £300,000, divided between track, excavations, an initial four stations, two tunnels and two iron bridges. Most of the cash was expended near Tintern, in burrowing beneath massive limestone outcrops and wooded hills. Delving beneath Tidenham Chase progressed at only two yards a day, requiring nineteen months' cutting.

Despite the rigours of blasting some of Britain's toughest rocks and working on precipitous forested slopes, the navvies' moderation of language and demeanour so impressed local clergy, periodically eavesdropping for levity, that they actually commended them in the print of their local press.

Though tourists were naturally expected to yield the line's chief income, in these early years they actually fell below expectations, as did freight consignments. Losses mounted quickly until in 1905 the little independent Wye Valley Railway gave up its struggle and capitulated to the omnipresent GWR, whose nationwide ability to balance the loss-making lines with highly profitable ones, financed operations for another forty years, through to BR ownership.

Under the GWR, tourism steadily increased. Low fares combined with through-excursions to breathtaking scenery glimpsed everywhere through the carriage windows brought the world flocking to the poets' 'Sylvan Wye', and to disturb the hallowed peace of Tintern Abbey. 'Summer Excursions to TINTERN via the Wye Valley Railway at REDUCED FARES from JUNE 4TH until further Notice' boasted the GWR's advertising department even before full ownership, in 1879. Customers were enticed with the bait of tours from Bristol at half-a-crown (12½p) return, Third Class (inexplicably, the same as from Ross, halfway there!), or all the way from Cheltenham for 3s. 6d. (17½p) Third, 5s. (25p) Second, or a lordly, luxurious 7s. (35p) First Class. The latter class was much patronised by wealthy retired Cheltenham colonels and their ladies in an age of fashionable spa sojourns.

Regular local services remained pretty constant throughout the WVR's lifetime, at four or five weekday services. Sunday trains were only added in the booming inter-war years of 1919–1939.

Travel was always inordinately slow (though who, apart from a few locals not out for pleasure, cared when the scenery outside the carriage windows was so magnificent?), there being but one passing loop, at Tintern, and a token-exchange signalling system in operation. To the end of its days the Wye train still took almost an hour to gasp barely fourteen miles between Monmouth and Chepstow, stopping at twelve wayside halts and stations to wheeze for breath.

The Great War meant economies in some directions, but expansion in others. The steeply graded, spectacularly scenic five-mile Wyesham–Coleford line had never seriously aimed at a practicable service; 'infrequent' was the politest term applied to its erratic timetable. War was an excuse for the GWR to evict passengers 'as a wartime measure' from December 31, 1916. However, in practice any notion of reopening was quickly scotched by lifting all tracks except a fragment near Coleford, useful to the GWR itself for removal of ballast stone for several more decades.

During both world wars, timber traffic on certain routes dramatically increased, over a quarter of Dean's timber having been felled for the war effort. Although the gaps are rarely discernible today, much was apparently used during World War II for fragile Mosquito aircraft built at Bristol and Gloucester.

After the war public road transport grew apace, as did private motoring, together conspiring to rob railways of some seventy years' monopoly. The Wye Valley proved vulnerable to car rivalry, picnickers much preferring to drive exactly where they wished – to the top of the viewpoint Yat Rock, instead of the station hundreds of feet below – and drink in the scenery feeling free to return home by a different way, unfettered by railway timetables. Chepstow racecourse, opened in 1926, drew some 70,000 punters annually, but mostly by road.

By 1952 trains from Monmouth, on weekdays only, were restricted to five each way through both halves of the line serving Ross–Monmouth–Chepstow, and only four on the crosswise Monmouth–Pontypool journey into South Wales. A few extras shuttled from Ross to Lydbrook Junction and Symonds Yat. Diesel railcars ousted the more picturesque valley 'puffers' both along the lower Wye and to Pontypool. The next stage, predictably, as patronage continued drifting to bus routes and home garages, was a succession of closures leaving Monmouth, once hub of a railway wheel, quite trainless.

Lydbrook to Lydney, and Cinderford to Speech House Road in Dean Forest, had indeed succumbed as far back as 1929, though Cinderford kept one GWR connection until 1958. Most of the other abandonments were packed into the universally fatal years of 1955–1965; Monmouth Troy to Usk and Pontypool in 1955; Lydbrook Junction to Speech House Road and Coleford in 1963; and from Monmouth to Ross-on-Wye in 1959, when the author and her mother travelled on some of the last trains.

The touristically important Wye Valley Line to Chepstow closed officially on January 4, 1959, but remained in operation for freight trains. Thus Tintern, the tourists's Mecca from the very first, kept a breath of life to the last, as the supposedly goods-only route was opened to special excursions to the famous Abbey in summer, through to 1963. After this the track was lifted and sold, unpoetically, for scrap.

Appropriately, therefore, it is Tintern station, minus tracks and trains, that still plays the most central role in directing and refreshing thousands of visitors today, in new guise and under Gwent County Council ownership.

Dean and the Wye Valley formed Britain's first official national forest park, incorporating thousands of acres of glorious Forestry Commission land. Today three county councils share with the FC in administering, mainly for public recreation, vast areas aptly termed, in total, the Wye Valley Area of Outstanding Natural Beauty. Of central interest is the carefully planned and signposted Wye Valley Walk, under Gwent County Council administration in close liaison with large private landowners, the FC and Wales Tourist Board. It follows the finest miles from Monmouth to Chepstow, along the same natural meander-

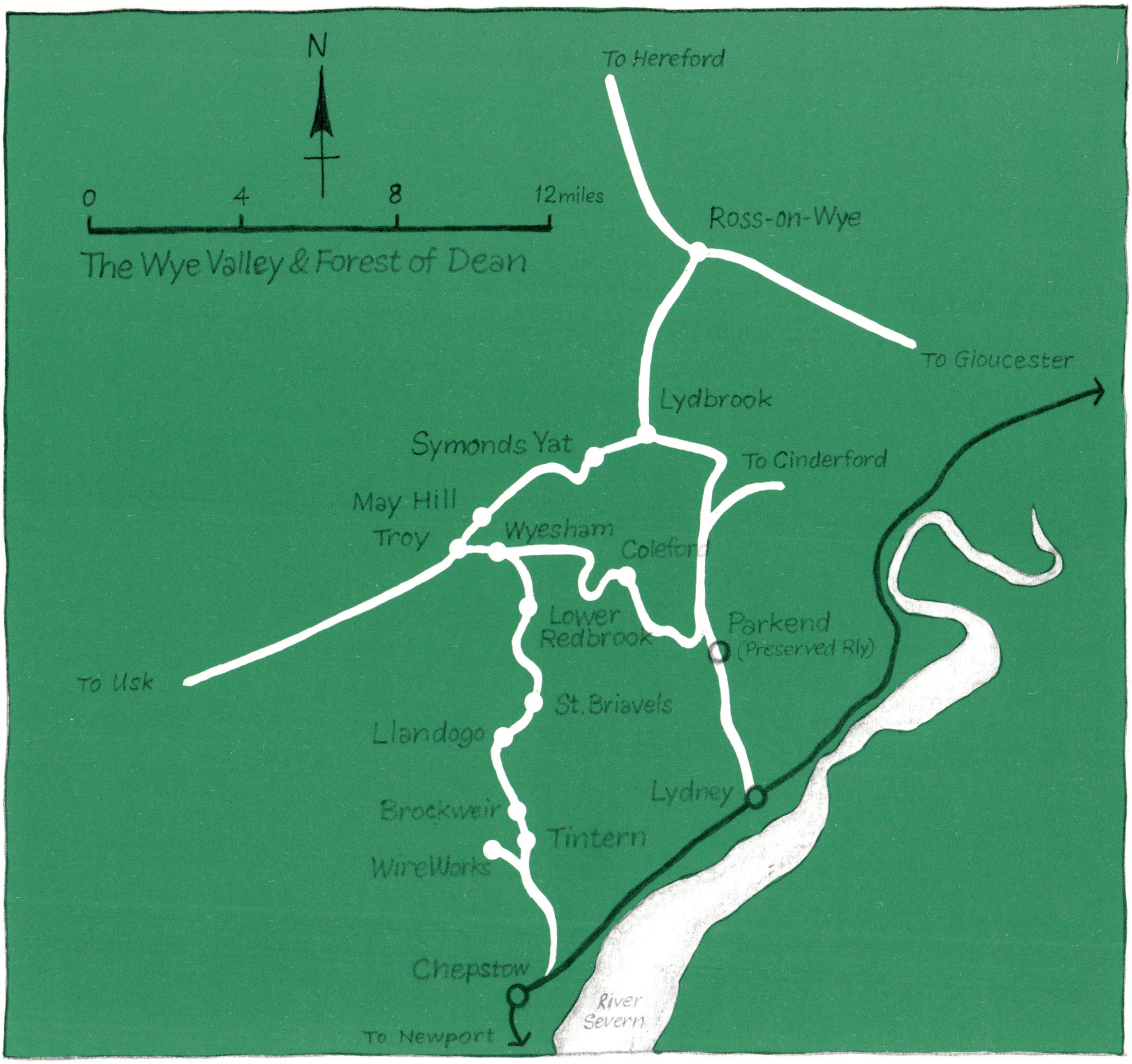

Monmouth Troy station showing both branches into the Wye Valley; Ross line leaving to left, lower Wye Valley Line forking right. *G Daniels*

145

ings as the former Wye Valley Line. Former trackbed is actually used for one long stretch, from Lower Redbrook to Whitebrook, south of Monmouth, before the Walk climbs higher above the river. At Brockweir it descends to rail and road level again, and thence to Tintern station, refurbished into very active life as a picnic, exhibition and control centre for the entire Wye Valley Walk.

Gwent Planning Department, with the Countryside Commission, have created a delightful resting place for ramblers and riders where their grandparents, somewhat less informally garbed, waited for their trains. Across the old goods yard and around the station, rustic picnic tables with incorporated wooden benches are dotted about, serviced with snacks and hot drinks from a station buffet. Inside the former booking hall, waiting rooms and staff quarters, an exhibition is maintained, depicting the Wye Valley Line in its full social, industrial, local and natural context.

From Tintern station officially organised parties depart on foot under the leadership of experienced Countryside Wardens enlisted jointly by Gloucestershire and Gwent County Councils (as this river touches several county boundaries as well as forming the one-time division between Wales and England).

The office of the Wye Valley Warden Service is very far removed from all that the word 'office' usually implies – day-long imprisonment within the hard walls of an impersonal block, surrounded by roaring traffic – being none other than the charming disused Tintern signal box, looking out on the glory the Wardens are there to protect and explain.

For railway archaeologists happier making their own discoveries, evidence remains near Tintern of Wireworks Junction, where the tramway ran over a small bridge. Outside Monmouth at deserted Wyesham Junction the derelict line to Coleford can be spied climbing steeply up the valley to disappear tantalisingly through forest trees. Unofficially, good walkers follow it for its glorious aspects, less familiar than the Wye tourist sights.

On the northern half of the Wye line, Gloucestershire and Herefordshire County Councils combined to acquire Stowfield viaduct near the Youth Hostel of Welsh Bicknor. Not only is this a fine example of

Tintern station with the Chepstow–Monmouth freight in August 1958.
G Daniels

Tintern station in 1905, personifying a forgotten age of travel.
Gwent County Council

Tintern station in spring 1978 after adaptation as a Wye Walk picnic and exhibition centre. On trackbed (right), grassed over and planted with saplings, rustic picnic tables have been laid. Authentic looking station nameboard, white palings and flower beds are all replicas of originals removed or decayed before Gwent County Council acquired the station in 1970.
Gwent County Council

← Crew of the 11.50 am Monmouth–Chepstow train pause to pose for a cameraman, in the leisurely way of country branch lines, in August 1958.
G Daniels

Primitive Penallt Halt near Tintern.
G Daniels

← No. 9745 arrives with a Down freight at Tintern.
G Daniels

Train from Monmouth Troy for Newport behind No. 1420. Wye Valley Line viaduct in background. *G Daniels*

11.50 am Monmouth–Chepstow crossing the river at Redbrook. River is almost obscured by piers of bridge and deep foliage. *G Daniels*

railway architecture blended happily with natural beauty, but a vital necessity; otherwise, there is no crossing for hostellers, except by several miles of scrambling on either side.

Not surprisingly, plans have been mooted for returning steam traction to the Wye. Private backers approached the Monmouthshire Railway Society for co-operation in laying a narrow gauge pleasure line, seated on the old standard trackbed, as at Bala. However, their chances of success were from the start slight, in face of so many powerful official bodies operating for preservation of the countryside. Planning permission seems most unlikely to be granted. In any case, costs of restoration have now risen to astronomical levels.

Only one preserved railway, to the writer's knowledge, has succeeded in opening commercially, not in Wye but in Dean; at Parkend where the Dean Forest Railway Preservation Society runs some picturesque rescued locomotives including the charming old saddle tank 0-4-0 *Uskmouth*.

But in the Wye Valley, whose superb panoramas were formerly completed for thousands of onlookers by tiny plumes of smoke moving as if disembodied in and out of the trees, round and round the snaking curves of the river, there is no restoration of steam.

We are left with only memory, vivid as yet but fading as years roll past. Sitting on the Yat Rock we imagine we can hear the familiar 'cuff-chuff-chuff-whooooooooo!' hundreds of almost vertical feet beneath, magnified by height and clear air, as it approaches, only to be cut dead as sharply as a turned-off railway-nostalgia record, as it plunges into its tunnel and is lost.

Line closed, but track still down. Seen from the dizzy edge of Symonds Yat many hundreds of feet above. *M V Searle*

Puzzle: find the lost line. A view typifying this glorious Area of Outstanding Natural Beauty after loss of its trains.
M V Searle

Graceful bridge remaining between Tintern Abbey and village.
M V Searle

CHAPTER 20

Exalted Valleys

SOUTH WALES

National industrial growth based on coal; the mid-nineteenth century population explosion which created our most crowded city terraces, every house using coal almost exclusively for heating and cooking; and the displacement of sail by steam, again dependant on coal, with the consequent expansion of river, coastal and ocean fleets on a previously unknown scale; all these developments came at about the time of the Railway Mania that drove trains into every inhabited cranny of the kingdom.

It was therefore certain that South Wales, resting on unlimited seams of 'black diamonds', should have developed one of our most complicated and concentrated networks of main, branch, mineral and pit lines by which wagons could roll out the precious paying commodity from valleys to the sea, gobbling up yet more local coal as they went.

The hinterland of Cardiff and Newport in particular presents a most intricate railway map, revealing at a glance how many lines were built for the sole purposes of transporting miners and their families, and the coal that bought their pittance livings. Maps reveal, too, how few remain active on today's BR scene.

In one short chapter, one can but mention a selection of these innumerable tracks, climbing fly-like up steeply twisting mountainsides whose peaks somehow remained beautiful despite the disfigurements of mining. Most of them were children of the GWR, either by birth or subsequent adoption.

Before steam came, industry was already beginning to grow. It inspired, as early as 1792, the Monmouthshire Railway and Canal Company to negotiate powers for bringing out iron from works at Blaenavon and Sirhowy, along tramways to level ground and then by canal to the seaboard.

Among South Wales' steam railways the oldest, most extensive and profitable to its shareholders was the Taff Vale, covering the country behind Cardiff to Merthyr Tydfil. Twenty-three branches, some penetrating entire vales, others only serving one or two collieries, totalled nearly 125 working miles, taking Glamorgan coal to Cardiff's docklands or the lesser Bristol Channel port of Penarth.

Brunel himself was the TVR's engineer, originally concerned with moving products of the big Dowlais iron works, far inland, to the coast. But between 1840, when Brunel laid it out, and the next year, when it opened, pit developments of extraordinary rapidity changed the TVR's prime work from iron to coal, and for which two branches were quickly added.

The South Wales Railway, even before addition of the Severn Tunnel enhanced its value, not only moved tons of coal from valley pits to the docks for use throughout England. It also carried much engine room coal for both Royal and merchant navy use. Deep under the palatial lounges of majestic liners, unseen by the wealthy minority able to sample the lavish First Class which dispelled all illusion of being afloat, teams of sooty faced men shovelled Welsh coal into the roaring maws of furnaces. Wealth relied on coal, and upon the derided poor who dug it, transported it, and fed it to their floating palaces.

The SWR, sanctioned in 1845 on broad gauge, fostered the realisation that every valley could be exalted, financially, by what lay under its pale turf.

Aberdare valley worked but seven smallish mines in the year of the broad gauge's arrival. By the time it passed Swansea, aiming west, their number had more than doubled, and another dozen were being hurriedly equipped. More miners, seeking work with regular pay, moved up to Aberdare, turning a village into a mining town; a process repeated from valley to valley, wherever trains brought work and workers. South Wales, to the credit of the SWR, was now more accessible from England than ever before. In return, it could give England what she wanted as never before: coal, coal and more coal.

1852 was another landmark year, when the GWR overcame the challenge of the Wye at Chepstow to open directly across from London to the coalfields. Unusually big tidal differences combined with unusual terrain – very hard Wye Valley limestone cliffs on the castle side, low swampy marshland on the other bank – to test Brunel's ingenuity to the full. He triumphed at a cost of £77,000, with his first major iron bridge. Welsh coal was now only about six hours' run from London, and transfer to ships for long coastal hauls was no longer the only way from city to city.

Floodgates of mine prosperity opened, in particular for Rhondda. Though large quantities of anthracite were tapped early in the Neath area, Rhondda had been relatively underdeveloped, still notable for the natural beauty of its mountains and streams, until its entire face and character were changed by the laying of rails.

In 1855 Rhondda's first coal train rumbled into Cardiff; the initial movement that set an avalanche of coal flowing into the nation's boilers. In one single decade, 1865–1875, twenty more mines opened, around which spread pit villages whose ugliness seemed to assert that beauty was routed for ever by industry and urbanisation, unless a man lifted up his eyes to discover that Rhondda's mountain setting was still magnificent at its higher levels. Chapels proliferated in Wales as fast as pubs in working communities elsewhere, centres for practice of the uniquely moving male-voice singing that went with the men down to the grimy pits. Tired almost to collapse, they trudged home again in groups, still singing hymns with the instinctive natural four-part harmony characteristic of the Land of Song. This phenomenon of throat-catching beauty among working men is still sometimes encountered today, where mining is followed, often quite unexpectedly on a street corner.

Mineral wealth of Merthyr, Rhondda and other Welsh declivities brought the GWR's constant rival and enemy, the LNWR, creeping up like the Big Bad Wolf to grab some of this wealth for itself, by 'topping' the heads of the valleys that ran so conveniently parallel to each other with a connecting line of its own.

Coming in across the border county of Monmouthshire from the Forest of Dean, was the Coleford, Monmouth, Usk and Pontypool Railway, authorised in 1853. Pontypool, with heaven above it in mountain scenery and untold riches to be scooped out in hellish conditions under its feet, was the eastern gateway to the South Wales coalfield. The CMUPR entered at a junction of the Newport, Abergavenny and Hereford Railway near Pontypool. In July 1860 the NAHR was taken over by the West Midland, and the CMUPR a year later. Further amalgamation added them to the growing GWR kingdom in Wales.

Rhymney Railway, among the best known to railway enthusiasts, opened in 1854. It comprised over fifty track miles; one main stretch made no less than eleven junctions with adjoining coal systems, both large and independent, reaching out like tendrils to grasp these stems on their way towards Cardiff, where the world's money was held out in exchange for yet more coal. The RR ran from an extensive locomotive works of its own, at Caerphilly.

In its heyday, the RR was to goods trains what a modern commuter line is to passengers: a seemingly eternal procession of train after train rumbling on each others' heels with little pause, helping Cardiff earn the title it was fast wresting from Newcastle of 'Metropolis of Coal'.

Only the Cambrian Railway consciously aimed at passenger revenue above freight income, by exploiting its access to the magnificent tourist scenery beginning where the coal valleys ended, stretching from Aberdare northwards into the Brecon Beacons and Mid-Wales. Significantly, the CR's prosperity was less than that of the valley railways.

Expansion continued through the later nineteenth century. Criss-crossing the lines that had by then penetrated most main valleys, lesser companies set up additional outlets wherever coal was likely to be found. And where was there *not* coal, in this land where a cottager's garden fork struck black only inches down, and gutters ran with black dusty waters after rain? Most of the companies, both greater and minor, found their way into GWR hands before Victoria made way for Edward. Sometimes the GWR had strategic railway reasons, as well as coal income, motivating its bidding, as when in 1865 it acquired the independent Vale of Neath Railway, running up to prosperous Merthyr Tydfil and Aberdare. By this move the equally eager LNWR and MR were prevented from pushing themselves into territory the GWR regarded as its own – the transport of coal from Aberdare to Swansea.

Over 21 million tons of coal had left South Wales by 1880. The population was rising swifter than anywhere else, even London, as men poured in to earn hard but good money, set up tiny mining village homes and breed big families. In tune with this, Cardiff grew apace. Its docks grew fivefold in forty years. The Severn Tunnel increased the district's exports still further.

Near the century's end new railways were still being built, such as the Barry Railway, of nearly ninety track miles. Started in about 1886 to divert some of Cardiff's income from coal into its own docks, it shamelessly played against the Rhondda line for custom. Cardiff's own dock railway, the Alexandra (Newport and South Wales) Docks and Railway Company, and the Cardiff Railway, also ran outwards to connect up with the numerous other companies converging on the port.

The Great War of 1914–1918 wrought the first major changes in South Wales' profitable fuel monopoly, beginning a long decline that went on until the intricate spider's web of coal lines was reduced to the pathetically few surviving strands left today. As steam had replaced sail, so now oil was beginning to supplant coal in both industry and ships' fuel. Exports overseas almost died in wartime. After 1918 those markets had less need for Welsh imports. Ruhr and Saar coal, extracted from Germany as war reparation, was more accessible.

This is not to say that Wales' great coal mining days were finished, but rather that she no longer had a monopoly. Output remained very considerable, as did its indigenous population made up almost entirely of miners, their wives, and those who succoured their bodies through food production, or their souls by organising the male voice choirs which occupied the leisure role in Wales which was assigned to darts in England. The Taff Vale Railway, alone, still carried about eight million passengers over a total network roughly equalling in mileage only one return run from London to Brighton.

Losses resulting from decreased coal production in the early twenties however, became more real and distressing. Just before the Great War, South Wales production had touched a never-to-be-equalled peak of 56 million tons. In 1921, it had come down by four-fifths, to ten million tons. The Taff Vale, despite its eight million passenger tickets, was desperately worried, when freight, its real *raison d'être*, slumped by about 55 per cent.

As the Twenties wore on, Welsh pits became increasingly drained of their black riches after seventy years of continuous digging. The best seams were more and more inaccessible, whereas Midlands coal was less dangerously placed. This and other areas began supplanting, instead of merely supplementing, the Land of Our Fathers. This GWR kingdom served by an incredible 445 stations, as well as pure pit lines, discovered the meaning of the word Depression. Railways felt the pinch doubly. Freight dropped as less coal was surfaced. Less coal meant fewer men required to mine it, creating mass unemployment and no money to fritter on unnecessary or frivolous rail travel. If it was, Mother or Father often went alone, leaving the rest at home, to save three or four half-fares. The GWR's losses were openly called 'unparalleled in the history of the Company'. Financial outlooks were no better in Swansea, Barry and Cardiff, where less coal coming down created idle ships and idle men.

At its worst, the Depression meant some 36 per cent of all adult males in South Wales being unemployed. Many left, to earn pittances in London and other cities, almost foreigners in alien surroundings but at least with a few shillings in their pockets. Meanwhile whole terraces – even entire villages – became half derelict back home.

No region of England, except perhaps for the area around Newcastle with its complicated interlace of lines comparable to Cardiff, would be left with so many lost railway lines for the future to either rescue for motor roads or, more commonly, leave to rot under rough vegetation choking tracks that once carried fortunes in nuggets.

Those lines with good passenger traffic, not entirely reliant on industry, somehow survived the Depression and another war before dying in a sudden rush as if an epidemic were among them. (Even earlier had been the closure of Brynmawr–Pontypool in 1941 and Rhymney–New Tredegar, which succumbed in 1930.) At the outward edge of the network, Pontypool clung on to its Usk and Monmouth service, truncated by about 1952 to four daily runs by diesel railcar.

Passenger closures set in thicker and faster during the fatal Fifties and Sixties, often after a last-hope period of reduction to diesel railcar working. In most cases they were also followed by a cessation of freight working. They were so numerous that listing and

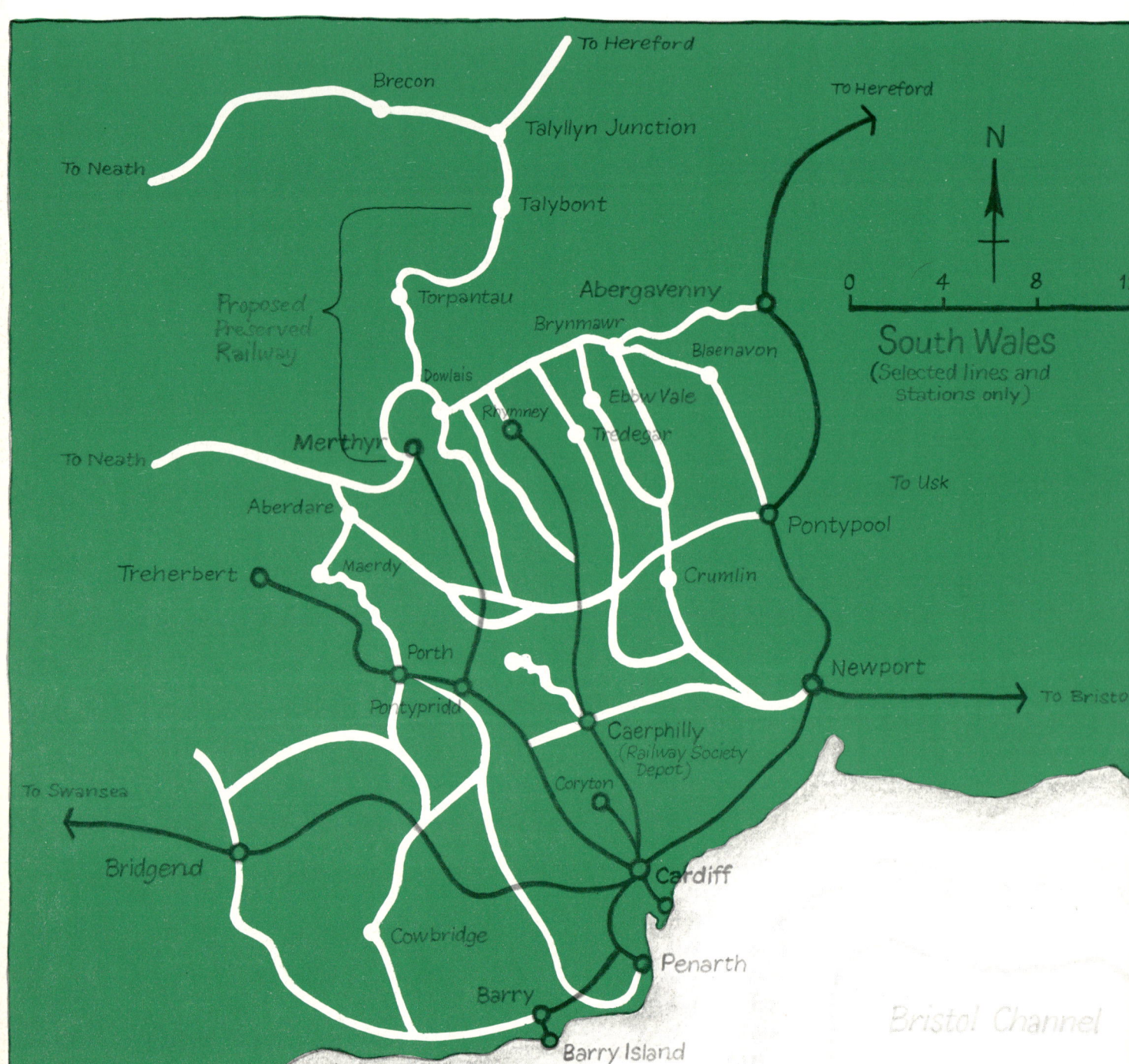

dating them merely becomes an exercise in self-generated depression. It is, indeed, simplest to list the handful still open today under BR: the lines across from Severn Tunnel Junction through Newport and Cardiff to Bridgend and beyond; from Newport to Pontypool and Hereford; and only three true mining valley lines, to Rhymney, Merthyr and Treherbert, plus a short modern branch to Coryton and those to the seaside suburbs of Penarth and Barry Island. That is all, out of scores. BR also uses, for freight only, the former mining valley lines serving Abertillery, Brynmawr, Blaenavon and Aberdare.

The latter station was reopened to passengers of a specialised sort for one single day in 1977 during a Jubilee year tour of South Wales by Charles, Prince of Wales, when it received the Royal Train direct from

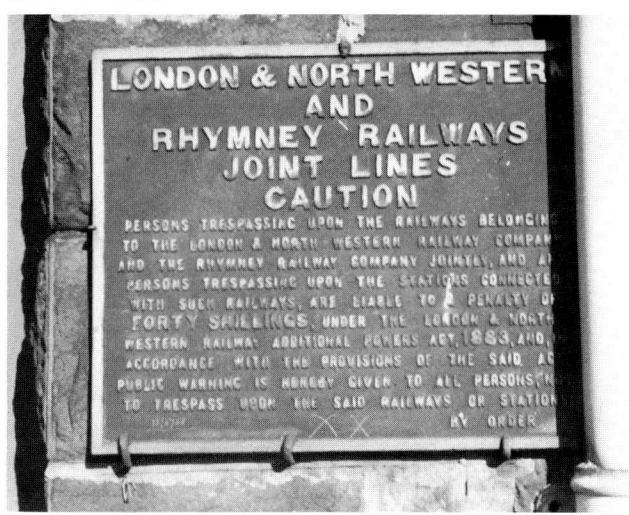

Rhymney Railway trespass notice, still *in situ* at Rhymney in 1957. *G Daniels*

6412 pauses to replenish water tanks on an evening train to Tredegar, 1960. *G Daniels*

Tredegar-bound service in Welsh mist and damp at Ynysddu. *G Daniels*

56XX No. 5676 climbs up towards Rhondda with returning Barry Island miners' pleasure excursion, 1960. *G Daniels*

Leaving Cwmavon en route from Blaenavon to Porthcawl, 1962. *G Daniels*

Balmoral. Many hours of track weeding, platform scrubbing and painting of flaking station walls were put into its revival, in keeping with the spirit that dressed the whole of normally sober Aberdare with Union Jacks and Welsh dragons. For all too brief a time, used as the Prince's base, Aberdare seemed like a town with a normal railway again.

Preservation societies have not so far been particularly active in this part of the Principality, less touristically minded than the north despite the magnificence of much of its inland scenery. However, mention should be made of the Gwili Railway, rather farther west, and the depot of the Caerphilly Railway Society, with six engines in steam through a short summer season.

'I will lift up mine eyes': the natural beauty surrounding most Welsh towns is captured in this picture of 1961. A plume of white smoke marks the passage of a valley steam train. *M V Searle* →

Mountain Ash (Oxford Street), looking towards Abercynon in 1963. *G Daniels*

Aberdare–Pontypool Road train at Mountain Ash (Cardiff Road) station in October 1963. *G Daniels*

At the present time one Birmingham enthusiast is at work on a short derelict stretch beyond the coal valleys, through the beautiful lakes and mountains north of Merthyr towards Talybont. Two engines, one American, one German, are hopefully being restored for this venture.

Otherwise destruction or adaptation rather than preservation is most usual, apart from the obvious alternative of letting old lines lie. The majority of them do.

Destruction of some of the better bridges raised a certain degree of public resistance, though not sufficient to save them. Chief of these were the Gamlyn and Dare viaducts on a mineral branch off the former

BRITISH TRANSPORT COMMISSION

BRITISH RAILWAYS (Western Region)

PUBLIC NOTICE

The British Transport Commission hereby give notice that on and from

MONDAY, 13th JUNE, 1960

the passenger train service operating between Risca and Nantybwch, including through trains to Newport, will be withdrawn. Parcels facilities will also be withdrawn from Ynysddu, Pontllanfraith H.L., Holly Bush, Tredegar and Nantybwch and freight facilities from Argoed Halt and Nantybwch.

THE FOLLOWING STATIONS AND HALTS WILL BE COMPLETELY CLOSED:—

YNYSDDU	MARKHAM VILLAGE HALT
WYLLIE HALT	HOLLY BUSH
PONTLLANFRAITH (H.L.)	BEDWELLTY PITS HALT
ARGOED HALT	NANTYBWCH

Buses are operated in the area by Messrs. Red & White Services Ltd., Western Welsh Omnibus Company, Ltd., Cardiff Corporation, Caerphilly U.D.C., and West Mon. Omnibus Board.

Collection and Delivery arrangements for parcels and goods "smalls" traffic will continue to be provided in the area and facilities for the handing in or collection of such traffic by the public will also continue to be available at Blackwood and Sirhowy Goods Depots.

Alternative facilities for dealing with freight traffic in full truck loads, including coal and coke, will be available at Sirhowy for Nantybwch traffic and at Blackwood in respect of Argoed traffic.

Special arrangements have been made for passengers using the alternative bus services who wish to avail themselves of Passengers Luggage in Advance Facilities. Luggage will be accepted upon senders undertaking to obtain a railway ticket from the nearest main line station. Alternatively passengers can obtain their tickets in advance at Blackwood or Sirhowy Stations or the British Railways Agency at Tredegar for the purpose of sending luggage in advance.

Any further information required in respect of these arrangements can be obtained upon application to:—

MR. W. J. MORRIS,
DISTRICT TRAFFIC SUPERINTENDENT,
NEWPORT.
Tel. No. Newport 58461 (Ext. 386).

STATION MASTER at:—

BLACKWOOD	Tel. No. BLACKWOOD 3218
SIRHOWY	Tel. No. TREDEGAR 72
PONTLLANFRAITH (L.L.)	Tel. No. BLACKWOOD 2263

PADDINGTON STATION, W.2.

J. R. HAMMOND,
General Manager.

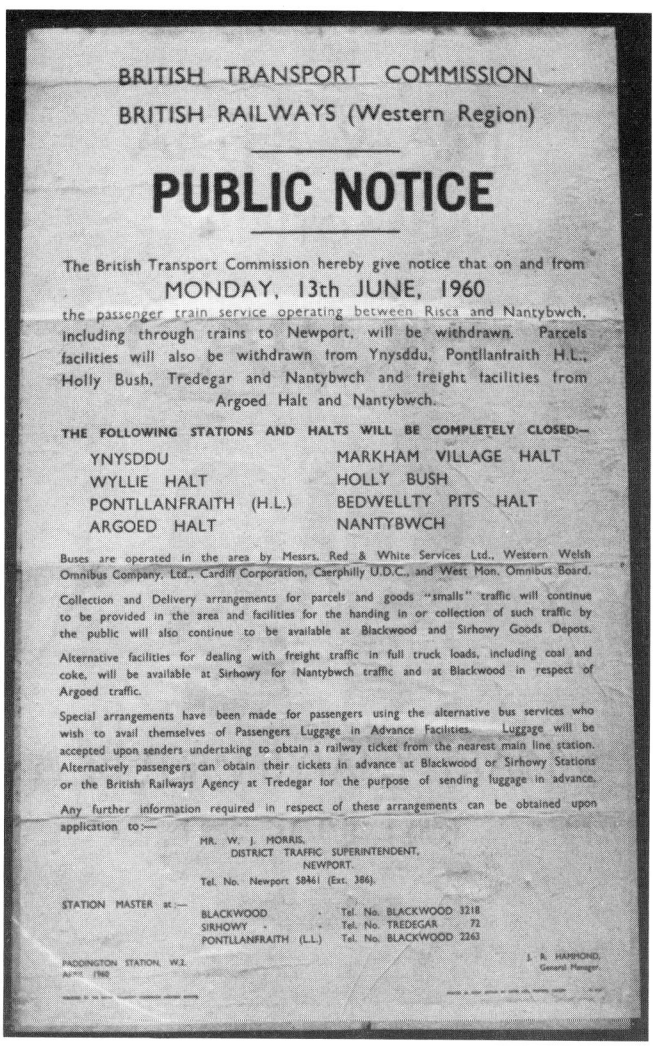

The beginning of the end for innumerable Welsh lines – the appearance of a funereally gloomy closure notice. This example announces closure of the Sirhowy Valley line in 1960. *G Daniels*

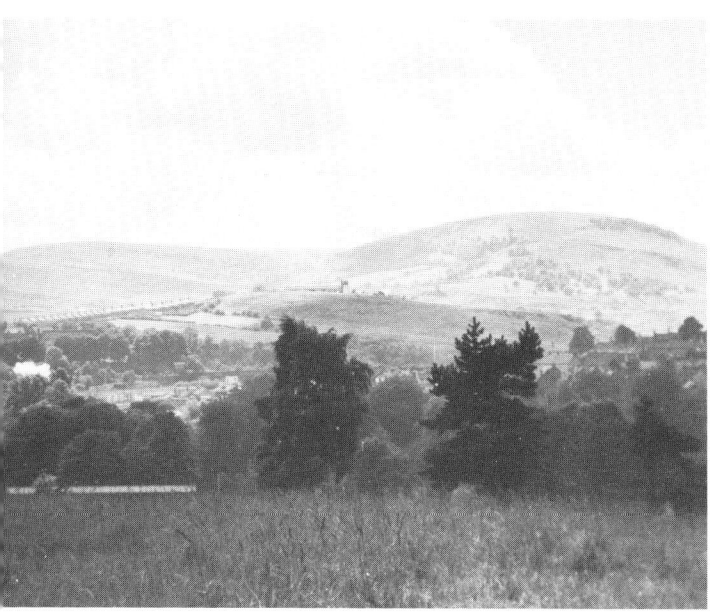

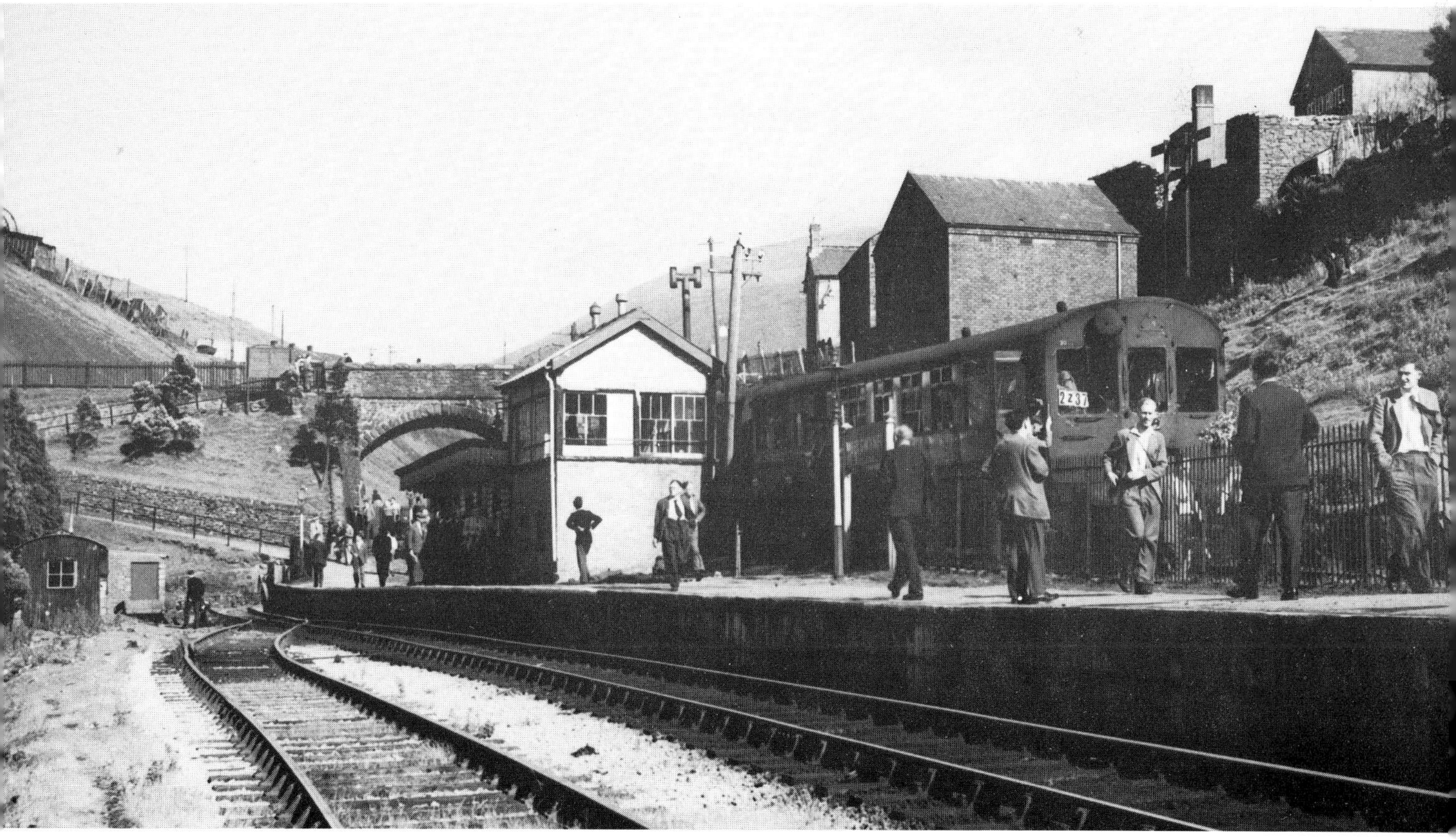

A locomotive enthusiasts' special, touring lines about to close, at Abergwynfi. The train is on colliery line behind railings. *G Daniels*

Vale of Neath Railway, lost in 1947; and the major Crumlin Viaduct crossing deep Ebbw Vale, a century old iron bridge. Crumlin, considered outstanding, was fiercely defended as worthy of preservation, but in vain.

Curious conversions are everywhere met, from a station yard turned into a caravan park (Aberbran) to a line serving as access for a Breconshire wild life park.

The old LNWR line 'topping' all the coal valleys is now, almost throughout, the busy Heads Of The Valleys Road; interlinking roads descend the many parallel valleys exactly as the old railway company did in the past. Ordnance maps, better than the eye carried too fast along the road, demonstrate how closely the Heads Of The Valleys Road sits on the trackbed, by the numerous railway cuttings and embankments marked as being still in place alongside.

Nevertheless, for every extant or re-used railway, several more lie unwanted. Nowhere outside industrialised Tyneside and Lancashire has the railway age left more deserted evidence of its passing, to intrigue archaeologists interested in the near-past as well as in ancient Rome.

Silent trackbed everywhere lies sinking under growing grasses and wild flowers of the Welsh hills, gaining rapid hold on ageing ballast. Nature, whose pure streams and unadulterated green valleys were raped by railways as the chief instrument of mankind's greed for gain through coal, seems to smile over their ruin with a certain satisfaction.

Torpantau station on old Newport–Brecon route being demolished in 1970. Being considered an eyesore to the Brecon Beacons National Park, the authorities obtained permission from its private purchaser to remove the derelict station, signal box and station house. As a training exercise by the Army Apprentices' College of Chepstow, destruction was completed without cost to the Park authority. Note two soldiers near platform remains. *Countryside Commission*

↖ Freight-only lines maintained in the Aberdare area, seen in the gloom of descending fine Welsh drizzle.
M V Searle

← Cameramen swarm round a club special at Nantymoel.
G Daniels

Grim lighting towards dusk accentuates the black depression of an overgrown halt, probably beyond Aberdare towards Rhigos.
M V Searle

Abandoned embanked trackbed at Rassa, before commencement of works for Heads Of The Valleys Road.
Rendel, Palmer and Tritton

Rassa: the same point near completion of road works, from Bridge No. 32. Note telegraph poles still in position.
Rendel, Palmer and Tritton

Contractor's work in progress on a disused railway wall during conversion of trackbed for a road. Tafarnau Bach, 1965.
Rendel, Palmer and Tritton

CHAPTER 21

Land Cruise
NORTH WALES

I have lived all my life with trains as integral everyday features, from within ten days of birth, close beside the main line to Dover, one of the world's busiest. From babyhood upwards I saw regularly everything worth seeing on the Southern, usually with only partial awareness despite the inevitable train-spotting phase, such is the undoubted contempt of overfamiliarity – the *Blue Train*; the *Golden Arrow* when she was truly golden, roaring through with French and British flags flying and great arrows on every Pullman, inscribed *Golden Arrow/Fleche d'Or*; Continental expresses when restaurants were Pullman and carriages bore destination boards; magnificent *West Country*, *Merchant Navy* and *King Arthur* monsters; Great Western *Kings* and *Castles*, summer visitors heading in on *Sunny South Expresses*; troop trains and fruit trains; the postwar extension of third-rail electrification that drove steam out of London, and ultimately out of our lives.

Unlike most enthusiasts, who travel miles to some point and there drink in every detail of locomotion and working, we linesiders only notice our trains when they stop, as on Christmas Day; by sound, when unfamiliar strangers intrude, such as Charing Cross diesel units invading our Victoria territory; or when a train is so different from everyday experience that even we cannot fail to notice it, particularly when visiting a different region.

Into the latter category fall European trains, met on holiday, and such unique experiences as the once famous *North Wales Radio Land Cruise*, entirely encircling Snowdonia in one day, a holiday highlight of 1961 that is now only a memory. It can never be repeated; closure of two of the most important segments of this unique circle ensures that.

A typical pattern of small independent Victorian railway companies building their own lines and then, gradually joining up and interlinking, made possible for holidaymakers of the 1950s and 1960s the Land Cruises. These were introduced to commemorate the Great Exhibition of 1851, that event which in the mid nineteenth century demonstrated the genius of British engineering to the world, recalled in the Festival of Britain a century later.

At the end of 1851 the Great Exhibition closed its doors. Four years later its extraordinary setting, the Crystal Palace, was rebuilt for permanent use. At about the same time the first plans for railway intrusion of the North Welsh coast and through the mountains (eventually to push right through to the west Welsh coast in a long diagonal line) were seriously mooted. They were set in motion in 1856 by a Local Act for the Vale of Clwyd Railway, a little ten-mile stretch towards the touristic castles, cathedral and scenery of that glorious long valley running inland from popular Rhyl. This single-track section was opened on October 5, 1856, followed by a little one-mile branch to Foryd Pier at the Clwyd river mouth.

The VOCR enjoyed only a short independent existence, being absorbed into the LNWR nine years after its opening, but it played a disproportionately important part in Welsh railway history, in opening up the first stage of this long inland route.

Joining onto this line at Denbigh, well into the valley, came the second company, the Denbigh, Ruthin and Corwen Railway, aiming, as its title implied, for the market town of Corwen, most important commercial and population centre of the area.

It was one of two companies with eyes on Corwen, this one approaching down the Clwyd from the north, the other across from Ruabon, from the east. They converged on that town at about the same time, forming an important junction.

The Denbigh, Ruthin and Corwen Railway, incorporated under an Act of July 1860, reached as far as Ruthin in 1862, where it stopped for about two years before continuing down to its goal of Corwen, opening on September 1, 1864. Considerable delay was caused by necessity of drilling and blasting through specially tough varieties of Welsh rock in the neighbourhood of Eyarth, near Ruthin, one of the few reasonable population centres apart from Denbigh, St Asaph and Corwen itself.

Like its neighbour, the little VOCR, the DRCR enjoyed only brief life as an individual entity, before being swallowed by that ever-hungry devourer of tasty small morsels of railway, the LNWR, in 1879.

Between them these two initial stages of the diagonal inland route past Bala Lake to the west coast served mainly local residents rather than tourists, who at this stage still approached such beauty spots as Llangollen and Bala by coach and carriage – a situation not long to remain unrailwayised.

Coming in from east to west, to and through Corwen, was the next stage of railway building. It extended the existing line both eastwards, to a point on a main route to Chester, and onwards and westwards past Bala to within a few miles of the coast, at Dolgelley (modernised as Dollgellau). This time the builders had behind them one of the big boys, the Great Western, anxious to reach through to the West coast of Wales as a consolidation of its ever-Westward policy, against LNWR opposition.

Four small component parts made up this long 44-mile stretch of mainly single track from Ruabon, across Corwen and almost to the sea: the Vale of Llangollen Railway, from Ruabon as far as Llangollen, opened on December 1, 1861 for goods, June 2, 1862 for passengers; the Llangollen and Corwen Railway, completing this short lap to the junction by May 1, 1865; the Corwen and Bala Railway, carrying on further west again between those points, opened in two sections during 1866 and 1868; and, for the final run, the Bala and Dolgelley Railway, incorporated in 1877 and opened to Dolgelley on August 4, 1868.

All these companies, each building one section of the same continuous line, were comparatively poor, operating under working agreements with the GWR and having no rolling stock to call their own. Soon, all were fully incorporated into the GWR, a logical development where one single continuous route was involved. Not least among their financial failings had been opening halts in places so remote that two sheep and three housewives were a crowd; yet these were sometimes quite expensive stations, out of all proportion to necessity. Carrog, near Llangollen, for instance, was given most impressive and solid offices more akin to a manor house than a country station, to serve nowhere in particular.

Tourists rather than residents would be the VOLR's salvation, it was hoped. When sketching became such a fashionable pastime, Victorians would undoubtedly flock out by train, just as they had by carriage. Certainly this proved true of the five-mile track completed out of Ruabon, convenient by main line to the larger Northern cities including Manchester. Tourists descended in satisfactory numbers, armed with fishing tackle and sketch blocks, to marvel afresh at the beauty of Wild Wales even in the tamed version presented by courtesy of the steam engine. So heavily used was this section, mainly by visitors, as to warrant doubling in 1898 and installation of special sidings for accommodating day excursion trains and other specials, as well as slate wagons.

From the Llangollen railhead before building continued, tourists eagerly went on into wilder Wales by coaching road until the Llangollen and Corwen Railway added its contribution, meeting up at Corwen with the Vale of Clwyd line. Further pleasure riding possibilities were thus opened up northwards through exquisite if not spectacular scenery to Rhyl. Corwen was now the most important station, complete with such refinements as refreshment rooms and networks of sidings. It remained a major centre to the end, with its large cattle market visible immediately adjacent to the platform when the Land Cruises paused there.

Stage three of the race to the west coast was in the hands of the Corwen and Bala Railway, aiming as its title implied for the scenic beauty of Bala Lake, where a junction was also built taking a further line up into the slate bearing mountains of Snowdonia to serve the huge quarries of Blaenau Festiniog (still accessible today, from the other side of Wales, via the beautiful Conway Valley line). This was constructionally the easiest part, alongside the pretty Dee, over flat ground with few gradients or blasting problems. It reached the intermediate Llandrillo in 1866, and Bala itself in 1868.

Fourth came the longest link in the chain from Ruabon – the Bala and Dolgelley Railway (August 4, 1868), bringing the total route within a short distance of the sea at Barmouth. It ran through about eighteen miles of superb scenery and followed immediately after the breathtakingly beautiful run along the glittering Bala Lake. Gradients were steep – up to 1 in 58 – and villages few. Tourists were the line's bread and butter, backed up by consignments of slate from the interior of Wales.

Only seven and a quarter miles still remained unlaid, the concern of yet another tiny company with a big name, the Aberystwyth and Welsh Coast Railway. This company was to be responsible for the final joining up from its own Barmouth Junction, near Barmouth itself, to Dolgelley. This section was opened on July 3, 1865 to intervening Penmaenpool, and on to Dolgelley in June 1869. The long, scenic, inland route from north-east to south-west, cutting diagonally right across the heart of Wales from one sea to another, was thus complete. It was absorbed before completion into the mightier Cambrian Railway, whose property it remained for half a century before the GWR finally won full passage through Wales at the 1923 Grouping.

Land Cruise trains of the latter years here rounded across the spectacular Barmouth Bridge into Barmouth, where they were stabled in a siding whilst passengers enjoyed several hours in that beautiful if excessively sandy resort, filling themselves with Wales' staple diet of fish and chips, and their clothing with flying white sand that penetrated every cranny. This was a small drawback to two or three hours in so lovely a place, by a sea as green-blue as on the Riviera.

Northwards from Bala the ride continued over track that still exists, reprieved by BR to serve Harlech, Criccieth and Butlin's highly profitable holiday camp at Pwllheli. At Afon Wen, some miles short of Pwllheli, the Land Cruise branched off inland again. Passengers had wonderful panoramas of the whole of distant Snowdonia after entering this other major lost line of north Wales, between Afon Wen on the coast up to Caernarvon and Bangor, where it again joined the main Holyhead track for return to clients' various resorts.

This twenty-eight mile Bangor and Caernarvon Railway of 1852 established the first of Caernarvon's three termini, and a line of sharp curves and gradients. Its early trains were in the hands of the adjacent Chester and Holyhead Railway and of the LNER, who took over the Bangor and Caernarvon as early as 1867.

With this line a complete circle was formed, from Rhyl up the Clwyd to Corwen, on past Bala to Barmouth, northwards to Afon Wen and again to Bangor, and finally eastwards along the coast back to Rhyl. Snowdonia was encircled by trains, as well as being actually climbed by the Snowdon Mountain Railway.

The middle years of this line brought tourism by rail to its height, before the incursion of charabancs, buses and cars drew off an increasing proportion of the railway's patronage. Even that process was a long time coming here, where lines twisted through countryside unkind to early and unreliable cars.

Cambrian Railways, in their 1906 advertising, encouraged the idea of land cruising, unashamedly christening Wales of the unpredictable weather 'The British Riviera' with 'delightful, Spring, Summer and Winter resorts'. Stations were advertised in the order in which they appeared on the circular route. Also mentioned were 'The Wells of Mid Wales'. Travellers were wooed with 'Tourist, Weekend and Ten-Days Tickets . . . from the Principal Towns in England' and with prospects of 'Numerous Rail and Coach Excursions from Cambrian Stations . . . also Cycling and Walking Tour Tickets at Reduced Fares'. Holidaymakers, not villagers, were Cambrian Railways' bread and butter, and they knew it.

Special events occasionally poured additional Welsh gold into their coffers, notably the Investiture in 1911 of the future Edward VIII as Prince of Wales, when over thirty specials converged on Caernarvon's stations in only three morning hours.

Public and private offshoots did good business, again benefitting the standard gauge lines, such as the attractive Glyn Valley Tramway near Chirk GWR station, gateway to a valley 'frequented by many lovers of the piscatorial art'. This little line was also an outlet for more mundane but paying products, among them slate and Welsh flannel. Big and little companies found it profitable to work together, as here at Chirk, near Ruabon: 'Open carriages are attached to the trains, which are timed to run to or from Chirk in connection with the GWR trains', went the Tramway's advertisement.

Rhyl, at the northern end of the route, enthusiastically advertised the Vale of Clywd line's attractions, with: 'Rhuddlan is the most convenient station from which to visit Bodelwyddan Marble Church'. And there was the charming miniature railway to Dyserth, east of Rhuddlan. 'A light railway on which a motor car runs', served that place, 'romantically situated on a very steep declivity commanding an extensive view'. Young ladies in muslin would go a long way in 1913 to paint, in wishy-washy watercolours, an 'extensive view'.

At first the advent of buses was a thing to be adopted by railway companies, rather than feared, extending their services outwards from suitable stations into the country, for usefulness or pleasure. Thus the following route was advertised from Corwen in 1913: 'Bettws-y-Coed: By GWR Motor Bus daily from Corwen (22 miles). . . . The road from Llangollen (33 miles) and Corwen follows the route taken by George Borrow and described in his Wild Wales Chapters xxiii and xxvi'.

The main development of the Great War was a new standard gauge military railway of about four miles, following the Clwyd route to a camp near St Asaph and used for army purposes until 1925, when – this being Wales – it became instead a quarry feeder.

Tourism reached new peaks between the wars, inspiring the GWR to erect a prodigious number of new halts serving no local purpose, in areas whose only fortune was their beauty; such truly Welsh names as Bonwm Llys, Llangower Wnion, Garneddwen and Dolserau were among the twenty or so which occured between Barmouth and Ruabon.

At the 1923 grouping this part of Wales went jointly to the GWR and LMS, resulting in such odd allocations of staff as four and a half Corwen men to the LMS and half a signalman to the GWR; hopefully, the upper half, with arms to operate his levers! Denbigh acquired a small locomotive shed of its own, housing the small Webb 2-4-2 tanks of the LMS. Passing places and other improvements were made to accommodate the GWR's more powerful 43XX *Moguls*, which thereafter dominated passenger working except for purely local stopping trains. Both big companies continued their tourist blandishments, the LMS offering in 1938 a 'Weekly Runabout Go-as-you-please Ticket' for only 10s. 6d. (52½p) right round the circle from Prestatyn up to Denbigh, through Bala and across to Afon Wen to Caernarvon; in effect, the classic Land Cruise route.

The North Wales Radio Land Cruise, as an officially titled train, was BR's hopeful counter thrust against the great surge in private motoring of the 1950s which, more than any other factor, spelled death within a few years to any rail line not able to keep its end up commercially, through main long distance express routes, or intensive commuter traffic. North Wales' industry was tourism, and its commuters a summer army of holidaymakers. It was these summer visitors who gave the marvellous circular route around Snowdonia a brief reprieve. Festival of Britain year (1951) provided a suitable gimmicky peg on which to hang the venture, which proved successful enough to last for ten years.

The cruise train, running Mondays to Fridays so as not to interfere with North Wales' still very heavy Saturday arrival and departure movements, and weekenders' specials, picked up at most popular north coast resorts, including Llandudno Junction, Conway, and Colwyn Bay. After Rhyl, and branching into the lovely Vale of Clwyd, the trip proper began.

'A Circular Rail Tour through some of Britain's finest scenery' ran the posters and handbills: 'A Commentator will supply information on the Principal Features of Interest, and Popular Music or BBC Radio Programmes – news items, etc – will be provided at suitable intervals during the Cruise.' The prospect of being a captive audience to continuous bombardment by semi-pop music or eternal courieristic chatter appalled the author and her mother, yet the lure of this rare opportunity to ride over lines that were already closed to normal traffic over several stretches, was too strong. We took the risk, and were picked up under the walls of Conway Castle.

Entering our carriage was like entering a new railway world. Or, rather, an old, forgotten world. A world of long open carriages with no fixed seating, with moderately comfortable, if venerable, individual armchairs ranged to face directly out of the windows, instead of sideways on, giving optimum viewing. Commentaries proved discreet and helpful without excessive chattering, merely drawing our attention in good time to some approaching feature: Rhuddlan Castle, St Asaph's spire, a glorious view, the widening Dee and ten miles of lakeland alongside Bala. Old fashioned courtesy and helpfulness were well in evidence among the crew; not least from the guard who firmly sat me on his lap and held me steady to film through the windows, full of information on when and where to shoot, but innocent of a Londoner's leer. Mile after mile we dawdled deliciously over those already half 'lost' lines, never normally used for passengers, through to Barmouth; up to Afon Wen, where passengers could enjoy superb views of the sea and mountains from the bridge and platform of a station so near the beach it was almost part of the sea wall. And so round the best of Snowdonia to Caernarvon and home. We will never do it again. Too much of the circle has gone for ever – and so has one of us.

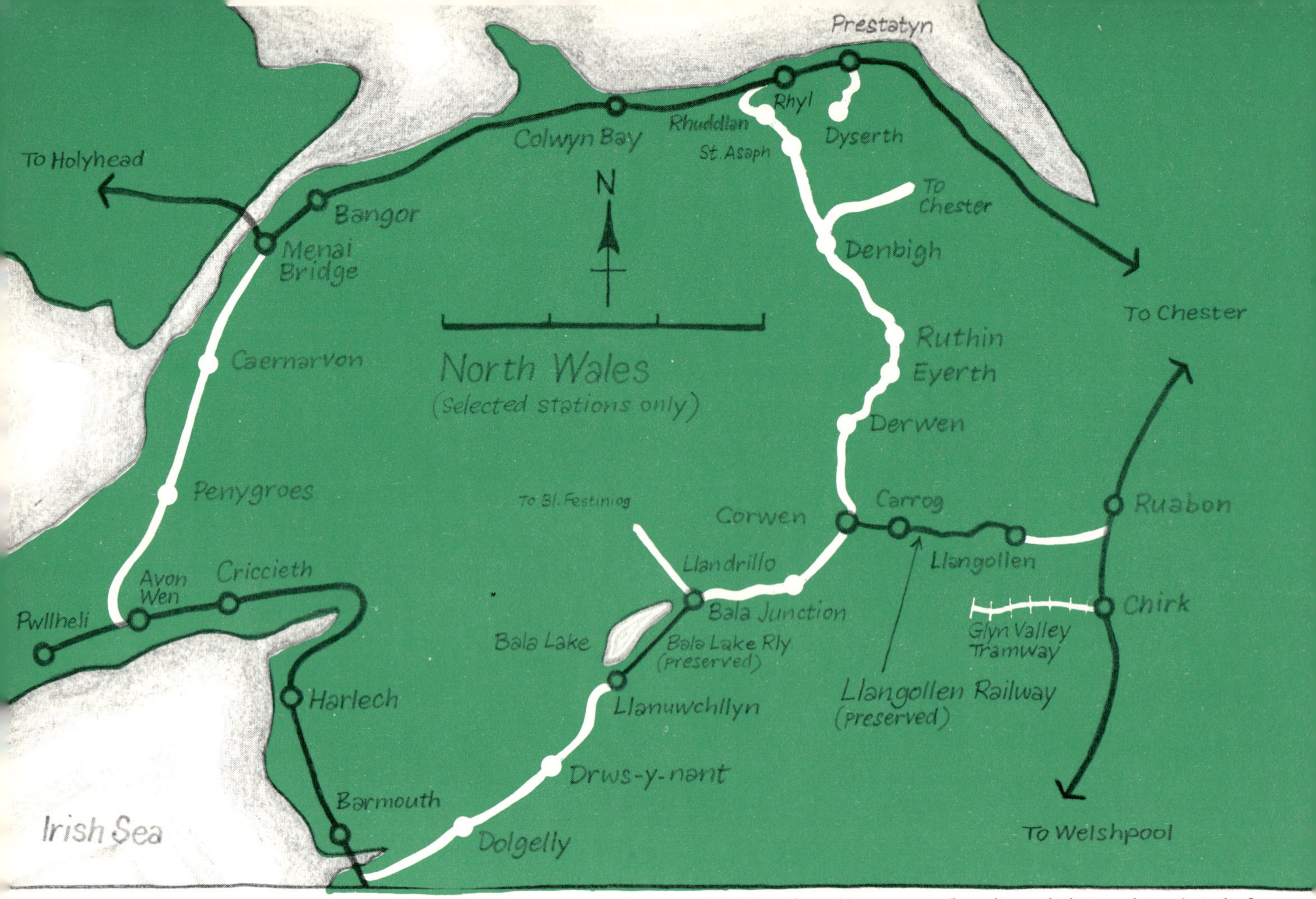

Running down in North Wales began soon after the first Radio Land Cruises began. As early as 1952 Denbigh shed was in effect a retirement home for locomotives declared redundant (it survives today, hemmed in on an industrial estate).

Closures are here detailed in geographical, and not necessarily chronological order. A circle built in fits and starts to suit the whims of growth, folded likewise somewhat erratically as business died here, lingered longer there. From Rhyl as far as Denbigh closed to passengers on September 19, 1955, together with Denbigh shed, but the little local Foryd Pier offshoot to the Clwyd mouth continued another four years. The line shut entirely, to both specials and goods, at the end of 1967. The next section, Denbigh on to Ruthin, ended on April 30, 1962, for passengers, remaining open to freight until 1965, when the whole stretch of Ruthin–Corwen also closed to freight.

Ruabon–Llangollen continued goods service as late as April 1, 1968. The long stretch from Llangollen forward across Corwen Junction to Bala and Dolgelley was partially closed ahead of schedule between Llangollen itself and Bala Junction (December 13, 1964), after disastrous flooding did Beeching's job for him in one night and day, washing away much of the single line track at Llandderfel; in any case, total closure right through to Dolgelley was planned for only five weeks later. In the event the undamaged Bala Junction–Dolgelley part functioned until January 18, 1965, but at the other end the little Ruabon–Llangollen fragment, though closed to passengers, functioned for freight through to April 1968.

No. 75034 heads the Cambrian Radio Cruise train round the day-long Caernarvon–Rhyl–Corwen–Bala–Barmouth–Afon Wen–Caernarvon circle in 1962. *M V Searle*

162

Snowdonia viewed from open window of Radio Cruise train (part of carriage at right) in 1962. *M V Searle*

Radio Cruise stops for passengers to admire sea and mountains in North Wales. *M V Searle*

The ex-Barmouth and Dolgelley Railway also lasted into the early Sixties, closing (unusually) for freight before human cargo; freight, December 14, 1964; passengers, January 18, 1965. Closure at about the same time of the long and scenically beautiful link northwards from Afon Wen towards Bangor lifted a second major segment from the once complete railed circle of Wales. Only a disastrous fire necessitating lengthy closure of Menai Bridge reprieved a fragment, when Caernarvon temporarily took over Irish traffic, replacing Holyhead.

What remains? That is the only question left to ask, when tracing the lifespan of a railway neglected for fifteen years or more. Over two such long routes as the Rhyl–Barmouth and Afon Wen–Bangor, the answer is a varied list: near Eyarth, a children's play-

Denbigh station in April 1954 with Chester train on left and Rhyl train on right. Already the southward run to Corwen had lost its passenger service. *H C Casserley*

A charming if not entirely accurate sketch of Bala lake in 1900.
Home Words

Cattle pens attached to Corwen station, still in use after closure of line.
M V Searle

ground in a disused cutting; bridges everywhere, some intact, others gaunt and half demolished, as near Ruthin; here a gradient post beside a bank where a track once ran; there a cornfield, where level track has been returned to farming; stations as private houses (Eyarth and several more); remains of stations, more or less vandalised; Berwyn tunnel; Penmaenpool engine shed. And, of course, many miles of grassy trackbed, only intermittently broken by new road works.

Again, much has been put to contemporary use, from housing on the station yard at Trefnant, to a large by-pass roundabout on the site of Ruthin station. Only recently have some landmarks been pulled down, among them Caernarvon station and the bridge at Port Dinorwic.

No trackbed remains in BR ownership, the whole having been sold to the appropriate County Councils, for re-use or disposal. Plans have been mooted, ranging from public amenities to industrialisation of special concern in some valleys. Where railway and road naturally followed closely the course of a river and riverside embankments have not been maintained, there is a danger of breaching during flooding of the Dee and other streams, and consequent land inundation. While there were trains, river and sea embankments acted also as dykes and dams. Now many are crumbling.

Selling railway land privately has, however, opened the door to a return of railways on a smaller scale, through the many preservation societies today climbing aboard the bandwagon manufacturing nostalgia for public pleasure.

Two short lines are the result, one in the middle of the main diagonal route, the other near its eastern extremity. Wonderful scenery, and the attraction of steam, promise them prosperity.

Already completed is the little Bala Lake Railway, a two-foot gauge track sitting on the old standard gauge bed and controlled from the revivified standard signalbox. It was partially opened in 1972 from Llanuwchllyn at the lovely lake's western end, and went on to Bala itself soon afterwards. In its rebirth, tiny Llanuwchllyn station, with its two platforms, sees more passengers in one summer week than in a year of its former sleepy existence.

Bridge over track near Ruthin, parapet filled in with wood. Note children's playground swings and slides in old cutting beneath. *F Lewis*

Level deserted trackbed near Ruthin, late 1977. *Fred Lewis*

Filling in of cutting on Rhyl–Corwen route, December 1977. *F Lewis*

Scooped out hollows and a stark central feature, all that survive of Ruthin station. A traffic roundabout occupies part of the site. *F Lewis*

An almost undamaged reminder of railway days by a deserted track on the Rhyl–Corwen line, 1977. *F Lewis*

Another enthusiast group, the Llangollen Railway, is presently tenant of that station and working towards lease of the old line as far as Corwen, whose scenery first brought railway tourists to this part of Wales a century ago. More grandiose future plans, at the mercy of available capital, even extend to linking onward again to join the Bala Lake Railway, repeating almost exactly the east–west movement of the original small companies. History, it is very true, does repeat itself.

Whether it could ever repeat itself on so grand a scale as to restore this whole line, or that north of Afon Wen, is a much more debatable point. One doubts very much that the joy of a completely circular cruise on land behind a fine steam engine around Snowdonia will ever again become possible.

The tidy, well kept station at Llangollen in 1949.
Locomotive & General

Dolgelley station, 1949.
Locomotive & General

Bala Junction, showing branch-off for Blaenau Ffestiniog, 1933.
Locomotive & General

Denbigh shed in 1952.
Real Photographs Ltd

RCTS special behind 42461 at Corwen in 1955.
Real Photographs Ltd

CHAPTER 22

The Signal in a Field
YORKSHIRE & HUMBERSIDE

If we compare Yorkshire railway maps of past and present, the county is revealed as a whole network of lost lines and lost causes. Scores of derelict railways crisscross the Ridings, inside the black outlines representing main lines and branches that are left. Only a complete volume could cover them all.

As representative of this cartographical pattern of 'then' encircled by 'now', we have taken the squashed circle formed by the Selby–York mainline, the eastward York–Scarborough route via Malton, the southward run thence to Driffield and Hull, and back towards Selby. Its central territory is now empty, and Market Weighton, former crossroads of four routes, lies disused. Leading off the circle's outer edges are more grassgrown lines of memory – to Hull's own local seaside resorts, Withernsea and Hornsea; across from Selby to Goole; and out from Selby by the forgotten Cawood, Wistow and Selby Light Railway. Trackbed even lies deeply buried under the walls of York itself.

The closed and lifted Hull and Barnsley Railway, intruding across this area and out again, is deliberately omitted, as a long early inter-city connection of quite different character from the localised railways under consideration.

Though authorised in 1879 on an initially expansive scale, the branch entering towards the river opposite stately Selby Abbey was still only a paper plan four years later, when yet more elaborate ideas were revived, to extend past Selby to the Hull and Barnsley, who would work the line. The NER, giant ruler of Yorkshire either directly or by numerous running powers, scotched both ideas, favouring a truncated Cawood, Wistow and Selby Light Railway, which would utilise a fraction of the route. The chairman's wife, without whom no Victorian ceremony was complete, cut the first sod on July 11, 1896. Within two years the single track CWSLR was complete; there was little to hinder progress over land flatter than the proverbial pancake, rich in farming communities, whose produce the line aimed to transport. In the event, 7,000 people and nearly 16,000 tons of cabbages, potatoes and beans rattled into Selby in the opening two quarters, to the CWSLR's own miniature terminus.

In its own right the locomotive stable consisted of exactly one small 0-6-0 saddle tank purchased in 1897, rather predictably christened *Cawood*; other rolling stock belonged to the NER (the lion having swallowed by takeover this intrusive flea) and consisted principally of a railcar of 1904 and a ramshackle but reliable Leyland bus remounted to run on train rails. More normal road vehicles, arising during the 1920s, caused passengers to dwindle alarmingly, forcing service withdrawal from January 1, 1930. However, goods patronage was sufficient for the line to continue for another thirty years until an increasing tendency to sling sacks onto lorries at farm gates for quicker despatch made the line an easy target for the Axe in the age of closure-mania. Track was lifted, and the CWSLR might never have been.

For about a century, the Selby–Goole offshoot provided passengers with a swift link between two important towns. In its final decades the line was much worked by G5 class and similar engines. But as we have found elsewhere motoring proved even more direct, and buses more frequent. Decline merged into closure and abandonment, as the Axe chopped away most of non-mainline Yorkshire. He who lacks a car must now travel halfway to Hull and change at Gilberdyke to reach the remaining line through Goole.

Two resorts, Hornsea and Withernsea, enjoyed railways from Hull, geared to what appeared at the time to be infallibly profitable two-way traffic; Hull businessmen to villages or coastal dormitory towns, growing under trains' influence; and Hull workers to their nearest seasides on weekends, Bank Holidays and half-days.

Withernsea branch, serving intervening villages, opened first, on June 27, 1854, as the Hull and Holderness Railway. It was genuinely independent, in territory made almost universally NER by ownership or running powers. Emphasising the difference, the H&HR maintained its personal rolling stock, locos and livery, without NER borrowings.

Initially trains shared the York and North Midland Railway station of Victoria Dock, for rent and shared running expenses, but the Y&NMR's star was waning in Hull's suburbs, and within months it abandoned its local service, leaving the little H&HR in a cock-a-hoop possession of the station. Not until 1860 did the NER breach this defiant independence by working some Withernsea services; the inevitable amalgamation came in 1862. Soon after, approaches to the larger TULL Paragon were completed, allowing Withernsea trains entry after 1864.

Withernsea gently developed as resort and residential town. So viable was business and seaside traffic as to warrant the doubling of most of the mileage. Not least of the seaside station's attractions for holiday crowds was its turntable, directly beside the platform barrier, an intriguing free entertainment.

The branch was no exception in losing out to cars after World War II. Expense-cutting schemes were tried, such as the introduction of diesel railcars (though steam lingered on, mainly in Class L1 locomotives) and travelling ticket collectors, replacing wayside station staff. Losses mounted, despite unmanned and unpainted stations, until closure became certain, announced for October 19, 1964.

Hornsea branch history is a similar tale of initial high hopes, a middle-period of undistinguished plodding, which was then overtaken by buses and cars, and final demise. Here yet another midget braved the giant NER, but briefly; before opening day, March 28, 1864, the Hull and Hornsea Railway was committed to NER working. Two years later, the North Eastern took full ownership. This was among the easiest lines ever built by railway navvies; twelve miles of marshland and meadow so level that the inland terminus stood only 16 feet higher than the seaward end.

Before completion of Hull Paragon, the H&HR terminated on the outskirts at Wilmington, there meeting the sister Withernsea line, but both transferred to Paragon from July, 1864.

Again, custom was two-fold; commuters and pleasure-seekers. At the height of localised seasidedom, in the Twenties and Thirties, so many extra excursions pulled out, packed out with crowds paying only a few shillings return, that motive power often ran short. Curious makeshifts were brought in, including unsuitable goods engines; anything, indeed, on mobile wheels.

At the other extreme of activity was Wassand, the so-called Market Day Only Station; from 1865 right through to closure a century on, Wassand never opened except on that one day, to one train out and one train back, overcrowded with country housewives.

Cars and buses, once again, ended the romance of steam-borne Market Day and allegiance to simple seaside pleasures near home. Despite staff economy experiments, like those tried on the Withernsea branch, Hornsea also lost its trains, on the same desolate day as Withernsea, October 19, 1964.

Inside the now deserted Humberside circle, Market Weighton was the hub of a four-line crossroads, from Selby across to Driffield, and crosswise from York to Beverley. Its principal taste of railwaydom came in 1846 with an application by the Y&NMR, against a rival, to build out from Selby a single track at the high cost of £156,000. Opening day was fixed for August 1, 1848. From the other side in 1885 came a company with the tongue-twisting name of Scarborough, Bridlington and West Riding Junction Railway, whose section from Driffield completed a continuous run, joining a major route at both ends. A further two-part line within the now railwayless circle created Market Weighton's position as a busy hub.

The latter York–Beverley service had been authorised in 1846, in the same year as the Selby–Market Weighton, taking suitable trains across country to avoid congested main junctions. Y&NMR pecuniary problems, however, allowed only for the northern half, opened to Market Weighton on October 3, 1847. Eighteen long years were to elapse before the final short stretch on to Beverley materialised. The double track via Pocklington cost £380,000, plus the expense of buying out the Pocklington Canal, whose owners demanded £18,000 despite its ailing financial condition. In addition the Market Weighton and Leven canals were bought out, ensuring a monopoly of freight carriage for the railway. Behind it all was George Hudson the railway-king, chairman of the Y&NMR, whose personal power bought the luxury of a private halt near Londesborough on the new branch, with a two-mile drive to his mansion, allowing ostentatious carriages to transfer guests from his own trains to his own house in one smooth operation.

Life on this unhurried route was peaceful and predictable. Trains wandered amiably from halt to halt. There was always a modicum of truth in the alleged early boardroom remark: 'This is a beautifully made line, but unfortunately without passengers to travel on it.'

Somnolence deepened into semi-desertion once buses speeded up rural travel, a gentle state of decay appropriate to a line strolling through places almost unheard-of outside the Ridings. Final traffic control experiments merely confirmed that a death certificate was the most appropriate document in the circumstances. Stations began closing, and the noble all-over roof at Market Weighton was removed in about 1948, a visible hint of things to come. These criss-crossing lines, in their youth, had liberated the general public in an undreamed-of manner from centuries of parochial imprisonment, when even York was a long way off; now the same ungrateful public climbed into its black Ford or Morris, and drove away.

One more abandoned line once ran inside our circular Yorkshire area, northwards from Driffield up to Malton on the more busy Scarborough route, and presented a stiffer engineering challenge than most of the others with its tunnels and cuttings. Quarry traffic helped keep it solvent, and for countrymen it was once the only regular link with the world beyond their own pastures.

Malton came into its own during holiday peaks, straddling main and branch lines and relieving York's congestion by an ingenious process of 'double reversal' in some Scarborough–Newcastle trains. Such a train on reaching Malton would have a pilot engine coupled to its rear end to drag it backwards through the triangular junction up the branch towards Wharram, still with its own locomotive at the leading end. Then, after clearing a second set of points, it was repositioned facing north onto another now lost country line up through Gilling, joining the main line about fifteen miles north of York.

Passengers were never the Malton–Driffield branch's prime revenue, its chief income being through stone. But the exceptional occasions when the future Edward VII, as Prince of Wales, came through via Gilling were long recalled, the handsome 2-4-2 T No. 1597 thereafter bearing the princely Feathers on her smokebox in remembrance of those events. Nor was the sight forgotten of a Royal wedding train headed by the streamlined No. 60015, when the aristocracy of locomotion carried the aristocracy of landed humanity on this normally humble little Malton and Driffield Railway, that was born in 1853 but adopted by the NER at one year old.

The line lasted until June 5, 1950, for passengers, served mainly by G5s, a ubiquitous local class. Freight, always more important, continued another

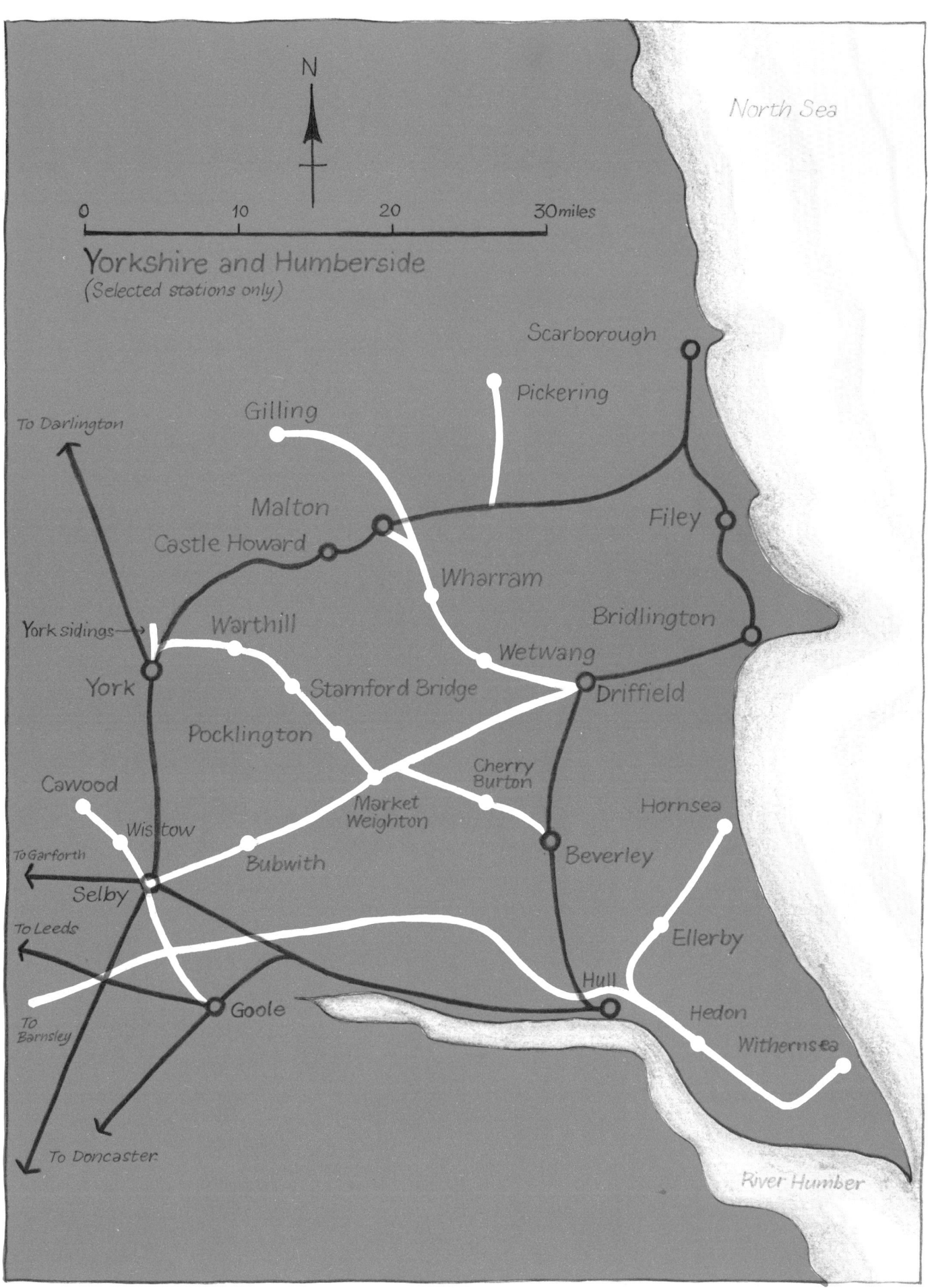

eight years, based on two large quarries yielding heavy building stone. When the trains stopped, the quarries fell into disuse; like Siamese twins, one was unable to survive without the other.

York itself has lines, which, hidden within its very walls, are the least identifiable of any in England. Who, walking those noble ramparts from the great station towards the Minster realises that buried under the artistically landscaped grassy banks are trackbeds of the former Y&NMR's lines and sidings? Or that the arches piercing supposedly impregnable defences are not medieval but Victorian work, arrogantly cut by George Hudson to let his trains inside. Public outcries mattered little to the Hudsons of the railway age; but in retaliation posterity has reinterred his unseemly sidings under beds of wallflowers.

Thus nothing is visible above ground of the tracks that desecrated York's ancient walls. However, of the region's other derelict lines signs remain in plenty even though on railway maps every track bears the single sad reference letter 'L', for 'lifted'.

Then . . . coaches parked in sidings under the walls of York around the turn of the century.

Last curve into Selby, approaching the river, all that survives of the old Cawood and Wistow line. *M V Searle*

The signal left in a lonely field that once was sidings. Selby, Yorks. *M V Searle*

Who would imagine sidings and lines in this same foreground? Trackbed filled in and sloped upwards to conform with historic walls' outline. But the main road, curved wall-top railings and low transverse wall immediately behind bus can all be identified in earlier picture.
M V Searle

Between Malton and Driffield is the waiting room of Sledmere station, transported to a playing field to serve as a cricket pavilion. Hudson's private station has gone, and his trees, but his long private drive down to the trains survives. Also long lived, if long disused, is Market Weighton engine shed; it ceased shedding engines 65 years ago, in 1917, but its solid Yorkshire stonework stands. Trackbed between there and Driffield is somewhat obscured, some banks having been levelled into cropping land, mingling their stone and chalk into something resembling the land's pre-railway state.

Hull's seaside branches likewise have their memories and their forgotten or converted stations. One, Hedon Speedway Halt, replacing Hedon Racecourse, opened only in 1948; now it is derelict.

Well walked is the pleasant old Cawood embankment, on its final curve towards the river at Selby, heavily explored by visitors to the Abbey seeking new camera angles. I tramped it one dismal November morning, and found its peace like balm to a London-assaulted soul. Returning, I looked down below the embankment, onto a small grassy meadow backed by willows. Alone in it stood one solitary signal gantry, complete with signal, as unexpected as a cow in Piccadilly. Never otherwise would I have looked again, and seen the meadow as deserted sidings, mute evidence that farm produce wagons were once the life of a little Yorkshire railway.

The signal in a lonely field seemed peculiarly apt; like a memorial left to mark a graveyard of dead endeavours.

Hornsea station in 1949. Class A6 No. 69759 with Hull relief train. *Real Photographs Ltd*

Driffield station in 1949. G5 Class No. 67330 with Malton–Driffield service.
Real Photographs Ltd

No. 67250, Class G5, heads a Goole train at Selby in 1949.
Real Photographs Ltd

Withernsea station in 1949, with Class L1 No. 67764 on Hull train. *Real Photographs Ltd*

CHAPTER 23

Easygoing Easingwold

THE EASINGWOLD RAILWAY

Beeching's Axe and the axe of time and changing requirements felled examples of every kind of British rail system, from complete cross-country services over fifty miles long, such as that crossing Scotland from Dumfries to Stranraer, or the Somerset and Dorset, to the shortest one-station lines.

Probably smallest of all the latter, as a self-contained entity rather than simply an extension branch off a bigger line, was the diminutive Easingwold Railway in Yorkshire, only about two-and-a-half miles long. Yet Easingwold's interest in railway enthusiasts' eyes is disproportionately large, and complete books have been written about it.

Into its brief mileage were fitted most of a full-sized railway's normal features: station; shed; a hotel; its own rolling stock; and a representative selection of engine design over the first half of the twentieth century, plus associated road vehicles.

Alne, the junction from which the ER ran off to its only other station, Easingwold itself, appeared on the mainline railway map nearly half a century before becoming the little Easingwold Railway's springboard. It was situated north of York on the Great North of England Railway, opened in 1841.

Ten years on, with much of the country embraced by trains, the existence of as yet train-less Easingwold, a cheerful small market town, was actually acknowledged in an important gazetteer of every town and village passed, if not physically served, by a railway. It was a curt and cursory glance, confined chiefly to mention of its principal landowner: 'Great North of England Railway . . . Right of railway from London . . . 221¼m Alne Station; 3m NE Easingwold, 2m from which is Bransby Hall; Francis Cholmeley Esq.' That was all the world at large knew of Easingwold, in the year of the first Crystal Palace.

Easingwold Railway, leaving the main line close to Alne station, was proposed as an independent company in 1887. Its mere two-and-half miles of standard gauge with modest installations and buildings cost its shareholders £17,000. Its main aims were to serve this rural market town's trade, and also open up mainline facilities forward from Alne to a populace previously reliant on sketchy road services.

The first trains pulled in from Alne on July 27, 1891, to a small single-platform terminus, beside which was soon built the regular landmark of most towns with train services, a Railway Hotel; in actuality, of course, usually not an hotel but an ordinary public house.

One solitary 0-4-0 saddle tank sufficed to maintain initial daily running between junction and terminus. Monotony was the worst problem encountered by its crews, eternally shuttling up and down so short a line with few if any challenges. Carriage stock was two ex-North Eastern four-wheelers, later replaced by another cast-off pair, also four-wheelers, bought secondhand from the North London Railway.

Soon after opening, an 0-6-0 ST appeared, the well remembered *Easingwold*, sold and replaced in 1903 by another of similar type (Hudswell Clarke) and name-plated *Easingwold No. 2* but usually referred to as *Easingwold the Second*.

Railway-operated road transport, extending services into surrounding country areas without actually laying track and installing stations, appeared in about 1910, when an NER *Londonderry* steam wagon began running out over the Plain of York via Easingwold and its neighbour, Bransby of the 1851 survey. It was a handy vehicle for conveying freight in small quantities from a railhead such as Easingwold, deeper into farming country, on its outward journey carrying fodder and supplies and returning with sacks of potatoes, crates of fruit, and net bags of vegetables. In appearance it was part locomotive, part traction engine at the leading end, and something resembling a modern lorry behind the driver's draughty open cab.

Easingwold followed an easygoing life from the Twenties into the Forties. Facilities were improved for passengers with reconstruction of its bay at Alne in about 1922. Motive power continued to be vested in the faithful 0-6-0 ST, but carriage accommodation went over to a more comfortable six-wheeler from the Great Central instead of the rattling older four-wheelers.

Not until forty-five years after building did little *Easingwold No. 2* finally lodge a protest against running year in, year out, over the same route, with only brief respites for overhaul. She was pronounced totally beyond repair, short of almost complete rebuilding, an unjustifiable expense for so limited a concern as the ER.

During its final decade or so before closure, when goods rather than passengers kept the line alive, the ER relied on loans from British Rail, mainly consisting of ex-NER 0-6-0 Ts of Class J71 or J72 borrowed from York depot. This was a policy found satisfactory on occasion in the past. Whenever the ER's one and only engine was overhauled, the NER or LNER had obligingly provided a substitute. The only problem was the fact that, whatever the class of locomotive loaned from whatever source, it rarely if ever fitted into the ER's own diminutive local shed and had to remain shedded at York.

Among borrowed locomotives seen at various times are recorded J1/1758 (1930s); LNER No. 8246 (the 1940s); and BR loans including Nos. 68313, 68246 and 68698 in the final years.

Easingwold's decline reflected events affecting inumerable other provincial railways throughout Britain during the years 1950–1966; adoption of more flexible road transport for goods, and the increasing reluctance of passengers to change after travelling only one or two stations and wait again for a train to a destination they could now reach direct by car.

Thus, two or three days after Christmas in 1957, J class No. 68698 pulled out for Alne with a string of final freight wagons. The last passenger train had left nine years before, on November 29, 1948.

The Easingwold and Alne had outlasted certain similar lines by some twenty years, no bad record for such a brief route leading to only one station. A year after departure of that last goods train, Alne itself was dropped from British Rail timetables. Subsequent track improvements removed all lingering traces of the former ER bay.

Class J71 No. 68313 at Alne in 1951; the toy-like Easingwold train waits in its bay.
Real Photographs Ltd

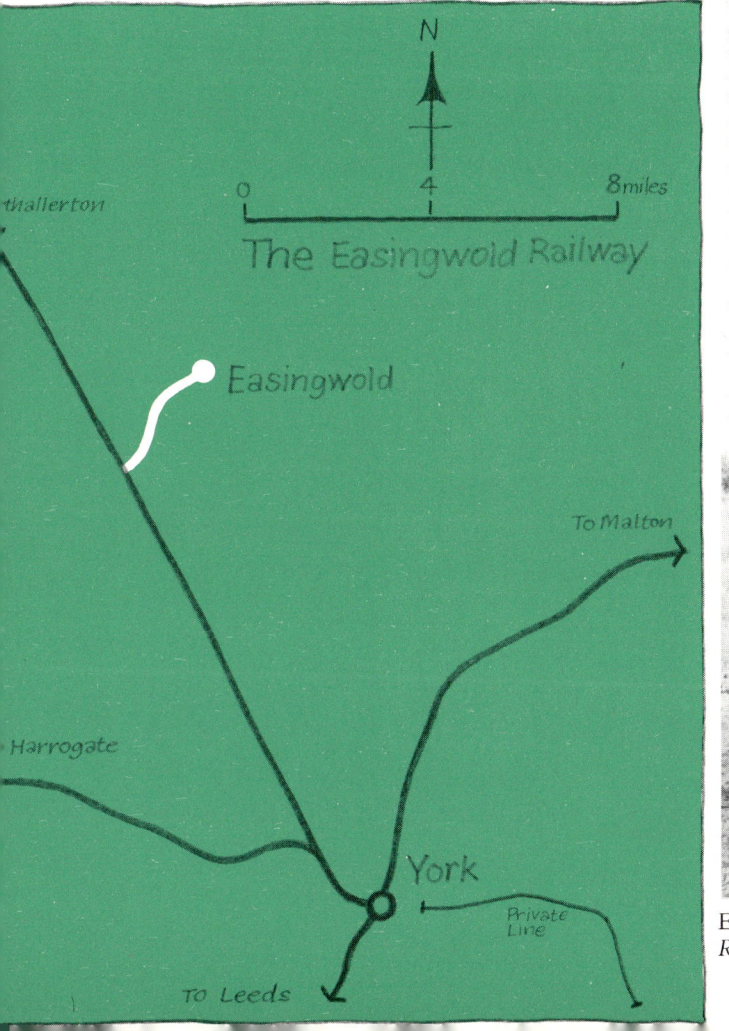

Easingwold shed with No. 68246, 1957.
Real Photographs Ltd

Easingwold station in 1931. Station hotel (still extant) on right. Rest of site is now occupied by agricultural buildings.
Locomotive & General

0-6-0ST No. 2, seen in 1931.
Locomotive & General

No. 2 at Easingwold in 1933.
H C Casserley

Expresses now thunder past Alne towards Northallerton, the rushing rivulets of County Durham, and the city of Newcastle, as if it did not exist. Inter-City moves too fast for us to catch a glimpse of the point where the Easingwold Railway branched off, unless one knows exactly where to look in the proverbial split second.

Bulldozers annually gobble up more and more traces along the line, though fire forestalled them at Easingwold station, whose remains became derelict. The tiny engine shed outlived it by a few years, and local historians could also still spot the place by the goods yard where once had stood the steam wagon shed, housing that cumbersome but useful extension service vehicle.

Modernity has obliterated most outward signs that Easingwold ever possessed a railway station, whose place is occupied by a new housing estate. At Alne, the trackway again vanishes under modern roads. Between the two points, not much is left. Former track has often been incorporated into adjoining fields, reverting to its original land use before trains came.

Very little remains of the tiny fragment of social and railway history which was the Easingwold Railway.

Old station buildings at Alne converted into a row of houses.
M & J Harris

Railway buildings at Alne, used by a haulage contractor. Track ran along left-hand side. April 1978.
M & J Harris

Only remaining lineside telegraph pole beside the track, now surrounded by foliage, 1978.
M & J Harris

Station Hotel, Easingwold – minus station. The station stood behind the hotel, on a site now occupied by farm buildings, visible at the extreme left. 1978. *M & J Harris*

Gate keeper's cottage by a crossing near Easingwold. Track ran to the right of the house, now planted as an orchard. April 1978. *M & J Harris*

CHAPTER 24

Murder on the Line
RAILWAYS OF BLAYDON & CONSETT

'A new suspension bridge . . . and near to it . . . another bridge, constructed of wood, and resting upon six short and stout piers, over which a prolongation of the Carlisle and Newcastle railway is to pass in its course to the very verge of the last mentioned city.' So commented a passing scribe of about 1839 on the works of railway mania as he drove by coach out of Newcastle towards the 'sequestered and insignificant' Shotley Bridge Spa. Continuing into the increasingly majestic scenery of forests, ravines and Devon-like burbling rivers that is the Derwent country, this horsedrawn group was again reminded that changes beyond imagining were underway to destroy their exclusive carriage-borne world. Into the observer's diary went another note: 'In the distance, a line of elevated ground bounds the view; it is the Stanhope Railway.' The scribe was Dr Granville, compiler of the monumental *Spas of England*.

By next season those words of Granville, chronicler of almost every watering place in England during what was still the spas' heyday, could be read up by travellers to Shotley Bridge, but prospects of trains intruding into the remote Derwent, or to Shotley itself, appeared absurd. They quickly dropped from conversation in favour of speculation on a more immediate topic: was Shotley Bridge, 'almost unknown outside Durham', on the brink of wide fame in the light of Granville's ecstatically favourable report? Granville had predicted that inside two decades all the world would come to Shotley Bridge and drive along the Derwent.

Dr Granville was right, to within about seven years. But the world did not come by coach, seeking solace for pale Society beauties whose only disease was boredom. It came en masse with heartier voice, by trains driven into this and other previously natural valleys, to forget Newcastle's grime and work in picnicking. In return, Derwent sent back by train, consignments of the iron of Consett for which the various railways in this quarter of the north-east had been planned and promoted (passenger traffic being a secondary consideration). To represent this once intricate network of North Eastern Railway, colliery and private lines we have selected two NER developments: the Blaydon and Consett branch (via Shotley Bridge) and the Lanchester Valley branch, via its nametown. Together these formed a complete route across from Durham to Consett, and on to Blaydon for Newcastle, a more roundabout way than the direct route but serving important industrial and residential districts.

July 13, 1857, the date of the NER's Lanchester Valley Branch Act, might be called the birthdate of this connection planned as two separate stages, bringing with it authority for that outlet for Consett's expanding iron ore industry.

With an eye to profit for itself through freight carriage, as well as passengers, the NER drew up plans for a twelve-mile single track, south-eastwards down from Consett to Durham. One main engineering feat was required, a long viaduct near Lanchester, and gradients became taxing in the vicinity of Consett, about 800 feet above sea level (roughly equivalent to Masbury Summit on the Somerset and Dorset), with stretches at 1 in 60 and 1 in 80. £70,000 of the company's funds went into the line's creation.

The early 1860s were characterised by a series of battles, common wherever rival companies coveted the same ground and its potential revenue; big issues of yesterday which time has dulled to half-forgotten bickerings. Because of the value of the Consett area's industry to whichever party won the right to carry its ore and products, these arguments flared with considerable heat.

Proposals for the second part of the route, northwards along the Derwent Valley from Consett down to the main Carlisle–Newcastle line at Blaydon, ran through many a boardroom storm as well as into Parliamentary wrangling among hopeful promoters before the very reasonable conclusion was drawn that the NER, already embarked on the Lanchester half, should build what was in practice a continuation of that line.

The Derwent route via Shotley Bridge was designated under its Local Act of 1862 the Blaydon and Con*side* branch, only later more familiarly entitled the Blaydon and Con*sett*.

When in 1862 the Lanchester Valley branch opened, its own Consett terminus was unfinished, and the final site still undecided in view of the uncertainty of the Blaydon and Conside plans. Not even its name was settled, for the same reason.

Clamour was growing for an alternative terminus at Blackhill, in the territory of the Shotley Bridge route, supposedly more accessible to the expanding sprawl of workers' houses which was rapidly making Blackhill and Consett into towns. Blackhill won its point and its station in 1867, and also a one-and-a-half mile extension to a local iron works, one of scores of such branches-off-branches which make the local map a spider's web of now disused railways.

Lanchester Valley branch opened first, on September 1, 1862, at too unholy an hour to inspire much jubilation at the Durham end. The 6.20 am for Consett carried exactly six passengers, and returned to Durham with about forty. Celebration specials for the 'opening' ran several hours after these trains physically opened the line, at an hour considered more appropriate for well-fed and well-bred city and railway notabilities.

Freight expectations were quickly realised. The line carried coal and coke, pig iron, bricks, timber, ironwork in finished state, and railway building materials such as rails and iron plates, making the NER in a practical sense a do-it-yourself company.

Traffic swelled satisfactorily into the ensuing decades, moving the NER to double as much track as possible. By about 1882, all had been doubled, but for the awkward stretch over Knitsley Viaduct, built to accommodate only single track and therefore a major problem. A new station was added in 1883 to serve another colliery town, and passenger trains were increased to seven each way soon after the turn of the century.

Shotley Bridge paper mill ('perhaps the most extensive in the country'), sited on the other half of this through system, paved the way to industrial transport expansion of the Derwent Valley before Victoria was enthroned. Indeed, the mill built the road along which Dr Granville came spa-scanning in 1839 by coach, as an outlet for its product.

Plans for a railway over the same ground were mooted as early as 1844, though nothing materialised until 1862, when serious intentions were proclaimed in the NER's aforementioned Blaydon and Conside Branch Act. Work was, as usual, delayed about two years during protracted inter-company wranglings over rival schemes, as well as by the upheavals of the 1863 NER/S&D Amalgamation Act. Tenders for construction were eventually invited in 1864 for an eleven mile course to Consett via Rowlands Gill and Shotley Bridge, an expensive business involving viaducts, bridges and excavations.

Blackhill station, changing its name to Benfieldside, became the chief station, rather than the goal of Consett itself. One stop was complete when the Blaydon and Consett branch opened on December 2, 1867 (June 18 for freight), with the customary junketings and self-congratulatory speeches for officials from Newcastle Central feted at Consett iron ore works.

A full passenger service was offered over the completed through route from Durham via Consett and on to Newcastle in a semicircle, the line as a whole being entitled the Consett Branch.

Blackhill station was renamed again, as Consett, and the LV original station shut down, forcing some passengers at that end of the town to walk up to one-and-a-half miles to the trains; little improvement on the days of carrier's cart and Shanks' pony. Three trains daily did the complete circuit, except Sundays.

During these formative years, Blackhill station inched its way into the record books of history as Britain's most turncoat station, changing from Blackhill to Benfieldside, then to Consett (1882), to Consett and Blackhill (1885) and finally back to plain Blackhill (1879) in anticipation of a new Consett station.

As well as, literally, carrying coals to Newcastle, and iron ore to the world in general, the B&C cashed in on local tourist potential with the scenery of the Shotley Bridge area and its attractive little non-medical spa. Special trains often brought visitors out, not for the cure – there never was a true cure at Shotley – but for the occupational therapy of strolling in peaceful beauty away from Newcastle's smoke. Saturday market specials took local folk in reverse, down to Durham and Newcastle, returning either at 4 pm (traditional teatime) or at seven. Passenger tariffs settled, soon after opening, to a full length fare from Newcastle to Benfieldside/Blackhill of 2s. 8d. (13p) First, 2s. (10p) Second, and 1s. 2½d. (6p) Third, one way. A new carriage shed was added to Blackhill in 1873.

Three years later Blackhill, as the principal station, acquired its own motive power depot, at first a tiny shed accommodating only two engines. It cost the Blaydon and Consett the appropriately miniscule sum of £961. Expanding over the years the depot's allocation eventually rose from only two 0-6-2Ts at about the time of World War I to as many as sixteen engines during World War II, when some other sheds shut down.

A Sunday service was introduced during the 1880s, as far as industrial Consett itself, but only two trains continued down the less heavily worked Lanchester valley section. Class 'O' 0-4-4Ts or BTP 0-4-0Ts became the staple locomotives until about 1907 when steam autocars were introduced. They were considered specially suitable for excursions of city dwellers coming out to enjoy the tumbling rivers and twisting wooded valleys of the non-industrialised section.

Another new engine shed opened as the century ended, at the Blaydon branching off point. At the same time, once viaducts and bridges were widened to accommodate a second line of permanent way, track on the B&C branch was doubled, eliminating the thirty-year-old problems of single track crowding; originally building these to only single width had proved an expensive mistake on this and many another provincial railway. Widening was completed by about 1908.

In its final form the B&C branch settled to a life of ferrying three classes of traffic; local people to town, townsfolk to the country, and a specially heavy freight service to the huge iron ore works of Consett, whose great furnace chimneys, massive roofs, quarries and associated housing intruded gauntly into the plateau between Derwent and Wear.

Routine, orderly, placid – that was the branch until October 1911, when the mystery of the Lintz Green murder briefly propelled that peaceful little station into notoriety, and added local import to the popular old subject of ghost trains.

Quietly walking from his platform to the station house after seeing out a regular train on a very ordinary journey, the Lintz Green stationmaster suddenly cried out, almost simultaneously with the crack of a

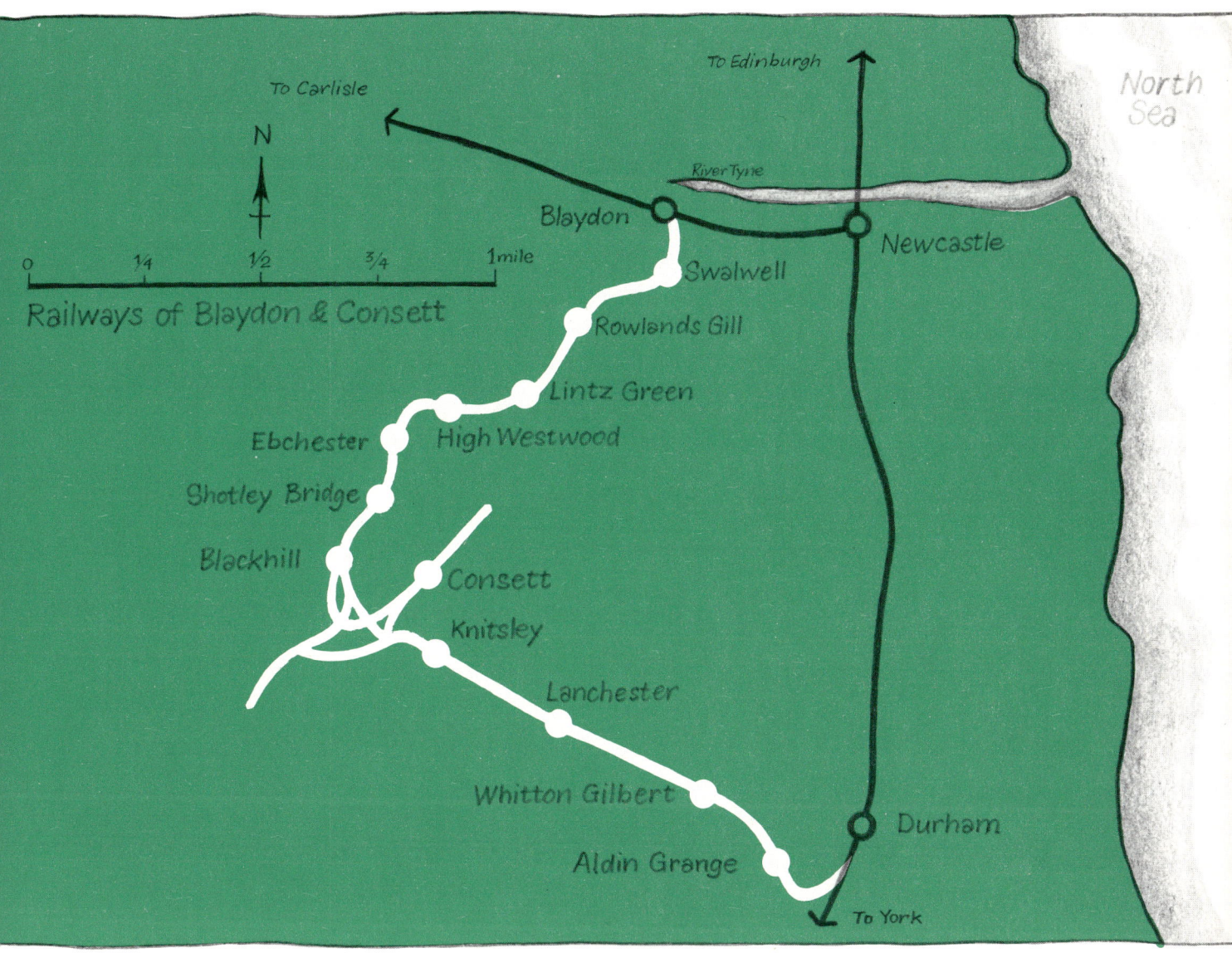

gun, and collapsed senseless on his own doorstep. Alerted by such unusual sounds in the stillness of Lintz Green, nearby miners ran to the scene, but the stationmaster was beyond help, shot by the proverbial unseen hand. The Lintz Green murder was never solved. Time gradually lulled rumours of an insane miner, armed with a loaded gun. But ever after, on wild stormy nights, it is said, a spectral train slipped without stopping past the fatal platform and vanished into the night; the ghost of the last train flagged away by the victim.

The decline towards demise by railways in Britain which reached an apparently sudden head in the 1960s, is often found to actually begin, in a small but ominous way, much farther back in time. Small closures (here a station, there a short branch) began paving the way as soon as motorised road traffic, particularly country buses and lorries, gained a hold. So it was on the Lanchester Valley branch. As an 'economy measure' Knitsley station was closed during the Great War; not until 1925 did it reopen, and then reluctantly. Passenger services began a slow but significant fall after the war as buses skipped in and out of village centres, which were nearly all of them a long way from the stations supposed to serve them. Building stations over a mile from their parent settlements spelled certain death on many a rural branch, once buses came to remove their isolation.

In barely two years (between about 1920 and 1922) passengers through Rowlands Gill, on the Derwent section, fell by a shattering 47,000, reflecting an all too universal trend. Freight continued heavy for a while after the Great War, despite closure of some smaller collieries, until it, too, became eroded by motor transport. Ore and coal gradually but surely transferred to lorries, with their more flexible working schedules.

Lanchester Valley branch succumbed earlier than its companion, the B&C. In 1929, about 29,000 passengers were carried, against 186,000 only ten years previously. The typical response to departing revenue was raised fares, driving still more onto the roads. Truncated services – only four a day by about 1930 – did nothing to tempt back patronage, and day excursions to the Yorkshire and Durham seaside resorts brought in only a little extra revenue. In the whole of 1932 one station booking office took little more than £100. Seven years later, the forlorn Lanchester Valley line closed to passengers.

Railway relics on the Newcastle & Carlisle Railway at Blaydon, terminus of the Blaydon and Consett branch, seen in 1956.
NCB

Class Q6 No. 63379 at Consett in 1956.
Real Photographs Ltd

Class N8 No. 69395 at Blaydon in 1952.
Real Photographs Ltd

A background of sidings and sheds for Class G5 No. 67316, photographed in 1952 at Blaydon.
Real Photographs Ltd

General view of Consett station in 1963, showing the extent of adjoining yards. Class Q6 No. 63939 and goods train.
Real Photographs Ltd

On the Blaydon and Consett branch, death came more slowly. High Westwood, last station to be erected (1909) was the first to shut, in 1942, a comparatively unimportant wooden affair in desperate need of the repairs which the LNER, owner of the line since 1923, declined to finance. It was an indication of official thinking about the line when much custom had gone to the buses.

Freight, always more important to this branch than most others, was the deciding factor in both its building and its running down. Once large scale colliery closures set in following the Second World War, precipitated by a move away from coal to diesel and other fuels, the end quickly came into sight. Falling passenger revenue forced a cut to only three trains daily, whilst buses ran every ten minutes. What dying railway could take such double desertion?

Running down began with pruning of individual stations: Shotley Bridge and Ebchester in September 1953; Lintz Green and Swalwell soon afterwards. Motive power through Blaydon was confined mainly to classes G5, N8 and Q6. All passenger movements through the remaining stations ceased from November 2, 1953, and another local route through to Black-

Hamsterley Mill Viaduct today, as part of the Derwent Walk.
Durham County Council

hill, the Pontop branch, ceased operations on May 23, 1955.

Only freight kept some blood coursing in the veins of this once prosperous network of railways great and small, but this, too, became increasingly drained by lorries until shut-down of the entire Blaydon and Consett line was announced for November 11, 1962. Blaydon locomotive shed shut its doors in 1965, and the old Lanchester Valley line, closed to passengers for over thirty years, bowed out of freight carriage the next year. Silence descended for the last time over the many railways sandwiched into the triangle formed by the main Durham–Newcastle and Carlisle–Newcastle lines, when the last secondary branches and sidings folded during the late Sixties.

Consett's giant iron ore works continued, reliant on roads for its ore, no longer local but imported, and dismantling overtook the Lanchester line, whose branching point, overgrown with stunted bushes, is still easily recognisable in disuse on the left from Inter City trains approaching Durham. The works themselves closed in 1980, generating acute unemployment and creating a local atmosphere of intense bitterness.

The Derwent Walk, over the old Blaydon and Consett branch trackbed, near Shotley Bridge, seen in about 1977.
Durham County Council

A happier fate overtook the Blaydon and Consett section than that which befell most disused railways, based on its original attraction to passengers: the impressive hilly scenery of the Derwent Valley. Out of the old line, phoenix-like, arose the Derwent Walk, following take-over of the grass-grown remains from BR by Durham County Council, for integration of its best ten miles into a larger 290-acre country park, opened in July 1972.

Rehabilitation was laborious. Masses of gorse, birch, willow, even fast-growing pine, almost obliterated trackbed in places. This vegetation was cleared, and the trackbed itself grassed over to provide pleasant walking and resting; four viaducts were repaired, drainage improved, and controlled tree planting instituted.

The cars that helped kill trains were welcomed back as friends, with parking places at access points, usually disused stations. Old stations took on new jobs. At Shotley Bridge, near magnificent viewpoints, the yard became a picnic centre, with the platforms left intact, and young birches were planted, sheltering the walk. Ebchester yard was also adapted for alfresco mealtimes and beautified for picnicking, though station buildings were reduced to rubble and buried with young trees over their graves. A fine surviving signal box became a public enquiry centre, staffed in season by Countryside Rangers.

Spectacular walking was opened across Foggoes and Hamsterley viaducts, letting walkers cross at dizzy heights above wonderful views previously seen only by engine drivers.

The companion Lanchester Valley branch, onwards to Durham, has been similarly converted, as another section of a very wide ranging scheme based on Durham County Council's enlightened realisation 'that former railway lines often offer unique access to the countryside'. As well as the Derwent and Lanchester Valley walks, the Council has tackled several other railways within its domain: Brandon to Bishop Auckland; Brandon to Waterhouses (The Deerness Valley); Consett to Waskerley (Waskerley Way). Work is currently in progress on one more, from Barnard Castle to Middleton in Teesdale. All are walkways, but are not integrated into bigger schemes as is the finest, the Derwent Walk.

County Durham has exceptionally lovely hill and riverside country, and a wealth of disused railways penetrating to many of its best areas. Few councils are making greater efforts to wed the two for public pleasure.

Thus life returns by day, particularly to the popular Derwent Walk. But when the last cars depart at dusk, there are no ore trains to keep it alive through the night, as before. Only one train may pass now, some believe, heard but never seen and needing neither the track nor signals that are no longer there, when, on the anniversary of a certain well remembered October night, the ghost train whispers through deserted Lintz Green.

CHAPTER 25

Into Lakeland

CONISTON BRANCH

'I know not . . . terms sufficiently expressive to describe this *infernal* road . . . let me seriously caution all travellers who may propose to travel this terrible country, to avoid it as they would the *devil*; for a thousand-to-one but they break their necks or their limbs by overthrows or breakings down.' So a traveller of about 1770 denounced the rough route from Preston towards the Lakes. Romance, the poets held, was in every lakeland ripple and blade of grass; but for mortal men, the effort of getting there destroyed all feeling of poesy and filled their coachmens' lips only with curses.

Only seventy years later the picture was changing drastically. Coaching would soon belong to the boneshaking past, as the next generation of travel writers pointed out: 'New lines of communication of . . . velocity . . . are shooting out in a northerly direction, one of which will reach Lancaster before the expiration of 1840, thereby affording the means of transport in ten short hours from London, to within twenty miles of the pure atmosphere of Winander-Meer and the other Lakes of the North. To a person of delicate health and susceptible nerves such a journey, with comparatively little or no fatigue, and less of adventure, must be a real blessing.' Windermere considered itself quite literally born of its railway. Birthwaite village, renamed Windermere to tally with its identifying station and lake, opened its arms to tourist profit, and shed few tears of sympathy for the sensitive souls of its Lake Poets, fleeing before steaming Progress.

'Is then *no* nook of English ground secure from this rash assault?' wailed Wordsworth. The answer seemed to be 'No!' Branch lines soon reached out from the Furness Railway-ruled coast towards the other major lakes, such as to beautiful Coniston.

Coniston branch was the child of a consortium of Furness directors, acting as a separate entity in this enterprise which was put into operation under an Act of August 10, 1857. Unfortunately their expertise as railwaymen was greater than their instinct for judging the reliability of their contractors. Exactly a year after obtaining their Act to build, the Coniston directors found themselves with a bankrupt contractor and an unfinished branch on their hands. Completion was achieved using more reliable localised contractors with official FR backing. The line, just under nine miles long, was opened on June 18, 1859, after eighteen months' stopping, starting, and heavy working. Gradients were severe at up to 1 in 49 over about half the route, inland from Broughton, climbing stiffly thereafter to a climax at Torver, one station from the lakeside.

Tourism was a growing but not entirely understood industry. Staple finance for the trains was initially, therefore, expected to be copper from local mines. It was hoped that in addition, the district's beauty would bring in worthwhile secondary income.

However, from being a secondary to a primary interest was but a matter of a few years, in the tourist field. The Furness Railway was quick to cash in with company-owned pleasure boats timetabled with trains (an offshoot of FR shipping interests centred on Barrow). In the line's opening year the FR launched *Gondola*, a craft much featured in subsequent tour advertisements, followed by her sister, *Lady of the Lake*. The FR organised direct excursions to Coniston from Barrow and elsewhere, without the Foxfield change, and in 1862 formally bought out the Coniston branch for itself.

In the same year discussions opened between FR and MR for joint running through from Bradford and Leeds to Barrow-in-Furness, and on through to Coniston, without changing. The introduction of summer tourist specials was planned, opening up the Lake District, once the private possession of moneyed carriage class gentry or wandering poets, to the world and his everyday little wife. At the other end of the scale, the wealthy director of the Furness Railway ran a private railway carriage, attached to his own trains, said to outdo in sumptuous comfort even that of the powerful Duke of Devonshire, also running over the FR of the 1860s; ducal indeed with its long picture windows, clerestory ceiling, and open end vestibules.

In 1872 the FR acquired steamers on Coniston's rival lake, Windermere, christened with avian appellations: *Teal*, *Tern*, *Swift*, *Cygnet*, *Raven* and *Swan*. They were direct precursors of the only railway-owned fleet in the Lakes today, British Rail's pleasure steamers on Windermere, which continue to use four of the original names.

Between the turn of the century and the Great War, the Furness Railway operated a wide tourist network by train, coach and ship. Many excursions were centred on the little Coniston branch. Among these was the 'Inner Circular Tour embracing Furness Abbey, Coniston Lake (*Gondola*), and Crake Valley; Fare from 3s. 3d. (16p)'; the scenic 'Four Lakes Circular Tour, viz. Coniston, Grasmere, Rydal and Windermere; Fare from 5s. 9d. (29p)'; and the 'Coniston-to-Coniston Tour via Red Bank, Grasmere and Ambleside, returning by coach to Coniston' at only 4s. 6d. (22½p).

Railway publishing followed in the wake of the tours, with the FR's *Tours Through Lakeland* advertised as 'To be had GRATIS at ALL Furness Railway Stations, or of Mr F J Ramsden, Superintendant of the Line, Barrow-in-Furness', owner of the aforementioned luxury director's carriage. Station booking halls likewise exerted themselves in their efforts to please the public, and augment their profits. Thus a 1906 FR advertisement proclaimed: 'Picture postcards of the Lake District may be obtained at any station on the Furness Railway, and on the Company's steamers . . . reduced price, 12 cards for 6d.' (2½p).

After the Great War, tourist traffic boomed again. The line's original dual purpose in carriage of tourists *and* copper was largely a thing of the past. Though in summer during the Twenties only one through trip ran to Coniston without the Foxfield interchange nuisance, local services from Foxfield were excellent by rural standards, if somewhat erratically scheduled for 9 am, noon, and 1 o'clock, with three closer together in afternoons. Returns ran up to 6.15 in the evening, plus a couple of regular freight trains. Who, trooping out at Coniston for picnics by the lovely lake, dreamed then of economic gloom, or another major war?

The Depression, when it came, hit the FR harder than most other railway networks, geared so much to the fortunes of the Barrow shipyards, from which came the incomes of many of its regular, as opposed to seasonal, passengers. Tourists, too, felt the monetary pinch as jobs folded all over the land, compelled to make do with a weekend at Cleethorpes instead of a fortnight exploring Coniston. Furness itself was declared a Distressed Area. The LMS, now owner of the Coniston line, felt compelled to truncate services passengers could not afford to use, and withdraw many locomotives.

When the economic situation as a whole improved, the railways did not. Bus development parallelled economic changes, sneaking in while trains were being axed to pick up families at lower fares and run them nearer to their actual destinations.

Branches less economic than Coniston and Windermere began closing. The closures of the Cleator and Workington line and Piel branch, were followed on the outbreak of another world war by the closing to passengers of the Sandside–Hincaster Junction line. The latter line has now been lifted after surviving for many more years for freight.

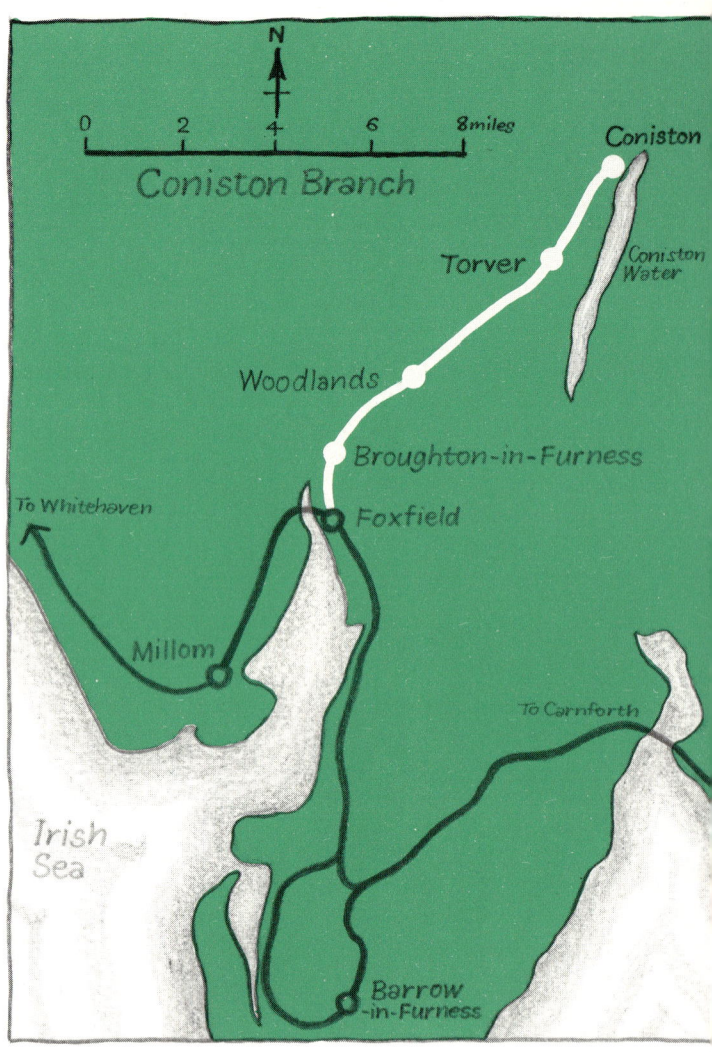

Steam railcar and trailer at Coniston just after the beginning of the twentieth century. *Locomotive & General*

Today only the touristically viable BR branch to Windermere penetrates the Lake District. Even the seemingly indispensable line through Keswick is closed, and most of its features dismantled.

Coniston branch, once offering those proud 'Twenty Coach and Steam Yacht Tours through English Lakeland' also lies silently disused, its metals lifted and trackbeds overgrown. Remnants of buildings and trackside features yearly slip further into disrepair, gaunt against a superb rural backcloth, whilst ramblers walk the track. For a while it seemed that this branch or a part of it, might join tracks in Durham, Scotland and the Wye Valley as an officially maintained public walk with picnic facilities, under the Lake District Planning Board. Coniston station was to become a chalet-style holiday centre.

Plans, however, fell through, chiefly because of the great cost of adequately maintaining several miles of fencing both sides of the old track. The Board also considered this to be one of the less interesting routes available for such treatment, only touching the lake at its terminus instead of running alongside its waters.

On another section, near Broughton-in-Furness, adaptation to forestry work has been considered, for carriage of timber. However, on a more cheerful note, the National Trust has been successful in restoring the graceful old *Gondola*, Lakeland's first railway owned steamship, featured in Furness Railway advertising for eighty seasons. Retired in 1940 and converted into a

Coniston, showing track layout from end of platform.
Locomotive & General

Coniston shed seen in 1954. *Real Photographs Ltd* →

'Furness Railway, The Gateway to the English Lakes'. An advertisement of about 1907 extolling the Coniston branch and other beauty spots. *Ward Lock Ltd*

Gondola, as the National Trust hope to restore her by 1980. *National Trust*

189

Coniston station, with its splendid mountainous background, in 1954. No. 41217 with Foxfield-bound service.
Real Photographs Ltd

Remains of Coniston station, in a glorious setting, in 1966.
Countryside Commission

houseboat, she was wrecked on Coniston Water and afterwards partially sunk by a far-sighted purchaser to preserve the remains of her hull. Fittings were stripped, including the lavish First Class saloon based on the FR Royal Train. They have been faithfully reproduced by modern craftsmen. Refloated after purchase by the National Trust in 1977, *Gondola* was ready for Coniston Water cruises under steam by 1980.

Thus the Lake District is reduced to only one internal operative railway, that to Windermere, in BR hands. But steam is still to be seen rising on the soft waterside air, on a fragment of the Lakeside Branch, a neighbour of both Coniston and Windermere lines. Here, between Haverthwaite and Lakeside stations, runs yet another fine, preserved steam railway, annually attracting more and more nostalgia-hungry holidaymakers for short runs into the railway world their grandparents knew. Indeed, this section has paid so well that the preservation society has been able to restore another closed station on its line, Newby Bridge.

But at Coniston no delicious smells of steam and oily rags assault he who comes to explore its deserted stations or walk its weedy trackbed. They can now only exist in imagination, unless he is old enough to remember puffing over Torver summit.

Fragmentary station remains at Coniston, photographed during the planning stage (unfulfilled) for chalet development. 1969.
Countryside Commission

CHAPTER 26

Across Scotland

DUMFRIES TO PORTPATRICK & STRANRAER

One of the longest stretches killed by a combination of thin population, uneconomic stations, lack of variety in sources of revenue, and increased motoring, was that joining three important onward transit points (Dumfries, Stranraer and Portpatrick) across the whole of South-west Scotland.

Its downfall was due to the fact that between these towns lay about sixty miles of expensively built and maintained track running through bleak wild hill country, whose remote stations attracted only handfuls of passengers, if any. Most travellers came through rather than into the area on their way to Ireland beyond, usually travelling by night and quite unconscious of the land through which they passed. Sea routes were the line's sole reason for birth and life. Had not Portpatrick, on a peninsula jutting out towards Ireland, been the nearest possible landing place from the Emerald Isle, railways would probably not have penetrated so sparsely populated an area for another forty years, nor would this line have ever acquired its famous train, *The Paddy*.

Lucrative Irish mails, troops, cattle and civilian passengers encouraged several small ponderously-titled but impoverished local companies to vie with each other in meeting these particular demands. As was quite common in such battles, the companies were forced to amalgamate for survival long before the great 1923 grouping. A tale whose ending was predictable, in a world without pity for uneconomic trains, remote halts, and vast tracts of hill and moorland requiring costly track maintenance out of proportion to possible revenue.

Early developments centred not on Stranraer but the more important Portpatrick, huddled into the only reasonable harbour on a cruel gale torn coast, within sight of Ireland in good weather. Half a century before trains, new steam packets had gone into service to cope with increasing passengers. Opening Portpatrick to greater days through rail connections therefore appeared a reasonable investment, despite having to take trains at great expense across sixty miles of bare unproductive uplands and alongside underdeveloped coasts and rivers, country which in itself would profit the shareholders almost nothing. It was also felt that Portpatrick, the port for Patrick's isle, should in itself justify the building of a line.

Railway developers based in Glasgow envisaged this line as completing a triangle, whose sides were formed on the east by Glasgow–Dumfries–Carlisle, and by the west coast stretch through Ayr.

First into the fray, setting up important opening mileage without actually tackling the most demanding section, was the Castle Douglas and Dumfries Railway, promoted under an Act of 1856 and opened on November 7, 1859. It worked under the auspices of a larger Scottish concern, the Glasgow and South Western Railway, who put up partial capital and supervised construction.

'A line of railway through Wigtownshire and Kirkcudbright to Castle Douglas and Dumfries' was the next scheme, which would embrace most of the remaining mileage and link up with the existing Castle Douglas railhead. Plans for duplicating services right through to Dumfries were dropped.

Rather than providing a service to scattered Scottish villages, the Portpatrick Railway aimed from the first at covering for the Irish traffic; the only possible justification for carrying costly track across, at one point, an area where thirty miles of nothingness held but one village.

An appalling winter for construction work delayed opening of the Portpatrick Railway until March 11, 1861, and allowed for second thoughts on stations. Two last-minute halts resulted, Palnure and Dunragit on the final section towards Stranraer, plus an elementary siding which eventually expanded into Castle Kennedy. A less practical offshoot was a station to 'serve' Gatehouse of Fleet, about halfway back to Dumfries – six miles from that village, by tracks so rough that railway money had to be diverted into approach roads to make it usable.

To both companies' credit, engineering of this difficult through route under two ownerships went well. Two-and-a-half years sufficed for the easier Dumfries–Castle Douglas part (CD&DR); and a mere three-and-three-quarter years for the PPR's challenging fifty-three miles across mountain, fell, moor and river to Stranraer.

Portpatrick Railway's opening day brought trains as far as Stranraer, the last stretch being incomplete. A delighted ballyhoo greeted the first one in from Castle Douglas, with a wooden crown wobbling precariously on each engine. Harbour shipping was bedecked with bunting; crowds cheered; ferry sirens blared; and a twenty-one-gun salute boomed. Delay of the great moment by unseasonable blizzards inland did nothing to dampen spirits, or expectations of future prosperity.

Next day the Portpatrick Railway Company welcomed its paying public with two trains daily to Castle Douglas, connecting there for Dumfries and so into England. Coaching was a memory of the comfortless past.

Two inside cylinder 2-2-2 locomotives ordered for opening not having arrived on time, loan was made of an LNWR 0-6-0 Class DX from Crewe, complete with LNWR driver. The bigger company eventually sold the engine to its borrower, and almost the driver with it. He was asked to continue with the PPR and his former charge, renumbered now as PPR No. 5; however, not surprisingly the man preferred to return to his native territory.

Within about eight months services were increased to three in each direction, at least one being mixed, with market day specials to bring modest non-Irish money into PPR coffers.

Not until August 28, 1862, did the PPR break through beyond Stranraer to Portpatrick village. Soon afterwards Stranraer Harbour branch also opened, giving that place two stations – harbour and town – while Portpatrick still lacked the Irish connections the line was created to serve. A day boat was inaugurated, Larne–Stranraer, and thence by rail to Castle Douglas.

Portpatrick Railway reached its destination and *raison d'être* on October 1, 1862. To celebrate, an improved packet service began. People of this tiny port declared a public holiday to cheer the day's events, backed up by 600 trippers off a special steamer.

From the other direction, Portpatrick in opening year was visited by a giant excursion train of twelve coaches, over the entire route from Dumfries, to which six more were coupled for the last lap from Stranraer, spectacularly double-headed over heavy gradients near intermediate Colfin.

Only one irony spoiled Portpatrick's rejoicing. It had been built to catch the lucrative Irish trade, but long before this the Mail had already deserted it for Holyhead. Future operations would therefore of necessity be geared to human freight. Improvements to the harbour were soon made, with financial help from the mightier LNWR, whose sights were set on thus gaining a foothold in the Irish boat-train traffic.

Once the cross country route was completed, two further untapped regions, south of this triangle baseline, caught speculative imaginations. A plan was mooted that Wigtown and Kirkcudbright, towns of some importance each governing a self-contained agricultural peninsula, should be joined to this outlet and thus to a new commercial world beyond Dumfries, by lines up to the PPR and CDDR respectively. In their favour were easier coastal terrain, and reasonable population centres in surrounding villages.

So, under an 1861 statute, another small independent local railway came alive, the Kirkcudbright Railway. It opened on February 17, 1864 from the increasingly important junction of Castle Douglas, now the meeting place of three systems (CDDR, PPR and KR). An age of railway rivalry had begun, with the bigger Glasgow and South Western, and the Caledonian's Dumfries, Lochmaben and Lockerbie Junction Railways on the sidelines.

Improvements to Portpatrick Harbour in 1865 and subsequently, and experiments in wooing more packet boat passengers, were insufficient to sustain its position in the overseas sea trade against expanding Stranraer. Two ports in one small locality, served by the same railway, were one port too many. In time the solution became apparent; to divert all Irish arrivals via Stranraer, instead of splitting them between both ports, and thus concentrate all funds and assets, and most receipts, into a single dock and station. The 'poor little port' of Portpatrick kept its trains, but was relegated to local branch status in about 1874.

As one door half closed, another was pushed tentatively open, exploring quite different ground off the PPR's main line. Newton Stewart, halfway between Stranraer and Castle Douglas, became the junction for a Wigtownshire Railway, whose first section entered Wigtown itself on April 7, 1875. In August rails reached Millisle to the south, preparatory to extending onwards to a terminus at Whithorn and outwards to the little resort of Garlieston or Garliestown. None of these could, in today's motorised world, support a railway; yesterday, enough local custom existed to bring the promoters modest profits.

Portpatrick Railway itself ran through a wide gamut of motive power during these formative years, ranging from 0-4-2 to 0-6-0, from 2-2-2 to 2-4-0, each class bringing some asset – or otherwise – to a demandingly hilly route.

Amalgamation saved many a rickety provincial company from extinction when railway mania occasionally blinded promoters to hard cash realities. This happened twice in southern Scotland, first in 1885 when the PPR and its offshoot the WR merged as the Portpatrick and Wigtownshire Joint Railway, in addition under the cumbersome auspices of the combined LNWR, Caledonian, Midland, and the Glasgow and South Western. Trains thereafter were worked mainly by the CR or GSWR, who took over among others the Wigtownshire's historic No. 1 (2-2-2 well tank), No. 2 (0-4-2T), and engines up to the former No. 6. All were used into the 1890s.

A second late nineteenth-century amalgamation brought the Castle Douglas and Dumfries Railway (the area's pioneer), together with the younger Kirkcudbright Railway, into the fold of the G&SWR.

The *Night Paddy* boat-train was always to remain the area's most impressive visitor, known to all by sight but rarely in actual experience, as she always flew non-stop past those who lived by the line.

Further branches into Scottish valleys (including one to Scotland's southernmost tip at Drummore) were proposed, and shelved once their financial potential was reduced from wishful thinking to hard truth. For this type of run the non-railed roadmotor was found more economic, able to stop and pick up 'anywhere . . . except on steep hills' without the expense of erecting stations and laying permanent way, and small enough to run solvently on scattered village patronage.

Passengers pouring through increasingly from London, Birmingham and Liverpool cared nothing for all these sideline trials and experiments in getting Mrs McLaren to market or Farmer McLaren to his supplier. All they were interested in was reaching Ireland comfortably, to which end the larger companies had laid on big improvements by the dawn of the luxurious Edwardian era. 'Sleeping saloons fitted with every modern convenience . . . Rugs and Pillows may be obtained by Passengers travelling by the Night Trains . . . charge 6d. for each Rug or Pillow', was advertised in 1906. Days were made correspondingly comfortable with 'Hot or Cold Lunches in Baskets, provided at the Principal Stations; 3s. (15p) *including beer or wine*' (!); or again, 'Tea Baskets containing a Pot of Tea, Bread and Butter and Cake, can be obtained at Preston, Lancaster etc. . . 1s. (5p) each'.

In an age when tourism became daily more widespread, Dumfries was proposed as a potential gateway to the scenic Burns Country, with such blandishments as: 'Passengers between Scotland and England . . . pass through the heart of the BURNS COUNTRY, and holders of Tourist Tickets to and from Glasgow, or North thereof, are allowed to travel via AYR (Burns' Birthplace). Tickets are also valid for break of journey at DUMFRIES (Burns' Burialplace).' Once thus attracted towards Dumfries for itself, instead of as a mere transit point, it was hoped that people might also be persuaded to sample the Stranraer line for its splendid scenery, bringing extra revenue to local ticket offices.

The GSWR constantly reiterated the benefit of its hotels when promoting such towns as Dumfries: 'The Company have fine Hotels at GLASGOW . . . AYR and DUMFRIES under their own management. These hotels will be found replete with all modern conveniences and comforts'.

The sea crossing nonetheless remained the real magnet of travellers, both over the straight cross-country line out of Dumfries, and down from the north via the west coast to the port where, it was advertised, 'steamboat connections are found to Ireland via Larne, the open sea passage being only 80 minutes'.

The GSWR played heavily on the advertiser's best loved word, ONLY, conveniently forgetting that sixty of those eighty minutes could be something approaching hell in an unstabilised steamer in weather often ranging from ferocious to terrifying off a squally coast. It was left to pharmaceutical advertisers to set passengers' minds at rest. 'There *is* a remedy for *mal-de-mer!*' crowed Roach's Seasickness Draughts. They might be pricey, at 4s. 6d. (22½p) for six doses, when £3 was a shop manager's weekly wage, but surely 4s. 6d. was a small price for a remedy 'never known to fail . . . totally efficacious both on the journey out and home', when faced with the Irish Sea in sullen mood.

As the Great War loomed, those who could afford to emulate ostriches buried their heads deeper into First Class comfort and good hotels. G&SWR advertising of 1913 reflected the trend, expanding its eulogy for the Dumfries hotel, a popular overnight stop en route to Ireland via Stranraer, to 'ALL modern Con-

Evening train from Dumfries, bound for Kirkcudbright, at Castle Douglas in May 1959.
NCB

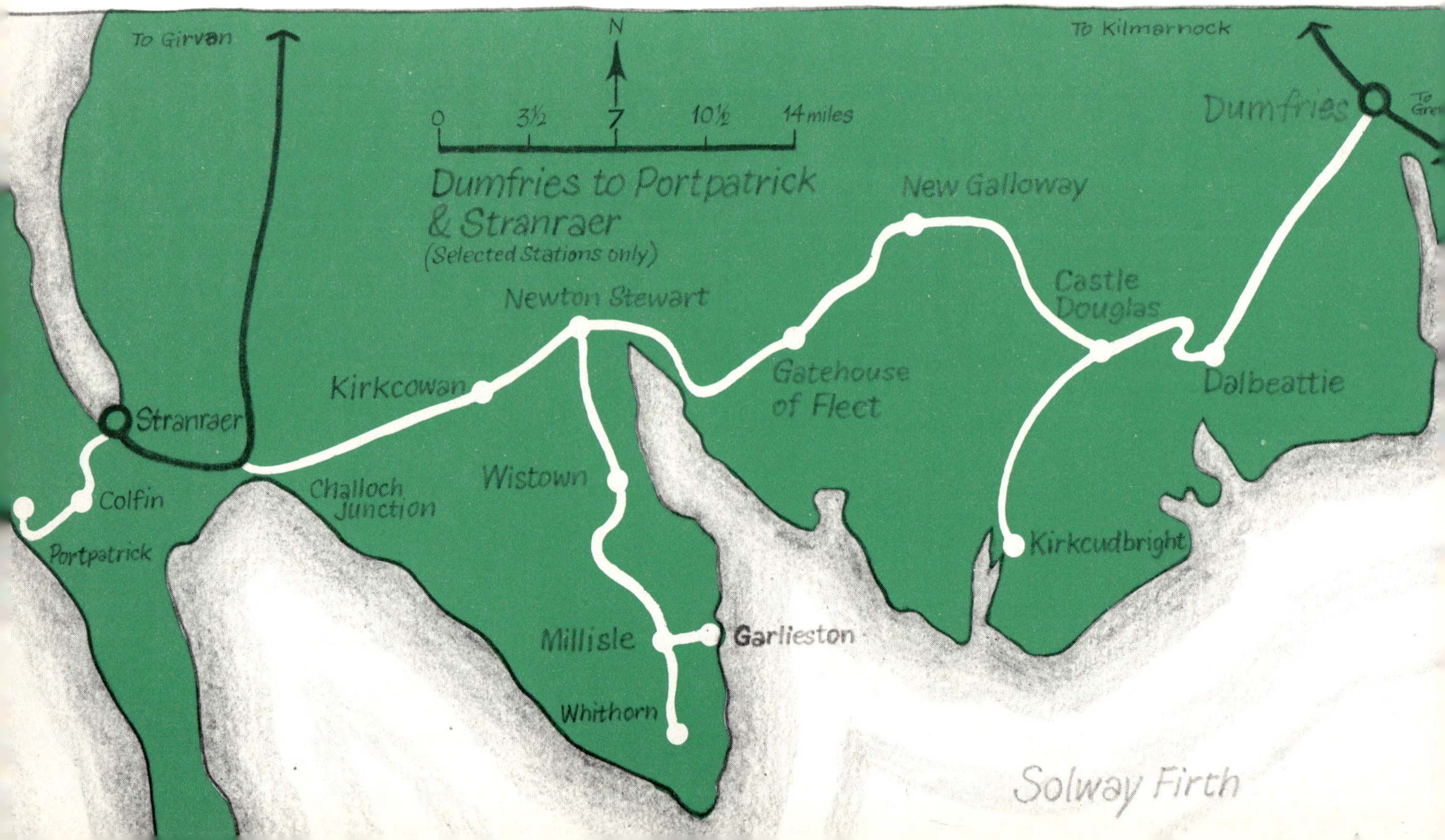

veniences and Comforts; Excellent Cuisine; Moderate Tariff'; an ostentatious idea of moderation to the man in a Third Class corner of a slow train, earning only £2 for a week's gruelling labour. The world took its pleasures and its travels almost frantically, as if conscious that they soon would cease.

They did, in 1914. The *Paddy* continued, behind such engines as G&SWR's 4-4-0 No. 152, but it was a risky trip, with the Channel submarine infested. Other sea routes halted altogether.

The Armistice found the Stranraer line in poor condition, battered by the always damaging weather of its mountainous route, as was attested by more than one accident attributed to track faults.

Life looked up again with merger into the LMS, though LMS engines did not actually appear until about 1929, when 2P class 4-4-0s numbers 618 and 619 came in, brand new, followed by others allocated in 1931. 2Ps now headed most southern Scottish trains.

The LMS attempted to boost holiday as well as through travel with such proclamations as 'The West Coast is the Best Coast'; Stranraer being prominently featured among its 'Best Resorts'. 'Fast and Luxurious Trains to take you, and LMS Monthly Return Tickets are only a penny-a-mile, with Weekly Holiday Contract Tickets (from as low as 7s. 6d.) you can explore your Holiday District to your Heart's Content' rhapsodised a typical LMS advertisement of 1937.

Just two years later, war was again to destroy old orders and old ways. *The Paddy* kept going, but on this long route normally thinly worked local trains often perforce gave way to long heavily laden troop trains, transporting boys in khaki. Wartime motive power relied chiefly on *Jubilees*.

A worse disaster occurred in peacetime than during six years of battle, when Galloway's greatest tragedy befell one night in 1953. In a gale of appalling ferocity, lashing waves into spume high above her decks, the car ferry *Princess Victoria* cast off. She was never seen again. Sledgehammer seas stove in her car deck doors, which being near the waterline, were the ferry's most vulnerable point. In the abandonment of the listing steamer 133 passengers and crew drowned. In disciplined seagoing tradition, *Princess Victoria*'s captain and officers went down with her.

Confidence in cross-channel travel inevitably wavered, temporarily driving uneasy travellers into the air via Glasgow, Manchester or London airports. Rumour, feeding on accounts of a half-empty daily *Paddy*, spoke of line closure. But public memory is notoriously short. Trade recovered, and the *Night Paddy* from London did as well as ever, a spectacular sight in the darkness with trails of flying red sparks, often double-headed with a 2P 4-4-0 piloting a magnificent *Jubilee*.

In 1959, anticipating things to come, the alternative west coast route to Stranraer from Glasgow went over to less romantic diesel multiple sets, whose tantrums on heavy inclines in early days aroused misgivings among footplatemen reared on steam since boyhood. Steam continued to be used for freight, handy also for hauling recalcitrant diesels back to the depot.

The dispirited little Portpatrick branch, on which original plans for all this lengthy lost route had hinged, closed to passengers as early as February 6, 1950, though a few miles out to Colfin lingered awhile for freight.

Newton Stewart to Whithorn ended on September 23, 1950, saying farewell with 2P class No. 40611 steaming into history.

Wigtown branch lasted until October 5, 1964 (its Millisle–Garliestown offshoot died long before, back in 1903). Track was dismantled with almost indecent haste.

Being straight from point to point, the base of our Scottish triangle might appear least dispensable of the two routes into Stranraer. However, its limited purpose outside boat-train services, and its long stationless hill country stretches, prohibitively expensive to maintain in suitable condition for their gradients, led to it being scheduled for closure on June 12, 1965, throughout its length.

Its funeral was a wake to remember, with huge crowds travelling prodigious distances by road from remote towns and villages to watch the last *Paddy* steam past, double-headed by two splendid Class 5 4-6-0 locomotives swathed in grand veils of steam. Thereafter, many extra miles and well over an hour were added to the journey from London, running well up towards Glasgow in order to reach the surviving west coast line and all the way back again to Stranraer.

Also closed in 1965 was the branch out of Castle Douglas down to Kirkcudbright, being cut off now from any junction outlet. A short stretch was allowed to remain, coinciding with the last few miles of the reprieved coastal route through Girvan. It was essential if trains were still to get through by that alternative line, but stations along it were closed, making it only a service road for non-stop services to the port. For local people, it might just as well not have been there.

Stranraer Harbour to Stranraer Town closed on March 7, 1966, the last of this series of closures progressively robbing a whole slice of Scotland of its railways, leaving only one station to serve both local transport needs and through custom.

Track rusted for several years unlifted, but for a fragment left near Dumfries maintained in order to serve a factory. Because of its continued presence, a few half-hearted schemes were floated for reopening, all killed by the hard financial truth that too many miles of track through difficult terrain touched too few human settlements. Those that did exist had in any case sworn allegiance to the more flexible personal car. Nevertheless, it was not until 1967 that BR finally made closure irrevocable by lifting all track from its beds of weeds and thistles.

That gesture seemed to confirm physically that no boat train could ever again demonstrate that the shortest distance between two points – such as Dumfries and Stranraer – can be a more or less straight line across country.

Glasgow & South Western Railway ('David Cooper, General Manager, Glasgow 1906') incites travellers to break journey at Burns' Dumfries; sample the S&SWR's Dumfries hotel; and to patronise Stranraer, where 'steamboat connections are formed to Ireland'. *Ward Lock Ltd*

Approach to Dumfries from the southern cross-country route: Dalbeattie, looking towards Dumfries in 1963. *G Daniels*

Railway Routes

GLASGOW & SOUTH-WESTERN RAILWAY.
SCOTLAND AND ENGLAND.

THE GLASGOW and SOUTH-WESTERN RAILWAY COMPANY gives a **Direct Route** between **Scotland and England**, connecting at **Carlisle** with the **Midland Railway**, the principal Termini being **St. Enoch, Glasgow**, and **St. Pancras, London**; and a Full and Expeditious Service is given between Glasgow, Paisley, Greenock, Ayr, Ardrossan, Kilmarnock, Dumfries, &c., and Liverpool, Manchester, Bradford, Leeds, Sheffield, Bristol, Bath, Birmingham, London, &c.

DINING CARS (First and Third Class) by the Morning and Afternoon Expresses, and **SLEEPING CARS** by the Night Expresses, in each direction, between GLASGOW (St. Enoch) and LONDON (St. Pancras).

New and Improved CORRIDOR CARRIAGES with LAVATORY Accommodation by all the trains.

Passengers between Scotland and England by this, the most **Picturesque Route**, pass through the heart of the **Burns Country**, and holders of Tourist Tickets to and from Glasgow, or North thereof, are allowed to travel *via* **Ayr** (Burns' Birthplace). Tickets are also valid for break of journey at **Dumfries** (Burns' Burial-place).

CLYDE WATERING PLACES.

The Glasgow and South-Western Line to Princes Pier Station, Greenock, is the most convenient for Visitors to the Watering Places on the Firth of Clyde and Western Highlands and the Islands of Scotland, to and from which places regular connections are maintained by the Company's magnificent Fleet of Steamers, "Glen Sannox," "Juno," "Jupiter," "Mars," "Mercury," "Neptune," "Minerva," "Glen Rosa," "Vulcan," "Viceroy," and new Turbine Steamer "Atalanta," as also by the "Columba," "Lord of the Isles," "Isle of Arran," and Turbine Steamers, "King Edward" and "Queen Alexandra."

All Passengers' Luggage is removed from the Trains to the Steamers, and *vice versa*, free of charge, by a special staff of attendants provided by the Company.

Passengers holding Through Tickets to or from England have the option of visiting Glasgow *en route*.

ISLAND OF ARRAN, MILLPORT, & CAMPBELTOWN.

The most direct and expeditious route to the far-famed **Island of Arran** is by the Company's new swift Paddle Steamer "Glen Sannox," *via* Ardrossan; and to Millport, Campbeltown, &c., *via* Fairlie, where the Company's Trains run alongside the Steamers.

AYRSHIRE COAST and THE LAND O' BURNS.

Passengers desirous of visiting the Ayrshire Coast Towns and places on the Company's Line, which are full of associations of the Poet Burns, and famous in history and romance, will find that the Company provide an excellent service of Express Trains from Glasgow and Paisley, composed of carriages of the most modern type, to Kilwinning, Stevenston, Saltcoats, Ardrossan, West Kilbride, Fairlie, Largs, Irvine, Troon, Prestwick, and Ayr, all of which places can be reached within the hour. There is also a service of Fast Trains to Maybole, Girvan, Pinmore, Pinwherry, Barrhill, New Luce, and Stranraer. From Stranraer Steamboat connections are formed to Ireland, *via* Larne, the open sea passage being only 8o minutes.

FAMOUS GOLFING LINKS.—Golfers will find Links of the highest order at Bridge of Weir, Kilmacolm, Johnstone, Stevenston, West Kilbride, Largs, Bogside, Gailes, Barassie, Troon, Prestwick, Turnberry, and Girvan. For descriptive notes on the various Links served by the Company's Trains, *see* the Guide to the Golfing Resorts, issued by the Company, free of charge.

HOTELS.—The Company have **Hotels** at **Glasgow** (St. Enoch), **Ayr**, and **Dumfries**, under their own management. These Hotels will be found replete with all modern conveniences and comforts. Excellent cuisine and a moderate tariff existing throughout.

GLASGOW, 1906. DAVID COOPER, GENERAL MANAGER.

Stranraer Town station, with No. 45081 prepared for the run to Dumfries. *Real Photographs Ltd*

Castle Douglas in 1956, with Dumfries–Stranraer service behind No. 41132. *Real Photographs Ltd*

No. 45588 *Kashmir* climbing from Big Water of Fleet viaduct into Gatehouse of Fleet with a railway enthusiasts' club special in April 1963. *G Daniels*

The magnificent viaduct left intact at Goldielea near Dumfries. *David Hope*

CHAPTER 27

Speyside

AROUND ELGIN

'Doing each others' dags' was a popular Victorian and Edwardian schoolboy expression for the sport of outdoing opponents' boasts and exploits, in half friendly, half earnest vein: topping a big conker with a bigger conker; dismissing sixty marbles with '*I've got seventy!*'; above all, getting there first wherever *there* might be.

In the Scottish Highlands contemporary railway rivalry showed a not dissimilar spirit. Commanding the playground (the important route from Aberdeen to Inverness via Elgin) were the two Big Boys, the Highland and Great North of Scotland Railways, alternately sharing, outdoing and frustrating each other. Looking on and entering in from the fringes was a group of smaller local companies, usually backed by one of the leaders, the small fry of railway-dom: the Morayshire Railway, Keith and Dufftown, the tiny Fochabers branch, and some coastal enterprises.

Doing each others' dags involved opening a railway to counter another, or sneaking around mountains by a different route to reach some place a bigger company had secured first. The immediate result was a web of small rural lines, more than any district could possibly need after the advent of cars and buses. The longer term outcome was a litter of disused tracks on modern maps, as far away as Fraserburgh, leaving only the original main Aberdeen–Keith–Elgin–Inverness line intact. Keith, centre of once bitter bargaining, is no longer a junction, except in name.

The Great North of Scotland, one of the two Big Boys, began this impressive major crossing of Scotland in 1854. They were aiming towards Keith but, being over ambitious, ran out of funds after forty miles at Huntly, leaving Inverness travellers to transfer there and continue by horse drawn coaches over jolting slow roads. Not until October 11, 1856 did the GNS's finances stretch to opening forward to Keith, soon to become a junction and centre of endless interchange squabbles. Drained by this further effort, the GNS rested at Keith without extending even to Elgin, not far but across difficult country, expensive to engineer. Thus passengers still had to suffer the contrast between trains and slow cramped coaches on to Inverness.

Completing this total artery was thus economically, socially and fiscally desirable to any company able to cope with it, reasons to encourage the entry of the big Highland Railway working out towards Keith and Elgin from the opposite geographical side. The two railways were always to exist uneasily together, though for passengers and freight their combined track, in one long city-to-city line, was eminently desirable.

The HR reached Nairn in November 1855, whilst the GNS doggedly excavated in from Keith. Cannily the GNS, faced with costly building including a Spey bridge, suggested that the HR might care to accept £40,000 to share the building of one unified route, the Inverness and Aberdeen Junction Railway. The matter was clinched, one of the few on which both parties settled reasonably amicably. The HR drew closer, reaching to near Forres on December 22, 1857, Elgin on March 25 of the following year, and Keith five months later still. Coach transfers became things of the jolting past.

Off this long line, the only one extant today, a network of disused offshoots and alternative routes gathers weeds or serves other purposes; testimony to decades of dag-doing by the HR and GSNR, regardless of the economic importance of their wandering around coast and country within the same district.

Ruler straight north from Elgin ran the local Morayshire Railway to Lossiemouth, later absorbed by the GNSR, opening it up as port and resort. The customary first sod was cut in 1851, and the route opened on August 10, 1852.

Continuing the same scheme southwards past Elgin, the MR delved deep into the beautiful but difficult country through Rothes down to Craigellachie. Powers were obtained in 1848 but lay dormant through financial disturbances until eight years later, when the idea was revived under MR auspices, then transferred to the Inverness and Aberdeen Junction, using that company's track as far as Orton. The rest opened in two sections: Orton–Rothes on August 23, 1858 and on to Craigellachie on Christmas Eve.

Disagreements bedevilled the MR and I&AJR on sharing the Elgin–Orton section, the MR asserting rights to transport stock not only over its own lines but over the whole, whilst only meeting expenses for its own half. The I&AJR counter-alleged that such special rights applied only to parts of the Lossiemouth-Craigellachie line. Huffily the Morayshire built itself another independent line to the Glen of Rothes under an 1860 Act, involving an awkward Elgin turn whereby trains had to be reversed from Lossiemouth into the hills. This line opened on January 1, 1862, a year after the MR obtained powers to run on again past Craigellachie, cross the Spey, and join the Strathspey Railway at Dufftown. Meanwhile, the small Keith and Dufftown Railway completed a deep triangular run, south from Elgin and north again to Keith.

Into most of these pies the powerful GNSR slipped its finger, jointly meeting costs for the theoretically independent K&DR and working its trains from the opening on February 12, 1862. In a similar way it backed the Strathspey with cash, loaned navvies, materials, and working after the opening ceremony of July 1, 1863, which opened up the line from Craigellachie to Nethy Bridge, Boat of Garten and Aviemore. Thus, through three interlinked sections of Dufftown, Morayshire and Strathspey metals, the GNSR sneaked by a backdoor into its real goal, Elgin. True, the mileage was nearly twenty-eight, against the Highland Railway's direct eighteen, but any entry was better than none and, before invention of the bus and car, passengers enough existed in these hilly communities to grant reasonable solvency.

Backdoor routes from Keith to Elgin, avoiding the already laid direct line, ran north as well as south along the north coast, where strings of small ports and resorts promised moderate revenue. The GNSR opened from Grange, near Keith, to Portsoy on August 2, 1859 after two years' navvying; but not until 1882 were powers finalised onwards via Portessie to Buckie – ironically, on the very day the rival HR got powers for a similar northwards cross route, from Keith to Portessie. It was a visible expression of the Highland's bitterness towards the GNR creeping along the seaboard to Elgin.

Eventually a schoolboyish swap granted the HR running from Portsoy to Buckie in exchange for powers enabling the GNSR to run from Elgin to Forres. They were paper pacifications; if one party failed to take up its option, neither could the other make its claim.

Coastal gaps closed: Portsoy to Tochieneal in April 1884; from the other side, Elgin to Garmouth on August 12, 1884; and the middle gap between Garmouth and Tochieneal in May 1866. These networks made Elgin increasingly important, sparking off further wrangling between the GNSR and the HR. Traffic initially exchanged at Keith, a facility coveted for Elgin. A wary seven-year agreement for routing some Aberdeen–Inverness services along the coast was signed in 1888, but this did little to ease problems for the only party never consulted in these years of rivalry, the passengers. What did they care if trains exchanged at Keith or Elgin, when the real problems were poor onward connections, delays, unnecessarily circuitous routes, and changes where trains surely could have continued 'through'?

Still unhappy in 1890, the GNSR applied for its own Elgin–Inverness line, foolishly sited almost alongside the existing straight route. The only moderately useful outcome of this move was the creation of a little branch up to Burghead and Hopeman, twin north coast ports.

Haggling continued between the two giants on scores both large and petty, to the twentieth century's dawn, when at last reason decreed agreement instead of cash-draining rivalry, and at last Elgin finally became the main interchange station.

As the district expanded to tourism, companies set about humouring passengers instead of treating them almost like side issues during operating squabbles. The HR enthusiastically promoted as 'Holiday Resorts in the Highlands' such inland stations as 'Aviemore, Carr Bridge, Boat of Garten' on the line northwards to Craigellechie, with 'Forres and Elgin'.

'For fishing, golfing, shooting, excursions by steamer or coach, or for quiet resting, the Highlands are unsurpassed. The scenery is delightful in variety; the climate bracing and wholesome' rhapsodised the Highland, luring holidaymakers not only with cheap Tourist Season Tickets but also with blandishments never met in modern advertising, such as (of railway hotels): 'Passengers can secure Apartments by Telegraph FREE OF CHARGE, by applying to any of the Station Officials on the Line and giving their Name and Address in writing'.

For the HR, war in 1914 replaced tourism with heavy traffic based on the Fleet at Scapa Flow. Around Elgin, conversely, line closures began with the uneconomic coastal route through Buckie, shut down from August 9, 1915, but for the Buckie–Portessie section, kept for freight until the next war, in 1944.

Nationwide amalgamation in 1923 precipitated further pruning and reorganisation. Second thoughts wavered over the old Keith–Portessie countryside branch, whose two ends remained for freight and fish but whose ten-mile middle section had been lifted in 1915. Preparations for its revival were well advanced when economic potential was again seriously investigated and found wanting. Reopening was abandoned.

Another casualty was the tiny Fochabers line, with only three stations in its three miles, served by one engine in steam, which died on September 14, 1931. It was highly sensitive to contemporary bus competition, with a station far from the town. On the same day Alves–Burghead–Hopeman closed, though freight used part of the route for another twenty-six years.

What of today, and the future, in this area crisscrossed by grass-grown trackways? As in scenic Derbyshire and Durham, rehabilitation by local councils is saving the best from oblivion. Moray District Council has worked on several derelict lines, most notably seventeen glorious miles of disused Speyside track intended for long distance hiking and pony trekking. Plans have now come to fruition for restoration, south of our map boundary, from Aviemore to Boat of Garten, with ten locomotives in steam. Otherwise most local lines remain studies in dereliction.

So many railways like these have been built and lost again since a traveller of 1840 described early 'inconveniences on the road . . . At one time it is a stray cow or sheep lying athwart the rails which the engine's scupper tosses into the air, being itself checked in its progress by that act . . . a supply of water to feed the boiler is required; the train reaches

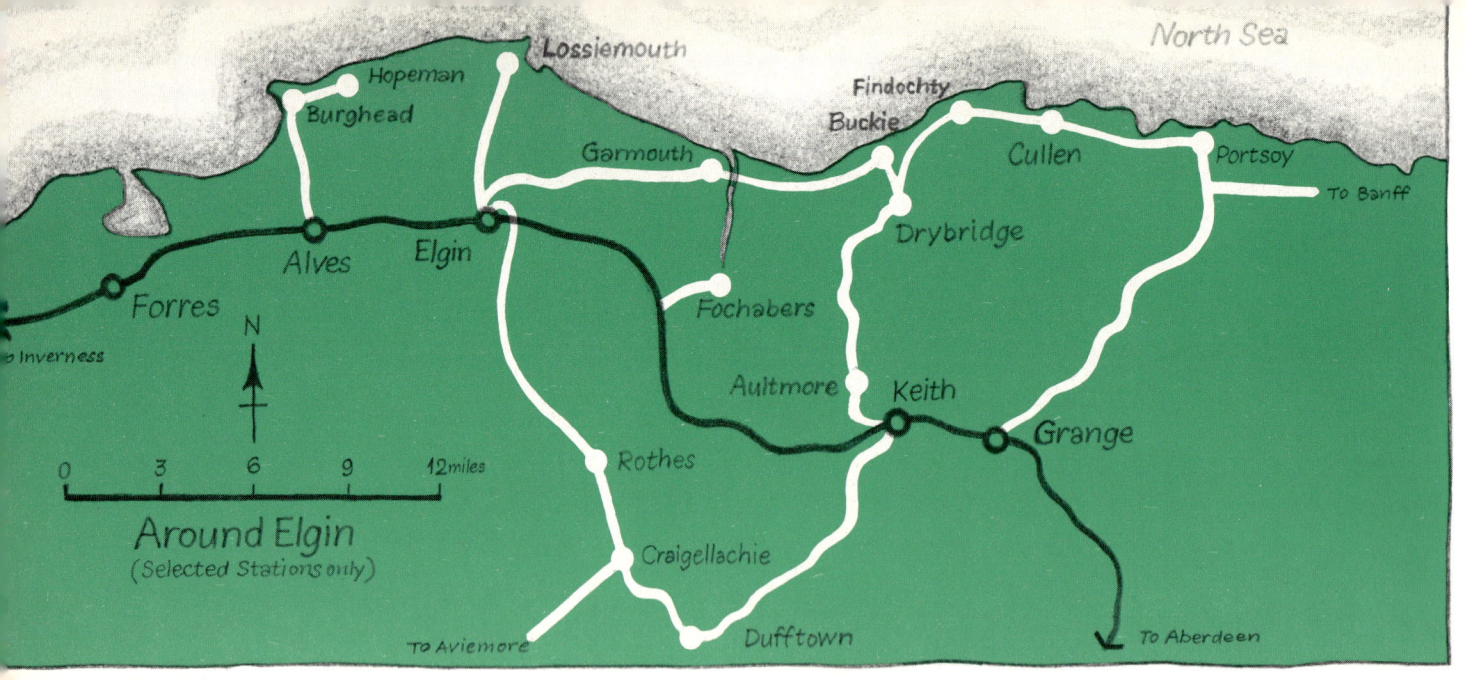

the pump at one of the stations, but the pump is frozen and refuses to work; the stoker who ought to be like Argus, ever vigilant, falls asleep now and then; the fire goes out and the locomotive which was to have conveyed the night mail at twenty-five miles an hour is standing stock-still. Here and there the rails will be covered with snow or be excessively wet, and the wheels refuse to bite, wasting their power in useless gyrations . . . a grand explosion takes place, and all power of locomotion is annihilated.' All the same, the writer concluded, 'The immense advantages . . . of this stupendous invention still remain'.

The advantages remain immense wherever viable main lines and branches have been spared, from Scotland down to Kent, where we began our pilgrimage. But for every operative route the average district often has several pathetic lost lines, abandoned in favour of cars, buses or faster Inter-City travel. In Yorkshire alone, enough lie grassy to fill a book as long as this necessarily arbitrary selection.

Unused, most are nevertheless still visible, often half a century after closure, where long-lifted sleepers pressed their outlines into ballasted trackbeds. They are not forgotten by those old enough once to have puffed along their leisurely miles. Nor by those too young to have seen steam up, but who enjoy 'walking the line' for pleasure, no matter whether their path is rough and unofficial, as between Canterbury and Whitstable, or superbly rehabilitated and fitted with every possible picnicking convenience, as on the Derwent Walk.

No. 62469 *Glen Douglas* with Speyside freight passes an Elgin–Keith train in 1958.
G Daniels

The little seaside Lossiemouth branch after arrival of the 5.10 pm from Elgin.
G Daniels

No. 55221 on the 6.0 pm from Elgin at Buckie in September 1958. *G Daniels*

No. 61783 *Loch Shiel* at Buckie with Keith Town to Elgin service. *G Daniels*

Cairnie Junction with the coastal and Craigellachie portions of an Elgin–Aberdeen train. *G Daniels*

Highland Railway advertisement of 1906 stressing as holiday resorts such places as Elgin, Nairn and Forres.
Ward Lock Ltd

Aberlour on the Speyside line. The sad dereliction of broken fences and a crumbling platform, vandalism and litter, seen in 1978. *Moray District Council*

Railway Routes

THE HIGHLAND RAILWAY.

Holiday Resorts in the Highlands of Scotland:—
Dunkeld, Pitlochry, Aberfeldy, Blair Atholl, Kingussie, Aviemore, Carr Bridge, Boat of Garten, Grantown, Forres, Elgin, Nairn, Inverness (the Capital of the Highlands), Beauly, Fortrose, Dingwall, Strathpeffer Spa, Garve, Achnasheen (for Loch Maree), Kyle of Lochalsh (for Portree, Stornoway, &c.), Tain, Lairg, Dornoch, Golspie, Helmsdale, Wick, Thurso, and Lybster.

For Fishing, Golfing, Shooting, Excursions by Steamer or Coach, or for quiet resting, the Highlands are unsurpassed. The Scenery is delightful in variety; the Climate bracing and wholesome.

All the above Stations are on the **Highland Railway**, and Passengers should obtain Tickets by the Highland Route, *via* **DUNKELD**. During the Tourist Season Tickets are issued at all the principal Stations in England and Scotland.

The Railway from SPEAN BRIDGE to INVERGARRY and FORT AUGUSTUS was opened in July, 1903, and provides new ground for Visitors in a most interesting and romantic part of the Highlands.

For Fares, Times of Trains, Through Carriages, &c., see the Company's Time Tables, sent to any address on application.

STATION HOTEL, INVERNESS

Belonging to the Company, is a First-class Family and Commercial Hotel. It adjoins the Station and occupies the most central position in the Town. Grill Room in connection.

The Company's Station Hotel at **KYLE of LOCHALSH** is convenient for Tourists *en route* to the **ISLE of SKYE, STORNOWAY**, and the **WESTERN ISLANDS**.

The Company's **NEW STATION HOTEL at DORNOCH, SUTHERLANDSHIRE**, is now open (**DORNOCH** is the paradise of the Golfer).

Passengers can secure Apartments by Telegraph, **FREE of CHARGE**, by applying to any of the Station Officials on the Line, and giving their Name and Address in writing.

INVERNESS, 1906.   T. A. WILSON, GENERAL MANAGER.

Rugged Scottish scenery flattens out towards the coast. →
Embankment and the distant Spey Bridge looking almost their old selves, but for the absence of track. *Moray District Council*

General view taken in 1978 of the fine old Spey viaduct on the Elgin–Cullen coastal line.
Moray District Council

A dramatic shot of the Spey viaduct today, complete except for rails and sleepers.
Moray District Council

Bibliography

The following publications on Britain's lost and extant railways, which the author has found both informative and interesting, are suggested for further reading:

Allen, P C   *Rails in the Isle of Wight* (George Allen & Unwin) 1967.
Anderson, C   *Forgotten Railways of the East Midlands* (David & Charles) 1973.
Appleton, A J   *Disused Railways in the Countryside of England & Wales* (HMSO) 1970.
Barrie & Clinker   *Somerset and Dorset Railway* (Oakhill Press) 1978.
Brown, G (and others)   *Lynton and Barnstaple Railway* (David & Charles) 1971.
Christiansen, R   *Forgotten Railways of North & Mid Wales* (David & Charles) 1976.
Course, E   *Railways of Southern England* (Batsford) 1974.
Daniels, G   *Passengers No More* (Ian Allan) 1980.
Gould, D   *Westerham Valley Railway* (Oakwood Press) 1974.
Joby, R S   *Forgotten Railways of East Anglia* (David & Charles) 1977.
Lincoln, E F   *Story of Canterbury* (Staples Press).
Rush, R W   *The Furness Railway* (Oakwood Press) 1973.
Smith, D L   *Little Railways of South West Scotland* (David & Charles) 1969.
Tolson, J M (and others)   *Railways of Looe and Caradon* (Forge Books) 1974.
Vallance, H A   *The Highland Railway* (David & Charles) 1969.
Warwick, A R   *Phoenix Suburb* (Blue Boar Press) 1973.
Whittle   *Railways of Consett & North West Durham* (David & Charles) 1977.
——   *Regional History of the Railways of Great Britain* (multi-volume) David & Charles.
——Lingard   *The Woodstock Branch* (Oxford Publishing Co) 1973.

Also consulted:
Beauties of England and Wales Vol X (1813)
Granville: Spas of England (1839)
The Rail-Road Book of Great Britain (1851)

Acknowledgements

Compiling a book like this, requiring so much verification as well as picture gathering and straightforward research, has shown the author just how helpful people can be, from nationwide and supposedly impersonal organisations to countrymen replying to local newspaper appeals. To them all, Muriel Searle extends sincere thanks.

In particular, she thanks the many regional, divisional, area and station managers of British Rail, from all corners of the system, for their prompt and informative answers to her probings for information on lost lines as they are today.

Thanks are also extended to the following:

The author's father, Noel Searle, for suggesting the chapter on Ramsgate Sands

Showerings/Babycham Ltd, of Shepton Mallet (S&DJR)

Gwent County Council, Planning Department (Tintern)

Mr S J Stevens; Mr F J Norris; Miss Amy Bright; Mrs F M Kite; Mr R A Holder; Mr W J Greer; Miss Pamela Williams; Mrs D Rowntree; Mrs Freda Miller; and in particular Mr Douglas Parker, all involved in the chapter 'Hayling Billy'

Dr J H Appleton (Isle of Wight and Derbyshire)

Pamlin Prints of Croydon

Mr J H Meredith (Ramsgate Tunnel Railway)

Railway Magazine (Dean and Wye Valley)

Sedgemoor District Council (Cheddar Valley Railway)

Eastern Evening News, Norwich

Portsmouth Evening News

Central Library, Great Yarmouth (Norfolk Railways)

Ward Lock Ltd, for permission to reproduce the old railway company advertisements from their 'Red Guides' series

National Railway Museum, York

Mr R Joby (Canterbury & Whitstable; Norfolk)

Durham County Council, for information and photographs for the Derwent Walk (Blaydon & Consett Railways)

Lyn Publicity Association (Lynton & Barnstaple Rly)

Mr R H Clarke (Norfolk)

Bromley Central Library (Westerham and Crystal Palace)

Miss P O'Driscoll (Port Victoria)

Director of Planning, Moray District Council (Elgin)

B P Oil, Kent Refinery Ltd (Port Victoria)

Dr E Course (Sheppey; Hythe)

Mr Fred Lewis (North Wales)

Rendel, Palmer & Tritton (South Wales)

Countryside Commission

Mr C Maggs (Weston Clevedon & Portishead Railway)

Michael & Janette Harris (Easingwold Railway)

Mr Peter Jennings (Heyling Island Branch)

Mr Peter Forbes (Blenheim & Woodstock Branch)

Apart from those obtained from commercial sources, and from the author's own collection, most of the illustrations were supplied by private individuals, often involving considerable effort. One couple braved attacks by angry geese, an example of the unexpected rigours often confronting those who penetrate the undergrowth of a truly lost line. Their contributions are individually labelled, but the author also thanks them again by name: Janette and Michael Harris, R S Joby; H C Casserley; Gerald Daniels; Edwin Course; F J Norris; Miss A Bright; W J Greer; S J Stevens; Miss Pamela Williams; Peter Jennings; Douglas Parker; Dr J H Appleton; John H Meredith; Peter Forbes; C Maggs; Fred Lewis.

A handful of illustrations come from the author's childhood collections, and their copyright holders have proved untraceable. (SDJR and York). It is hoped that this acknowledgement will be accepted for them.